Move α

Current Studies in Linguistics
Samuel Jay Keyser, general editor

Move α:

Conditions on Its Application and Output

Howard Lasnik and
Mamoru Saito

The MIT Press
Cambridge, Massachusetts
London, England

First MIT Press paperback edition, 1994

This book was set in Times Roman by Asco Trade Typesetting Ltd., Hong Kong
and was printed and bound in the United States of America.

Library of Congress Cataloging-in-Publication Data

Lasnik, Howard.
  Move [alpha]: conditions on its applications and output / Howard Lasnik and
Mamoru Saito.
      p.   cm.—(Current studies in linguistics series; 22)
  Includes bibliographical references and index.
  ISBN 0-262-12161-1 HB, 0-262-62091-X (PB)
  1. Generative grammar. 2. Grammar, Comparative and general-Syntax.
I. Saito, Mamoru. II. Title. III. Series.
P158.L375   1992
415—dc20   91-24170
                                                                    CIP

Contents

Contents

Preface

The goal of this monograph is to elaborate a "principles-and-parameters" framework in which the similarities and differences among languages with respect to WH-questions can be captured. We will be particularly concerned with bounding requirements on movement (Subjacency) and proper government requirements on traces (the Empty Category Principle). We hope to show that these and other general conditions on derivations and representations can bring linguistics closer to a theory in which there are no ad hoc statements involving particular syntactic rules, that is, toward the theory envisaged in Chomsky and Lasnik 1977, where the entire transformational component consists of the single process "Move α."

Chapters 1 and 2 include a detailed discussion and extension of the ideas in Lasnik and Saito 1984, out of which this monograph developed. In chapter 1, we propose an account of the differences between languages with and without syntactic WH-movement in terms of interaction between universal and parameterized properties of COMP. Along the lines proposed by Huang (1982), we examine a range of complement-noncomplement asymmetries in both types of languages and propose definitions of two modes of proper government—lexical government and antecedent government—to explain these asymmetries.

In chapter 2, we confront an asymmetry internal to the set of non-complements, one between subjects and adjuncts. We conclude that for traces of syntactic movement, antecedent government determination ("γ-marking") takes place at different levels for subjects (arguments in general) and adjuncts, S-structure for the former and LF for the latter. Ultimately we show how this γ-marking asymmetry follows from a plausible interpretation of the Projection Principle. In the course of the discussion, we take advantage of the possibilities available in the general rule Move α, and, indeed, we propose generalizing it even further to Affect α: "Do anything (move, delete, insert) to anything."

In chapters 3 and 4, we examine Chomsky's (1986a) modification of the theory of proper government and show how a merger of Chomsky's theory with the one proposed in chapters 1 and 2 can handle all of the phenomena considered thus far plus seemingly problematic facts of topicalization. In chapter 3, we first present arguments for the hypothesis, originally due to Ross (1967) and motivated in detail by Baltin (1982), that topicalization can involve adjunction to S. We then propose a simplified definition of *barrier* on the basis of the topicalization data.

In chapter 4, we first point out circumstances in which traces of topicalized phrases seem, unexpectedly, not to be antecedent-governed, and we propose an explanation for this fact. We then explore the consequences of our proposal for A-movement as well as Ā-movement, which leads us to a generalization of Chomsky's (1986b) Uniformity Condition.

Chapter 5 is concerned with remaining problems and alternative approaches. In particular, we discuss those facts that motivated alternative approaches to the ECP phenomena and speculate on how we might extend our theory to account for them. As we were completing this research, two important new works appeared on topics related to our own: Rizzi 1990 and Cinque 1990. We regret that we are unable to consider their analyses here.

Our intellectual debt to Noam Chomsky and to Jim Huang will immediately be clear to the reader of this monograph. It was their work that first interested us in the topics explored here, provided the foundation for most of our analyses, and proved a constant inspiration as we struggled toward explanations.

We are indebted to a great number of people, too numerous to mention individually, for valuable comments and suggestions. We would like to thank Chris Collins, Steven Franks, Masa-yuki Ikeuchi, Masaru Nakamura, and especially Noam Chomsky, Sam D. Epstein, and two reviewers for detailed comments on earlier versions of this monograph.

The material in this monograph benefited from presentations in seminars at the University of Connecticut, the University of Southern California, the University of Texas, Tohoku University, Universidad del Pais Vasco, and the University of Arizona, and in colloquia at the University of Arizona, Universitat Autònoma de Barcelona, the University of California, the University of Texas, Tohoku University, Universidad del Pais Vasco, and the University of Arizona, and in colloquia at the University of International Christian University, MIT, and the University of Southern California.

We thank Jun Abe, Yasuo Ishii, Yinxia Long, Keiko Murasugi, and Daiko Takahashi for their comments and their extensive assistance in the preparation of the manuscript, Anne Mark for her usual excellent editorial work, and Larry Cohen for his encouragement and his patience. The research reported here was supported in part by grants from the University of Southern California (Patricia Clancy, principal investigator), the Sumitomo Electric Company, the University of Tsukuba (Takeo Saito, principal investigator), and the University of Connecticut.

Move α

Chapter 1
WH-Movement in Syntax and LF: Preliminary Assumptions

1.1 Some Properties of COMP

As is well known, there is substantial superficial diversity among the languages of the world with respect to WH-questions. Given the principles-and-parameters approach to linguistic theory, this diversity must follow from settings of a small number of parameters.[1] One example of such diversity is that some languages, such as English, seem to have obligatory syntactic WH-movement, whereas others, such as Japanese, do not:[2]

(1) a. what_1 did John buy t_1
    b. *John bought what

(2) John-wa nani-o   kaimasita ka
    John-top what-acc bought   Q
    'what did John buy'

In fact, syntactic WH-movement is not only not obligatory in Japanese, it does not seem to exist at all. There are also languages, such as French, which, like English, allow WH-movement, but which, unlike English, do not require it (in the matrix):

(3) a. qui as-tu vu
    b. tu as vu qui
        'who did you see'

Thus, WH-movement can be obligatory, optional, or nonexistent, depending on the language. In this section, we will briefly summarize the account of this phenomenon in Lasnik and Saito 1984 (henceforth L&S) and reiterate the relevant principles and parameters proposed there.

1.1.1 Languages with Syntactic WH-Movement
Above, we spoke loosely about WH-movement being "obligatory." But of course it is not clear that this term has any precise meaning in the pre-

sent context. It clearly cannot mean that all WHs must be in COMP at S-structure. (4a) is allowed, and in fact (4b) is ungrammatical.

(4) a. what$_1$ did you give t_1 to who
    b. *who$_1$ what$_2$ did you give t_2 to t_1

Neither could "obligatory" mean that every COMP in a WH-question must be occupied by a WH-phrase, as shown in (5).

(5) a. who$_1$ t_1 thinks (that) John bought what
    b. *who$_1$ t_1 thinks what$_2$ John bought t_2

In (5a), the embedded COMP does not contain a WH-phrase, even though *what* could conceivably be eligible to move to this COMP. The sentence nevertheless is grammatical, and in fact the sentence would be ungrammatical if *what* moved to the embedded COMP, as shown in (5b).

A close look at the distribution of sentential complements in English immediately reveals that whether or not the COMP contains a WH-phrase depends on the matrix predicate. Consider the following examples:

(6) a. I believe that John saw Mary
    b. *I believe who$_1$ John saw t_1

(7) a. I know that John saw Mary
    b. I know who$_1$ John saw t_1

(8) a. *I wonder that John saw Mary
    b. I wonder who$_1$ John saw t_1

Suppose, as a first approximation, that the embedded COMP in (8) has a feature requiring that the embedded sentence be a question. Let us, following Chomsky (1973), call such a COMP a [$+ WH$] *COMP*. Analogously, suppose, again following Chomsky (1973), that the COMP in (6) is [$-WH$]—in other words, that the sentential complement must not be a question. Finally, suppose that the COMP in (7a) is the same as the COMP in (6), in relevant respects, and that the COMP in (7b) is the same as the COMP in (8). Evidently, there is a dependency between the [WH] feature of the embedded COMP, on the one hand, and the matrix predicate, on the other. This dependency seems essentially selectional in nature. (See Grimshaw 1979 and references cited there.) If we assume, following Stowell (1981), that COMP is the head of S' (i.e., that S' is a projection of COMP), then this selectional dependency is a head-to-head relation of just the same type as the selectional restrictions proposed by Chomsky (1965). *Believe* selects a [$-WH$] complement, *wonder* selects a [$+WH$] complement, and *know* allows either. In effect, there are two verbs *know*, one with the selectional restriction of *believe*, the other with that of *wonder*.

Though these selectional restrictions seem well motivated, they do not, by themselves, account for the distributional facts presented in (6)–(8). We need, in addition, constraints that make reference to the selectional features [± WH]. Whether a COMP is [+ WH] and whether that COMP must contain a WH-phrase are two independent questions. Aoun, Hornstein, and Sportiche (1981; henceforth AHS) propose the following S-structure filter (their (34)) as a statement of the constraint operative in English examples such as (8a):[3]

(9) *COMP, unless it contains a [+ WH] element.
     [+WH]

An analogue to (9) could be introduced to handle (6b):

(10) *COMP, if it contains a [+ WH] element.
      [−WH]

Another well-known fact about English COMP is that it cannot contain two WH-phrases, or a WH-phrase and a lexical complementizer. Thus, the examples in (11) are all ungrammatical.

(11) a. *I know who$_1$ what$_2$ John gave t_2 to t_1
      b. *I know who$_1$ that John saw t_1
      c. *I know that who$_1$ John saw t_1

Chomsky and Lasnik (1977), following Keyser (1975), posit the following filter to account for such facts:

(12) *[$_{COMP}$ X Y], X and Y lexical.[4]

We propose that the effects of this filter are to be derived from the assumption that COMP contains only one position, which is its head position. If adjunction to COMP is prohibited in the syntax, then the ungrammaticality of (11a–c) follows from this assumption.

(9) and (10) can accordingly be reformulated as follows:

(13) A [+ WH] COMP must have a [+ WH] head.   (= L&S's (183))

(14) A [− WH] COMP must not have a [+ WH] head.   (= L&S's (184))

Let us first illustrate (14) using (6b), repeated here as (15).

(15) *I believe who$_1$ John saw t_1

If COMP has only one position, the head position, and adjunction to COMP is prohibited in the syntax, then *who* in (15) must be in the head position of the embedded COMP. But the matrix verb is *believe*, and the embedded COMP is therefore [− WH]. Thus, the example is ruled out by (14).

(13), on the other hand, accounts for the fact that the embedded COMP in (8), repeated here as (16), must contain a WH-phrase.

(16) a. *I wonder that John saw Mary
    b. I wonder who John saw

The embedded COMP in (16) is [+ WH] because of the matrix verb *wonder* and hence, according to (13), must have a [+ WH] head. Thus, (13) correctly accounts for the contrast between (16a) and (16b).

Note that our account of this contrast directly extends to examples such as (17).

(17) *I wonder (that) John saw who

(17), too, is ruled out by (13): the embedded COMP must be [+ WH] because of the matrix verb *wonder*, but this COMP does not have a [+ WH] head.

However, our account does not directly extend to the examples in (1), repeated here as (18).

(18) a. what$_i$ did John buy t_i
    b. *John bought what

The ungrammaticality of (18b) (except as an echo question) clearly cannot be a consequence of selectional requirements for the COMP, since here the S′ is patently not a complement. But if (13) is to explain (18b), the matrix COMP in (18) must be [+ WH], even if not for selectional reasons. We will assume that this is the case, leaving aside the question of why it is so. Notice that it is not unreasonable that (17) and (18b) should receive partly divergent accounts, since there are languages in which the two cases pattern differently. The French example (19) is no better than (17), but, as we saw earlier, (20) is grammatical.

(19) *je me demande (que)   tu   as vu qui
     I wonder   (comp.) you saw who

(20)   tu   as vu qui
     you saw who

Presumably, selectional restrictions demand a [+ WH] COMP in (19) as they did in (17). In both (17) and (19), (13) must be violated. The mechanism (as yet unspecified) requiring a [+ WH] COMP in (18b) must be absent in French.

1.1.2 Universal Constraints on COMP

Aside from the difference between English and French illustrated in (18b) and (20), both languages seem to obey the filters in (13) and (14) strictly. However, there are languages that do not obey (13), because they lack syntactic WH-movement altogether.[5] Consider the following Japanese examples (see Huang 1981/82, 1982 for a detailed discussion of parallel Chinese examples):[6]

(21) a. Mary-ga [$_{S'}$ John-ga hon-o katta to]   sinzite iru koto
         Mary-nom   John-nom book-acc bought COMP believe   fact
         'the fact that Mary believes that John bought a book'
   b. *Mary-ga [$_{S'}$ John-ga nani-o katta ka] sinzite iru koto
         Mary-nom   John-nom what-acc bought Q believe   fact
         Lit. 'the fact that Mary believes Q John bought what'

(22) a. Mary-ga [$_{S'}$ John-ga hon-o katta to]   kiite iru koto
         Mary-nom   John-nom book-acc bought COMP heard   fact
         'the fact that Mary heard that John bought a book'
   b. Mary-ga [$_{S'}$ John-ga nani-o katta ka] kiite iru koto
         Mary-nom   John-nom what-acc bought Q heard   fact
         'the fact that Mary heard what John bought'

(23) a. *Mary-ga [$_{S'}$ John-ga hon-o katta to]   siritagatte iru
         Mary-nom   John-nom book-acc bought COMP want-to-know
         koto
         fact
         Lit 'the fact that Mary wants to know that John bought a book'
   b. Mary-ga [$_{S'}$ John-ga nani-o katta ka] siritagatte iru
         Mary-nom   John-nom what-acc bought Q want-to-know
         koto
         fact
         'the fact that Mary wants to know what John bought'

The verb *kiite iru* 'heard' allows for, and the verb *siritagatte iru* 'want-to-know' requires, a [+WH] complement. But the WH-phrases are in situ in (22b) and (23b). Thus, the filter (13) is violated.

An embedded sentence in Japanese is interpreted as a question if and only if it is followed by *ka*. Thus, we may consider *ka* as a phonetic realization of the [+WH] feature.[7] As shown in (24)–(25), although an embedded question must appear with *ka*, a matrix question can, but need not, appear with *ka*.[8]

(24) a. Mary-ga [$_{S'}$ John-ga nani-o katta ka] siritagatte iru (koto)
         (= (23b))
   b. *Mary-ga [$_{S'}$ John-ga nani-o katta (to)] siritagatte iru (koto)

(25) a. John-wa doko-ni ikimasita *ka*
         John-top where-to went   Q
         'where did John go'
   b. John-wa doko-ni ikimasita

If a COMP is [+WH] just in case it contains *ka*, as we assume here, then the facts in (24)–(25) indicate that the distribution of [±WH] COMPs in Japanese is exactly like that in French. In Japanese, embedded COMPs are either [+WH] or [−WH] for reasons of selection. Nothing forces matrix COMPs of WH-questions to have the feature [+WH] at S-structure.

We noted earlier that there are languages that clearly violate (13), namely, those without syntactic WH-movement. One might ask whether those languages completely ignore this filter, or whether they obey it at another level of syntactic representation, namely, Logical Form (LF). Following a long tradition, we assume the existence of WH-movement in the LF component.[9] A WH that was not already raised in the syntax moves in LF to the COMP where it takes scope. Under our assumptions, the S-structure and LF representations of (26) are as shown in (27a) and (27b), respectively.

(26) I wonder who saw what

(27) a. I wonder $[_{S'}[_{COMP}$ who$_1]$ $[_S$ t_1 saw what$_2]]$
     b. I wonder $[_{S'}[_{COMP}$ what$_2$ $[_{COMP}$ who$_1]]$ $[_S$ t_1 saw $t_2]]$

(27b) results from the LF adjunction of *what* to the embedded COMP. Given that there is only one position in COMP, adjunction is the only available option in this case.

Whereas some WH-movement happens in LF in English, all WH-movement happens in that component in Japanese. Thus, (28a) and (29a) have roughly the LF representations shown in (28b) and (29b).

(28) a. John-wa doko-ni ikimasita ka
        Johm-top where-to went   Q
        'where did John go'
     b. $[_{S'}[_S$ John-wa t_1-ni ikimasita] $[_{COMP}$ doko$_1]]$

(29) a. John-ga $[_{S'}$ Mary-ga   doko-ni itta ka] siritagatte iru koto
        John-nom   Mary-nom where-to went Q   want-to-know fact
        'the fact that John wants to know where Mary went'
     b. John-ga $[_{S'}[_S$ Mary-ga t_1-ni itta] $[_{COMP}$ doko$_1]]$ siritagatte iru koto

Similarly, the Chinese sentences (30a) and (31a), from Huang 1981/82, have the LF representations shown in (30b) nad (31b).

(30) a. ni   xihuan shei
        you like   who
     b. $[_{S'}[_{COMP}$ shei$_1]$ $[_S$ ni xihuan $t_1]]$

(31) a. wo xiang-zhidao $[_{S'}[_S$ Lisi mai-le sheme]]
        I   wonder   Lisi bought what
     b. $[_S$ wo xiang-zhidao $[_{S'}[_{COMP}$ sheme$_1]$ $[_S$ Lisi mai-le $t_1]]]$

The principle assumed here can be stated as follows:

(32) All WHs are in COMP at LF.

However, it is clearly not the case that a WH in situ can move to any COMP in LF. For example, as noted by Chomsky (1973), a WH in situ in English can move only to a COMP that already contains a WH. Thus, (33a) can have the LF representation in (33b), but not the one in (33c).

(33) a. John knows $[_{S'}[_{COMP}$ who$_1]$ $[_S$ t_1 bought what$_2]]$
    b. John knows $[_{S'}[_{COMP}$ what$_2$ who$_1]$ $[_S$ t_1 bought $t_2]]$
    c. $[_{S'}[_{COMP}$ what$_2]$ $[_S$ John knows $[_{S'}[_{COMP}$ who$_1]$ $[_S$ t_1 bought $t_2]]]]$

That is, (33a) must be an embedded double question, as in (34a), and not a matrix question plus embedded question, as in (34b).

(34) a. John knows [for which person x, and for which thing y] x bought y
    b. [for which thing y] John knows [for which person x] x bought y

This fact indicates that (32) should be strengthened as follows:

(35) All WHs must be in a [+WH] COMP at LF.   (= L&S's (186))

Given (35), *what* in (33a) cannot move to the matrix COMP at LF. Since the matrix COMP does not have a WH-phrase as its head at S-structure, it must be [−WH] by (13). Hence, by (35), no WH-phrase can be in this COMP at LF.[10]

Evidence for (35) can also be found in languages without syntactic WH-movement. Consider the following Japanese example:[11]

(36) John-ga $[_{S'}[_S$ dare-ga $[_{S'}[_S$ Mary-ga nani-o katta] $[_{COMP}$ to]]
    John-nom   who-nom   Mary-nom what-acc bought [−WH]
    omotteiru] $[_{COMP}$ ka]] siritagatteiru (koto)
    think   [+WH] Q   want-to-know fact
    Lit. 'the fact that John wants to know who thinks that Mary bought what'

Without (35), *nani* could move in LF either to the most deeply embedded COMP or to the COMP containing *ka* in LF. However, this example is not ambiguous. It can have the interpretation in (37a), but not the one in (37b).

(37) a. the fact that John wants to know [for which person x and for which thing y] x thinks that Mary bought y
    b. the fact that John wants to know [for which person x] x thinks [for which thing y] Mary bought y

This indicates that *nani* in (36) can move to the COMP containing *ka*, but not to the most deeply embedded COMP, as correctly predicted by

(35). Given that (35) applies to languages with or without syntactic WH-movement, the filter (14) will be satisfied by both types of languages at LF. (14), repeated here as (38), states that a [−WH] COMP cannot be headed by a WH-phrase.

(38) A [−WH] COMP must not have a [+WH] head.

This filter is automatically satisfied at LF, since (35) implies that no WH can be in a [−WH] COMP at LF.

Let us now return to our original question, that is, whether the filter in (13), repeated here as (39), applies universally at LF or not.

(39) A [+WH] COMP must have a [+WH] head.

This filter is satisfied at S-structure in English either by WH-movement, as in (40a), or by a base-generated [+WH], as in (40b).[12]

(40) a. I wonder [$_{S'}$ [$_{COMP}$ what$_1$] [$_S$ Mary saw t_1]]
$\qquad\qquad$ [+WH]

$\quad$ b. I wonder [$_{S'}$ [$_{COMP}$ whether] [$_S$ Mary saw Bill]]
$\qquad\qquad$ [+WH]

And it rules out examples such as (41), in which a [+WH] COMP contains no WH.

(41) *I wonder [$_{S'}$ [$_{COMP}$ (that)] [$_S$ Mary saw Bill]]
$\qquad\qquad$ [+WH]

The Japanese counterpart of *whether*, *ka dooka*, can be base-generated in COMP as shown in (42).

(42) John-wa [$_{S'}$ [$_S$ Mary-ga $\quad$ kuru] [$_{COMP}$ ka dooka]] siritagatte iru
$\qquad$ John-top $\quad$ Mary-nom come [+WH] whether $\quad$ want-to-know
$\qquad$ 'John wants to know whether Mary is coming'

Ka dooka has a short form *ka*, which is to be distinguished from the pure question marker *ka*. Thus, we can freely substitute *ka* for *ka dooka* in (42) without changing the status of the example. On the other hand, *ka*, when it is not interpreted as 'whether', must mark scope for a WH-phrase. Consider the following examples:

(43) a. John-ga $\quad$ [$_{S'}$ [$_S$ Mary-ga $\quad$ nani-o $\quad$ katta] [$_{COMP}$ ka]]
$\qquad$ John-nom $\quad\quad$ Mary-nom what-acc bought [+WH] Q
$\qquad$ siritagatte iru koto
$\qquad$ want-to-know fact
$\qquad$ 'the fact that John wants to know what Mary bought'

$\quad$ b. John-ga $\quad$ [$_{S'}$ [$_S$ Mary-ga $\quad$ sono hon-o $\quad$ katta] [$_{COMP}$ ka]]
$\qquad$ John-nom $\quad\quad$ Mary-nom that book-acc bought [+WH] Q
$\qquad$ siritagatte iru $\quad$ koto

want-to-know fact
'the fact that John wants to know whether Mary bought that
book'

In (43a), *ka* as a question marker marks the scope of *nani*, whereas in
(43b), *ka* must be understood as a short form of *ka dooka*. In our terms, *ka*
in (43) indicates that the COMP is [+WH]. Hence, a WH-phrase must
move into the COMP, as in (43a), or *ka* must itself be a WH-item *whether*,
as in (43b).

If the above description of [+WH] COMPs in Japanese is correct, then
they seem to be subject to the filter in (39) at LF. A [+WH] COMP
must contain a lexical item corresponding to *whether* or must contain a
WH-phrase at LF. Thus, we conclude that languages without syntactic
WH-movement are subject to (39) at LF, exactly as languages with
WH-movement are subject to this filter at S-structure.

(39) applying at S-structure distinguishes between languages with and
without syntactic WH-movement. The next question is whether (39) applying at LF also makes such a distinction, that is, whether (39) applies at
LF only in those languages without syntactic WH-movement. The answer
appears to be negative. That is, there is evidence that (39) must hold at LF
even in English. Consider the following example:

(44) who_1 [$_S$ t_1 knows [$_{S'}$ who_2 [$_S$ John saw t_2]]]

The lower COMP must be [+WH], or it will violate (38) at S-structure.
The S-structure representation (44) can be translated directly into a well-
formed LF representation, then, with who_1 taking matrix scope and who_2
taking embedded scope. There is another possibility, however. Suppose
that LF movement raises who_2 to the higher COMP, yielding (45).

(45) [$_{COMP}$ who_2 [$_{COMP}$ who_1]] [$_S$ t_1 knows [$_{S'}$ (t_2') [$_S$ John saw t_2]]]

Clearly, this possibility must be excluded. (44) cannot be a matrix double question. (39) applying at LF will give the desired result. As we
have shown, the embedded COMP, must be [+WH], hence must have a
[+WH] head. This requirement was satisfied at S-structure, yet that did
not suffice. Apparently, (45) is excluded as an LF representation for (44)
by (39).[13]

There is one further detail to be investigated before this analysis of (44)
is complete. It concerns the status of t_2' in (45). This intermediate trace
must not be [+WH], or the explanation fails. If t_2' in (45) is [+WH], then
the example satisfies (39). But in fact there is ample evidence that intermediate traces are not [+WH]. Consider (46).

(46) who$_1$ [$_S$ do you think [$_{S'}$ t_1' [$_S$ t_1 won the race]]]

There must be an intermediate trace in (46) at S-structure, or the subject trace will violate the Empty Category Principle (ECP), which demands a local antecedent for an initial trace in this configuration. (See section 1.3 for extensive discussion.) But if that intermediate trace were [+WH], then (38) would be violated at S-structure. Hence, the intermediate trace in (46) cannot be [+WH]. We can reach the same conclusion from the opposite direction as well. Consider (47).

(47) *who$_1$ [$_S$ do you wonder [$_{S'}$ t_1' [$_S$ t_1 won the race]]]

If t_1' were [+WH], it is not clear what would be violated, either at S-structure or at LF. On the other hand, if intermediate traces are [−WH], then (47) is straightforwardly ruled out by (39). Thus, the ungrammaticality of (47) once again argues that intermediate traces are not [+WH].

There is one final example to consider in this connection. As Baker (1970) observes, an example such as (48) is two ways ambiguous, rather than three.

(48) who wonders where we bought what

Obviously, (48) cannot be a matrix triple WH-question, since that would violate the LF requirement of the embedded [+WH] COMP. But (48) obeys a stricter requirement: *who* must take matrix scope and *where* must take embedded scope. The ambiguity lies solely in the scope of *what*. Thus, *where* must be prevented from undergoing LF movement. But notice that even if *where* were to raise, LF requirement (39) could apparently be satisfied if *what* were to take its place as head of the embedded COMP. To prevent this, we must guarantee that nothing other than *where* can be the head of this COMP. Suppose, then, that at S-structure, the embedded COMP receives the index of its head, *where*, via index percolation, and that an index once assigned to a category is permanent. If *what* were later to become the head of this COMP, then the result would be a category, COMP, contraindexed with its head, *what*. We assume that this is impossible.

(49) *[...Head$_j$...]$_i$, where i ≠ j. (= L&S's (76))

Thus, by (49), when a WH-phrase is the head of a COMP at S-structure, nothing else can be the head of that COMP at LF, precisely the desired result.

We demonstrated in this section that the filters (13)–(14), repeated here as (50)–(51), are crucial at S-structure in languages with syntactic WH-movement, and at LF universally.

(50) A [+WH] COMP must have a [+WH] head.

(51) A [−WH] COMP must not have a [+WH] head.

In addition, we proposed (35) and (49), repeated here as (52)–(53), as LF filters.

(52) All WHs must be in a [+WH] COMP at LF.

(53) *[...Head$_j$...]$_i$, where i ≠ j.

As far as we can tell, all of (50)–(53) apply universally at LF. On the other hand, (50)–(51) as S-structure filters are parameterized; that is, they apply at S-structure in and only in languages with syntactic WH-movement.[14] We can state this more precisely in the form of an implicational universal as in (54).

(54) If a language L has syntactic WH-movement, (50) and (51) apply at
      S-structure in L.   (See L&S (178).)

Now (50)–(54) are all universal principles, and the parameter is whether a language has syntactic WH-movement or not. This is a desirable result since evidence for the setting of this syntactic parameter is presumably readily available to the child, in the form of grammatical sentences. It is considerably less clear that LF properties will be directly available as evidence.

1.2 Constraints on Movement

So far, we have discussed syntactic and LF WH-movement in relation to its landing site—positions that a WH-phrase can, or must, move to in syntax and LF. We now turn to constraints on WH-movement itself and on the trace produced by WH-movement.

1.2.1 Constraints on Syntactic Movement

One of the widely assumed constraints on syntactic movement—or alternatively, its output—is Subjacency. Chomsky (1973, 1977a) has argued that a variety of "island" constraints can be subsumed under one general constraint prohibiting one step of movement from crossing two bounding nodes, where the bounding nodes are S and NP. In particular, violations of the WH-island constraint, (55), and the complex NP constraint, (56), both involve movement over two bounding nodes: two Ss in the former case, and one NP and one S in the latter.

(55) ??what$_1$ [$_S$ do you wonder [$_{S'}$ whether [$_S$ John saw t_1]]]

(56) ??what$_1$ [$_S$ did you read [$_{NP}$ a report [$_{S'}$ that [$_S$ John bought t_1]]]]

There seems to be parametric variation in the bounding nodes for Subjacency. (See Rizzi 1980, Sportiche 1981/82, Torrego 1984 for important discussion.) Thus, in Spanish, extraction from a WH-island is possible:

(57) que libro$_1$ no   sabes por que$_2$ te   han regalado t_1 t_2
      what book neg (you) know why   to-you have given
      'what book don't you know why they have given to you'

Note that the English translation of (57) has the usual marginal status of an example like (55). It has been proposed that those languages that allow extraction out of WH-islands have S′ and NP as bounding nodes, whereas those that obey the WH-island constraint have S and NP. (See Rizzi 1980.)

Another constraint prohibits extraction out of adjuncts.

(58) ?*which book$_1$ did John go to class [after he read t_1]

Huang (1982) groups this constraint with the subject condition and proposes a more general condition that requires an extraction domain to be properly governed (his Condition on Extraction Domain (CED)).[15] In effect, this condition allows extraction out of maximal projections that are complements, but prohibits movement out of noncomplements (i.e., subjects and adjuncts). It correctly predicts the contrast between (59) and (60), where the former is an instance of a subject condition violation.

(59) ?*who$_1$ [$_S$ did [$_{NP}$ friends of t_1] hit Bill]

(60)   who$_1$ [$_S$ did you visit [$_{NP}$ friends of t_1]]

Because the subject NP is not a complement, the movement in (59) violates the CED. As shown in (60), if the same NP that constitutes the relevant extraction domain in (59) is a complement, extraction is permitted, as predicted.[16]

Huang (1982) argues explicitly that both Subjacency and the CED are limited to the syntactic component and are not relevant to the LF component. The following examples indicate that LF WH-movement exhibits neither Subjacency effects nor CED effects.[17]

(61) [$_{S'}$ who$_1$ [$_S$ t_1 wonders [$_{S'}$ whether [$_S$ John saw what]]]]

(62) [$_{S'}$ who$_1$ [$_S$ t_1 read [$_{NP}$ a report [$_{S'}$ that [$_S$ John bought what]]]]]

(Compare (61), (62) with (55), (56), respectively.)

(63) [$_{S'}$ who$_1$ [$_S$ t_1 went to class [$_{S'}$ after [$_S$ he read which book]]]]

(64) $[_{S'}$ who$_1$ $[_S$ t_1 said $[_{S'}$ that $[_S[_{NP}$ friends of who] hit Bill]]]]

(Compare (63), (64) with (58), (59), respectively.)

Following Huang, we will assume that Subjacency and the CED are operative only in the syntactic component.

If our assumption is correct, then as Huang (1982) argues, WH-movement in languages without syntactic WH-movement should not be constrained by Subjacency or the CED. The grammaticality of Japanese examples such as the following indicates that this prediction is borne out:[18]

(65) $[_{S'}[_S$ John-wa $[_{NP}$ nani-o   katta   hito]-o   sagasite iru no]
       John-top   what-acc bought person-acc looking-for
    Lit. 'John is looking for the person who bought what'

(66) $[_{S'}[_S$ John-wa [dono hon-o   yonde kara] dekaketa] no]
       John-top which book-acc read   after went-out
    Lit. 'John went out after he read which book'

It has more recently been suggested that LF WH-movement in Japanese in fact obeys Subjacency and that in examples such as (65), the whole complex NP containing *nani* moves to COMP in LF. (See Nishigauchi 1986 and Choe 1987, among others.) As far as we can tell, even if this pied-piping analysis turns out to be correct, it does not affect the specific proposals made in subsequent chapters, although it provides alternative analyses for some of the examples. For this reason, we will continue to assume that LF WH-movement is not subject to Subjacency, and we will postpone discussion of the pied-piping analysis until chapter 5.

1.2.2 A Preliminary Discussion of the ECP

Although LF WH-movement does not seem to be constrained by Subjacency or the CED, it is not the case that LF movement is totally unconstrained. In this section, we will briefly summarize what we may call the classical ECP analysis of some examples involving LF WH-movement. In this classical ECP analysis, some assumptions are made that are different from ours. For example, it is assumed that S' is a projection of S and that COMP is a maximal projection. The inconsistency between those assumptions and ours will disappear as we revise the ECP in subsequent sections.

Let us first consider the following contrasts noted by Huang (1981/82, 1982):[19]

(67) a.   who$_1$ t_1 saw what
     b.   *who$_1$ t_1 left why

(68) a.   why$_1$ did you buy what t_1
     b.   *what$_1$ did you buy t_1 why

Huang attributes these contrasts to the ECP. The classical formulation of this principle is shown in (69), where *proper government* and *government* are defined as in (70)–(71). (In section 1.3.2, we will show that these definitions must be modified.)

(69) A nonpronominal empty category must be properly governed.
     (Chomsky 1981)

(70) α *properly governs* β iff α governs β and
     a. α is a lexical category X^0 (lexical government), or
     b. α is coindexed with β (antecedent government).

(71) α *governs* β iff every maximal projection dominating α also dominates β and conversely. (Aoun and Sportiche 1982/83)

In addition to (69)–(71), the following COMP-indexing algorithm (from AHS) is called upon in the standard account of certain ECP effects:[20]

(72) [$_{COMP}$...X$_i$...] → [$_{COMP}$...X$_i$...]$_i$ if COMP dominates only i-indexed elements.

   Given (69)–(72), the contrasts in (67)–(68) follow immediately from the ECP, provided that this principle constrains LF representations. The LF representations of (67a–b) are as in (73a–b) respectively.

(73) a.   [$_{S'}$[$_{COMP}$ what$_2$ [$_{COMP}$ who$_1$]$_1$]$_1$ [$_S$ t_1 [$_{VP}$ saw t_2]]]
     b.   [$_{S'}$[$_{COMP}$ why$_2$ [$_{COMP}$ who$_1$]$_1$]$_1$ [$_S$ t_1 [$_{VP}$ left] t_2]]

Let us first consider (73a). Since the COMP contains only *who* at S-structure, it receives the index *1* at that level by COMP indexing. In LF, *what* is adjoined to the COMP by LF WH-movement. The trace of *what*, t_2, is properly (lexically) governed by the verb, *saw*, and thus satisfies the ECP. The other trace, t_1, is properly (antecedent-) governed by COMP, which governs the trace, S not being a maximal projection, and has the same index as the trace. Hence, no trace in (73a) violates the ECP. Let us now turn to (73b). The COMP has the index *1* because *who* is the only WH in that COMP at S-structure. The other WH, *why*, is adjoined to the COMP in LF. The trace of *who*, t_1, is properly (antecedent-) governed by the COMP. However, the trace of *why*, t_2, is not properly governed. It is not lexically governed by the verb, *left*, since it is outside the maximal projection, VP. It is not antecedent-governed by *why*, because, as noted above, we are assuming here that COMP is a maximal projection. It is not antecedent-governed by the COMP, because it does not have the same index as the COMP. Hence, t_2 is not properly governed, and the example violates the ECP.

The contrast in (68) is accounted for similarly. The LF representations of (68a–b) are as in (74a–b) respectively.

(74) a. $[_{S'}[_{COMP} \text{what}_2 [_{COMP} \text{why}_1]_1]_1 [_S \text{you} [_{VP} \text{bought } t_2\, t_1]]$
     b. $[_{S'}[_{COMP} \text{why}_2 [_{COMP} \text{what}_1]_1]_1 [_S \text{you} [_{VP} \text{bought } t_1\, t_2]]$

The trace of *what* is properly (lexically) governed by the verb, *bought*, and satisfies the ECP in both (74a) and (74b). The trace of *why* in (74a), t_1, is properly (antecedent-) governed by the COMP. The COMP and the trace have the same index, and the former governs the latter, S not being a maximal projection, under the assumptions considered at this point. Thus, this trace also satisfies the ECP, and (74a) is well formed. On the other hand, the trace of *why* in (74b), t_2, violates the ECP. It is neither lexically governed by the verb nor antecedent-governed by the COMP. Hence, (74b) is ruled out by the ECP.

As Huang (1982) points out, if the ECP is a constraint on LF representations, as assumed to be the case here, then WH-movement even in languages without syntactic WH-movement must be subject to this constraint. This prediction is borne out, as also noted by Huang. Consider the following Japanese examples:[21]

(75) John-wa $[_{S'}$ Mary-ga   nani-o   katta $[_{COMP}$ ka dooka]]
     John-top   Mary-nom what-acc bought   whether
     siritagatte iru no
     want-to-know
     Lit. 'what does John want to know [whether Mary bought *t*]'

(76) *John-wa $[_{S'}$ Mary-ga   naze sore-o katta $[_{COMP}$ ka dooka]]
     John-top   Mary-nom why it-acc bought   whether
     siritagatte iru no
     want-to-know
     Lit. 'why does John want to know [whether Mary bought it *t*]'

In both (75) and (76), the WH in situ moves to the matrix COMP in LF.[22] In the case of (75), the trace of *nani* is lexically governed by the embedded verb *katta*, and hence there is no ECP violation. However, in (76), the trace of *naze* is not lexically governed and hence must be antecedent-governed. The LF representation of (76) is as in (77).

(77) $[_{S'}[_S \text{John-wa} [_{S'}[_S \text{Mary-ga } t_1 [_{VP} \text{sore-o katta}]] [_{COMP} \text{ka dooka}]]$
     siritagatte iru] $[_{COMP} \text{naze}_1]_1]$

The trace in question, t_1, is not antecedent-governed by the embedded COMP, since the latter does not have the index *1*. It is not antecedent-governed by the matrix COMP, since it is clearly not governed by this COMP. Thus, t_1 is not properly governed and violates the ECP.

Huang's (1982) account of asymmetries such as those in (67)–(68) between adjuncts and complements was an extension of the traditional ECP analysis of subject-object asymmetries. In fact, as Huang observes, lexical government essentially distinguishes between complements and noncomplements. Thus, the ECP predicts an asymmetry between complements on the one hand and subjects and adjuncts on the other. The original subject-object asymmetry that led Chomsky (1979) to propose the ECP was the *that*-trace effect exhibited by syntactic WH-movement. Consider the following contrast:

(78) a. $[_{S'} \text{who}_1 [_S \text{do you think} [_{S'} \text{that} [_S \text{John} [_{VP} \text{saw } t_1]]]]]$
     b. *$[_{S'} \text{who}_1 [_S \text{do you think} [_{S'} \text{that} [_S t_1 [_{VP} \text{saw John}]]]]]$

(78a) is perfect, since the trace of *who*, t_1, is lexically governed by the verb, *saw*. On the other hand, the trace of *who* in (78b) is not lexically governed and hence requires an antecedent governor. Exactly as in the case of Japanese (77), the matrix COMP cannot be the antecedent governor, since it does not govern the trace. The embedded COMP governs the trace, but does not have the index *1*. Hence, the trace in (78b) violates the ECP.

Note that even if there is an intermediate trace in the lower COMP in (78b), as in (79), antecedent government still does not obtain.

(79) $[_{S'} \text{who}_1 [_S \text{do you think} [_{S'} [_{COMP} t_1' \text{ that}] [_S t_1 [_{VP} \text{saw John}]]]]]$

Since the presence of *that* prevents the application of COMP indexing to the lower COMP, the trace t_1 still cannot be antecedent-governed by this COMP. On the other hand, antecedent government does obtain when *that* is absent from the lower COMP. (80) is grammatical.

(80) $[_{S'} \text{who}_1 [_S \text{do you think} [_{S'} [_{COMP} t_1']_1 [_S t_1 [_{VP} \text{saw John}]]]]]$

This time, COMP indexing applies to the embedded COMP, since this COMP contains nothing but the intermediate trace t_1'. Thus, the embedded COMP has the index *1* and antecedent-governs the subject trace t_1.[23]

Another type of subject-object asymmetry that has been attributed to the ECP is shown in (81). (See Kayne 1981a, Chomsky 1981, and Jaeggli 1982.)

(81) a. who$_1$ t_1 saw what
     b. *what$_1$ did who see t_1

The traces in (81a–b) are properly governed. The trace in (81a) is antecedent governed by the COMP, and the one in (81b) is lexically governed by the verb, *see*. Thus, neither (81a) nor (81b) violates the ECP at S-structure, even if the principle applies at this level. However, the two examples diverge with respect to the proper government of traces at LF. The LF representations of (81a–b) are as in (82a–b) respectively.

(82) a. $[_{S'}[_{COMP}$ what$_2$ $[_{COMP}$ who$_1]_1]_1$ $[_S t_1$ $[_{VP}$ saw $t_2]]]$

　　 b. *$[_{S'}[_{COMP}$ who$_2$ $[_{COMP}$ what$_1]_1]_1$ $[_S t_2$ $[_{VP}$ saw $t_1]]]$

In (82a), t_1 is antecedent-governed by COMP, and t_2, the trace created by LF WH-movement, is lexically governed by the verb, *saw*. In (82b), t_1 is lexically governed by the verb *saw*. But t_2 is neither lexically governed nor antecedent-governed. In particular, it is not antecedent-governed because the COMP has index *1*, not index *2*. Hence, (82b) is ruled out by the ECP.

Note here that the offending trace t_2 in (82b) was not present at S-structure, but was created by LF WH-movement. Kayne (1981a), who first proposed the analysis of (81b) making use of the trace of *who*, argued on the basis of this fact (among others) that the relevant constraint applies to LF representations. Chomsky (1981) proposed that the relevant constraint is the ECP and hence that the ECP applies at LF. Huang's (1982) analysis of the adjunct-complement asymmetry outlined earlier was in fact based on this conclusion.

1.3   On the Nature of Proper Government

We have noted how syntactic WH-movement is constrained by Subjacency and the CED, and how both syntactic and LF WH-movement are constrained by the ECP. In this section (and the following chapter), we will present details of the analysis developed in L&S, and a precise formulation of the ECP as proposed there.

1.3.1   COMP Indexing

As mentioned earlier, AHS propose the following COMP-indexing rule to account for certain ECP effects:

(83) $[_{COMP}\dots X_i \dots] \rightarrow [_{COMP}\dots X_i \dots]_i$ if COMP dominates only i-indexed elements.

This rule makes antecedent government possible in examples such as (84).

(84) $[_{S'}[_{COMP}$ who$_1]_1$ $[_S t_1$ left]]$

Since COMP is assumed to be a maximal projection, *who* does not govern

t_1 and hence does not antecedent-govern the trace. But given (83), the COMP containing *who* is coindexed with the trace. Thus, the trace is antecedent-governed by the COMP and therefore satisfies the ECP.

Now, recall that we proposed in section 1.1 that COMP has only one position, the head position, and that COMP receives the index of its head. COMP indexing here is thus considered as an instance of a general index percolation process from a head to the node that dominates it. We will argue in this section that this is the correct way to interpret the COMP-indexing rule of AHS. That is, we will show that once we assume index percolation to COMP from its head, the COMP-indexing rule is no longer necessary, and further, that the index percolation approach makes the correct prediction for some data that have not yet been considered.

Let us first consider the examples in (85).

(85) a.   Bill wonders [$_{S'}$[$_{COMP}$ why$_1$]$_1$ [$_S$ John bought what t_1]]
       b.   *Bill wonders [$_{S'}$[$_{COMP}$ what$_1$]$_1$ [$_S$ John bought t_1 why]]

The embedded COMP in (85a) must antecedent-govern t_1 and hence must have the index *1*. It can be assigned this index by (83), since it contains only *why* at S-structure. Note that index percolation from the head does the work equally well. The COMP in (85a) is [+WH] and hence, by (50), must have a [+WH] head. This implies that *why* must be in the head position of this COMP. Thus, by index percolation, the COMP receives the index of *why*.

(85b), on the other hand, violates the ECP, since the trace of *why* in LF fails to be properly governed. This result is also obtained with index percolation. Since the embedded COMP in (85b) is [+WH], *what* must be in the head position of this COMP. Thus, by index percolation, the COMP receives the index of this WH at S-structure. If *why* adjoins to this COMP in LF, the LF representation of (85b) is as in (86).

(86)   *Bill wonders [$_{S'}$[$_{COMP}$ why$_2$ [$_{COMP}$ what$_1$]$_1$]$_1$ [$_S$ John bought t_1 t_2]]

(86) violates the ECP since t_2 is not antecedent-governed. On the other hand, the LF representation of (85b) will be as in (87) if in LF *what* adjoins to the embedded COMP and *why* moves into the head position of the COMP.

(87)   *Bill wonders [$_{S'}$[$_{COMP}$ what$_1$ [$_{COMP}$ why$_2$]$_1$]$_1$ [$_S$ John bought t_1 t_2]]

(87), like (86), is ruled out by the ECP. The trace t_2 violates this principle, since the embedded COMP, having a different index, fails to antecedent-govern it. (87) also violates the filter (53), repeated here as (88).

(88)   *[...Head$_j$...]$_i$, where i $\neq$ j.

The head of the embedded COMP, *why*, has index 2, whereas the COMP itself has index 1. Thus, index percolation makes the correct prediction for the examples in (85).

Let us next consider the Japanese example in (89).

(89) ?kimi-wa nani-o   naze sagasiteru no
     you-top what-acc why looking-for
     'why are you looking for what'

(89) is somewhat marginal for some speakers but clearly does not have the status of an ECP violation. The LF representation of this example is as in (90a) or (90b).[24]

(90) a. $[_{S'}[_S$ kimi-wa t_1-o t_2 sagasiteru] $[_{COMP}[_{COMP}$ naze$_2$] nani$_1$]]
     b. $[_{S'}[_S$ kimi-wa t_1-o t_2 sagasiteru] $[_{COMP}[_{COMP}$ nani$_1$] naze$_2$]]

Neither of the two WHs in (89) is in COMP. Thus, they both move to COMP in the LF component. If *naze* 'why' moves into the head position of COMP, the LF representation of (89) is as in (90a). Alternatively, if *nani* 'what' occupies the head position, then we obtain the LF representation in (90b). Here, if we assume the COMP-indexing rule in (83), both (90a) and (90b) are ruled out by the ECP. The COMP contains no WH at S-structure, and it contains two WHs with different indices at LF. Thus, the COMP-indexing rule does not apply, and consequently the COMP cannot be the antecedent governor for t_2, an incorrect result. On the other hand, if we assume index percolation, (90a), though not (90b), satisfies the ECP. In (90a), *naze* 'why' is in the head position of the COMP, and hence the index of this WH, 2, percolates up to the COMP. As a result, the COMP qualifies as the antecedent governor for t_2, and this trace is properly governed. Thus, with index percolation, we correctly predict that (89) does not violate the ECP.

1.3.2 Antecedent Government

In the preceding section, we left open the status of intermediate traces with respect to the ECP. We now turn to this issue.

Let us first consider (91).

(91) *who$_1$ $[_S t_1$ thinks $[_{S'}[_S$ Mary left why]]]

This example seems precisely as bad as the ECP violation (67b), repeated here as (92).

(92) *who$_1$ $[_S t_1$ left why]

Hence, if (92) is to be ruled out by the ECP, as we assume here, then the ungrammaticality of (91) should also be attributed to this principle. We

immediately get the desired result if the LF representation of (91) is as in
(93).

(93) $[_{S'}[_{COMP}$ why$_2$ $[_{COMP}$ who$_1]_1]_1$ $[_S$ t_1 thinks $[_{S'}[_S$ Mary left $t_2]]]]$

In (93), the trace t_1 is antecedent-governed by the COMP. But the trace of
why, t_2, is neither lexically governed nor antecedent-governed. The matrix
COMP cannot be the antecedent governor for t_2 since it does not govern
this trace and furthermore does not have the right index. Thus, (93) violates the ECP.

However, there is an alternative LF representation for (91) that must be
considered. Suppose that *why* moves in LF from COMP to COMP, leaving a trace in the embedded COMP. Then, the LF representation of (91) is
as in (94).

(94) $[_{S'}[_{COMP}$ why$_2$ $[_{COMP}$ who$_1]_1]_1$ $[_S$ t_1 thinks $[_{S'}[_{COMP}$ $t_2']_2$ $[_S$ Mary
    left $t_2]]]]$

Here, the initial trace of *why*, t_2, is antecedent-governed by the lower
COMP, which obtains the index of the intermediate trace by index percolation. Thus, neither the trace of *who* nor the initial trace of *why* violates
the ECP. Yet, by assumption, (94) must be ruled out by the ECP, since (91)
has the same status as (92), an ECP violation. Hence, we conclude that the
intermediate trace t_2' violates the ECP in (94). This conclusion implies the
correctness of the null hypothesis: that intermediate traces, just like initial
traces, are subject to the ECP.[25]

Note that the LF representation in (94) points to a more specific conclusion as well, namely, that an intermediate trace must be antecedent-
governed. It has been proposed (for example, in Kayne 1981b and Stowell
1981) that intermediate traces are subject to the ECP. But in those works it
is proposed at the same time that bridge verbs can govern traces in COMP.
Under such an analysis, the matrix verb *think* in (95) governs—and furthermore, properly governs—t_1'.

(95) who$_1$ $[_S$ do you think $[_{S'}$ t_1' $[_S$ t_1 left]]]

The fact that (94) must be excluded indicates either that such government
is unavailable or at least that it is not sufficient for the purpose of the ECP.
Since t_2' in (94) violates the ECP, it cannot, in particular, be properly
governed by the matrix verb, *think*. And given that *think* cannot properly
govern the intermediate trace in (94), we conclude that such proper government is impossible in (95) as well.

Now, compare (94) with the grammatical structure (96).

(96) $[_{S'}$ why$_1$ $[_S$ do you $[_{VP}$ think $[_{S'}$ t_1' $[_S$ Mary left $t_1]]]]]$

Here, as in (94), the initial trace of *why*, t_1, is antecedent-governed by the embedded COMP. In addition, the intermediate trace, t_1', must be properly governed in (96) since the example is grammatical. But this trace is not properly governed by the matrix verb, *think*. If such proper government were possible, (94) would be well formed. The difference between (94) and (96) with respect to the intermediate trace is that only in the latter is the trace coindexed with the matrix COMP. Thus, we conclude that t_1' in (96) is antecedent governed by the matrix COMP, despite the fact that the latter does not govern the former. Such antecedent government is impossible in (94) since the matrix COMP and the trace do not have the same index.

The well-formedness of (96), as opposed to (94), thus indicates that government is not a necessary condition for antecedent government. We concluded that the intermediate trace in (96) is antecedent-governed by the matrix COMP, since it is subject to the ECP and cannot satisfy this principle by virtue of lexical government by the matrix verb. Hence, contrary to the definition in (70), VP is not a barrier to antecedent government, despite the fact that it is a maximal projection.[26] More precisely, antecedent government must be allowed in the following configuration:

(97) $[_{S'} \alpha_i [_S \ldots [_{VP} \ldots [_{S'} t_i [_S \ldots]]]]]$ (order irrelevant)

However, this does not mean that any maximal projection is transparent to antecedent government. Discussing example (98) (= (78b)), we have already noted that antecedent government is blocked in the configuration in (99).

(98) $^*[_{S'}[_{COMP} who_1]_1 [_S do you think [_{S'} that [_S t_1 saw John]]]]$

(99) $[_{S'} \alpha_i [_S \ldots [_{S'} \ldots [_S \ldots t_i \ldots]]]]$ (order irrelevant)

If t_1 could be antecedent-governed by the matrix COMP in (98), then this example would not be ruled out by the ECP. The point made here is in accord with our discussion of the Japanese example (76), repeated here as (100a).

(100) a. *John-wa $[_{S'}$ Mary-ga   naze sore-o katta $[_{COMP}$ ka dooka]]
          John-top   Mary-nom why it-acc bought   whether
          siritagatte iru no
          want-to-know
          Lit. 'why does John want to know [whether Mary bought it *t*]'
     b. $[_{S'}[_S$ John-wa $[_{S'}[_S$ Mary-ga t_1 sore-o katta $[_{COMP}$ ka dooka]]
        siritagatte iru] $[_{COMP}$ naze$_1]_1]$

The LF representation (100b) is ruled out by the ECP, since the matrix

COMP fails to antecedent-govern t_1. And (100b) has exactly the configuration in (99) in relevant respects. It seems that an $[_{S'}[_S$ sequence constitutes a barrier for antecedent government.

In addition, the following contrast indicates that a complex NP also constitutes a barrier to antecedent government:

(101) a. ??what$_1$ do you believe $[_{NP}$ the claim $[_{S'}$ that John bought $t_1]]$
       b. *why$_1$ do you believe $[_{NP}$ the claim $[_{S'}$ that John left $t_1]]$

Both (101a) and (101b) violate Subjacency, but the latter is much worse than the former. This contrast is typical of the adjunct-complement asymmetry due to the ECP, indicating that antecedent government, which is necessary in (101b), fails to obtain.

In this case also, a similar contrast can be found in Japanese:

(102) a. Mary-wa $[_{NP}[_{S'}[_S$ John-ga   nani-o   nusunda]] koto]-o
           Mary-top   John-nom what-acc stole   fact-acc
           mondai-ni siteru no
           problem-to make
           Lit. 'what is Mary making an issue out of the fact that
           [John stole t]'
       b. *Mary-wa $[_{NP}[_{S'}[_S$ John-ga   naze sore-o nusunda]] koto]-o
           Mary-top   John-nom why it-acc stole   fact-acc
           mondai-ni siteru no
           problem-to make
           Lit. 'why is Mary making an issue out of the fact that
           [John stole it t]'

In both (102a) and (102b), the WH moves to the matrix COMP in LF. (102a) is grammatical since LF WH-movement is not subject to Subjacency, and the trace of *nani* 'what' satisfies the ECP by virtue of lexical government at LF. The LF movement of *naze* 'why' in (102b), on the other hand, results in an ECP violation. If *naze* moves from COMP to COMP in LF, the LF representation of (102b) is as in (103).

(103) $[_{S'}[_S$ Mary-wa $[_{NP}[_{S'}[_S$ John-ga t_1 sore-o nusunda] $t_1']$ koto]-o
       mondai-ni siteru] naze$_1]$

(103) is straightforwardly ruled out by the ECP, if (complex) NPs are barriers to antecedent government. Then, the intermediate trace t_1' fails to be antecedent-governed by the matrix COMP and thus violates the ECP.

The well-formed configuration in (97), repeated here as (104), indicates that neither S nor VP is a barrier to antecedent government.

(104) $[_{S'} \alpha_i [_S \ldots [_{VP} \ldots [_{S'} t_i [_S \ldots]]]]]$ (order irrelevant)

On the other hand, the ill-formed configurations, instantiated by (98) and (103), have the following structures:

(105) a. $[_{S'} \alpha_i [_S \ldots [_{VP} \ldots [_{S'} \ldots [_S \ldots t_i \ldots]]]]]$ (order irrelevant)

     b. $[_{S'} \alpha_i [_S \ldots [_{VP} \ldots [_{NP} \ldots [_{S'} t_i [_S \ldots]]]]]]$ (order irrelevant)

Thus, if we assume that NP is a barrier to antecedent government, and also that S' is a barrier for traces that are not in the COMP immediately dominated by the S', the distinction between (104) and (105) follows. Given that S and VP are not barriers to antecedent government, the trace in (104) is antecedent-governed, since it is in the COMP immediately dominated by the S'. On the other hand, the traces in (105) are not antecedent-governed. The embedded S' blocks antecedent government in (105a), since the trace is not in the COMP immediately dominated by that S'. In (105b), antecedent government is blocked by the NP. Thus, the ungrammatical examples (98), (100a), (101b), and (102b) are correctly ruled out by the ECP.

Why is S' not a barrier to antecedent government for a trace that is in the COMP immediately dominated by it? Recall that we have been provisionally assuming, contrary to the discussion in section 1.1, that S' is a projection of S. We made this assumption because government is a necessary condition for antecedent government in the classical definition of proper government given in (70). An S node clearly does not block antecedent government, for otherwise (106) would violate the ECP.

(106) $[_{S'} who_1 [_S t_1 left]]$

Given the definition of proper government in (70), this implies that S is not a barrier to government, which in turn implies that S is not a maximal projection. Hence, we have been led to the assumption that S' is a projection of S. However, we argued above that VP is not a barrier to antecedent government and hence that—contrary to (70)—government is *not* a necessary condition for antecedent government. This conclusion enables us to maintain that S is a maximal projection and yet is not a barrier to antecedent government. And it enables us to readopt our assumption in section 1.1 that COMP is the head of S'.

Once we assume that COMP is the head of S', there is a straightforward account of the fact that S' is not a barrier to antecedent government in (104). Kayne (1980), Belletti and Rizzi (1981), and Stowell (1981), among others, argue that a head can be governed from outside its maximal projection. Elliott (1982), in particular, argues that this is the case for antecedent government as well. We can now adopt this assumption for antecedent government and maintain that the embedded S' is not a barrier to antecedent government in (104) because the trace is in the head position of the

S'.[27] Thus, we formulated the definition of *antecedent government* in L&S essentially as follows:[28]

(107) α *antecedent-governs* β if
   a. α binds β, and
   b. there is no γ (γ an NP or S') such that α c-commands γ and γ dominates β, unless β is the head of γ.

By (107), NP and S' are absolute barriers to antecedent government in the sense that only the head is accessible to such government from without.

Assuming the discussion above, let us once again consider (67b), repeated here as (108) with its LF representation in (109).

(108) *who$_1$ t_1 left why

(109) *[$_{S'}$ [$_{COMP}$ why$_2$ [$_{COMP}$ who$_1$]$_1$]$_1$ [$_S$ t_1 left t_2]]

Neither t_1 nor t_2 is lexically governed in (109). But t_1 is antecedent-governed by the COMP. The COMP now does not govern t_1 since S is a maximal projection. But that does not matter at this point since only NP and S' are barriers to *antecedent* government. On the other hand, t_2 is not antecedent-governed. It is not antecedent-governed by the COMP because they are not coindexed. In the classical ECP analysis of (108) discussed above, t_2 is not antecedent-governed by *why* because COMP is a maximal projection and blocks government of this trace by the WH. This analysis can no longer be maintained here, since according to our assumptions, S' is a projection of COMP, and hence, COMP is not a maximal projection. Given (107), *why* fails to antecedent-govern t_2 not because it does not govern the trace (even though it does not) but because it does not bind it. This is so because, being adjoined to COMP, *why* does not c-command the trace.[29] Thus, (107) correctly excludes (108) as an ECP violation.

1.3.3 Lexical Government

Definition (107) was proposed as a revision of part of the standard definition of proper government shown above in (70)–(71) and repeated here as (110)–(111).

(110) α *properly governs* β if α governs β and
   a. α is a lexical category X^0 (lexical government), or
   b. α is coindexed with β (antecedent government).
   (See Chomsky 1981, Aoun and Sportiche 1982/83.)

(111) α *governs* β if every maximal projection dominating α also dominates β and conversely. (Aoun and Sportiche 1982/83)

As mentioned above, in the standard definition, the relation "proper government" is defined on the basis of the relation "government." Both "lexical government" and "antecedent government" are subcases of the relation "government." On the other hand, in (107) the relation "antecedent government" is not a subcase of "government," and is more similar to "Subjacency" than to "government." Also as mentioned above, antecedent government into a WH-island or complex NP from without is blocked by (107). On the other hand, S and VP, despite the fact that they are maximal projections, are not barriers to antecedent government. So far, our discussion has centered around the relation "antecedent government," since this was the relation relevant to our crucial examples. In what follows, we will briefly discuss "lexical government" and, more generally, the relations "government" and "proper government."

We have tacitly accepted (110a) and (111) as the definition of lexical government. However, all of our examples involved simply the core case of lexical government, namely, the relation between a head and its complement. As is well known, the definition encompasses additional cases as well. First consider raising, as in (112).

(112) $[_S \text{John}_1 \, [_{VP} \text{seems} \, [_S t_1 \text{ to be intelligent}]]]$

On the standard account, t_1 in (112) satisfies the requirements for lexical government given in (110a) and (111). This is so since S'-deletion is operative here and S is assumed not to be a barrier to government.[30] Thus, the X^0, *seems*, governs t_1 and hence properly governs it.

Note that under our formulation of antecedent government in (107), t_1 is also antecedent-governed. *John* (and the matrix INFL) bind t_1, and there is no NP or S' containing t_1 and c-commanded by *John* (or INFL). At this point, we want to raise the question of whether t_1 in (112) should in fact be properly governed in both ways. In particular, we will question whether t_1 is lexically governed.

Recall from our earlier discussion that *why* in situ in English is always ungrammatical. For a wide range of cases, we showed how this follows from the ECP. For (113), repeated from (91), even if *why* moves from COMP to COMP in LF, the intermediate trace violates the ECP, as shown in (114).

(113) *who thinks Mary left why

(114) $[_{S'} [_{COMP} \text{why}_2 \, [_{COMP} \text{who}_1]_1]_1 \, [_S t_1 \text{ thinks} \, [_{S'} [_{COMP} t_2']_2$
$[_S \text{Mary left } t_2]]]]$

The matrix COMP could not antecedent-govern t_2' since the index of that COMP is *1*. Thus, the ungrammaticality of (113) is accounted for. But now consider (115), with the LF representation (116).

(115) *who believes Mary to have left why

(116) $[_{S'}[_{COMP}$ why$_2$ $[_{COMP}$ who$_1]_1]_1$ $[_S$ t_1 believes $[_S$ Mary to have left $t_2]]]$

Again, t_2 cannot be antecedent-governed, since the matrix COMP does not have the index 2. But by the definitions in (110) and (111), this trace can be lexically governed. *Believe* is an X^0, and it is separated from t_2 only by S. Thus, (116) seemingly violates nothing, an incorrect result since (115) is ungrammatical. We conclude that lexical government must be blocked in the configuration in (116). Suppose that θ-role assignment is a necessary condition for lexical government, an idea originally proposed by Stowell (1981). Then, (116) will be correctly excluded, since clearly there is no θ-relation between *believe* and the trace of *why*.

As noted in L&S (fn. 56), one further consequence of this proposal is that so-called super-raising, as in (117), is excluded by the ECP.

(117) *John$_1$ seems $[_{S'}$ that $[_S$ it is likely $[_S$ t_1 to win]]]$

The trace t_1 is not antecedent-governed since it is separated from its nearest binder *John* (or the INFL associated with *John*) by an S'. Further, by the hypothesis now under consideration, t_1 is not lexically governed either, since *likely* assigns no θ-role to the trace of *John*. Now, the contrast between (112) and (117) is attributed to the ECP. In neither example is the trace t_1 lexically governed. Antecedent government obtains for t_1 in (112), but not for t_1 in (117). Hence, the latter, and only the latter, violates the ECP. This is clearly a desirable conclusion. Although the derivation that would give rise to (117) is excluded by Subjacency as well (since the movement of *John* from the position of t_1 crosses two Ss), (117) is far worse than a simple island violation.[31] Given the formulation of the binding conditions in Chomsky 1981, (117) does not count as a Condition A violation either. The governing category for t_1 is the matrix clause, since *it* and AGR in the intermediate clause, being coindexed with the embedded infinitival clause, are not accessible to t_1. Note that an anaphor in basically the same position as t_1 in (117) can at least marginally have as its binder an NP in the position of *John* in (117):

(118) ??the men believe that it is important for each other to succeed

The contrast between (117) and (118) confirms Chomsky's claim that (117) should not be handled by Condition A.

There is one difficulty with the proposal that lexical government crucially involves θ-marking. Although the proposal allows us to account for adjunct traces as in (114) and super-raising traces as in (117), this limitation on lexical government seems too strong in certain circumstances involving exceptional Case marking (ECM). Consider (119).

(119) ??[$_{S'}$ who$_1$ [$_S$ do you know [$_{S'}$ whether [$_S$ John believes [$_S$ t_1 to have
        won]]]]]

(119) is marginal, being a Subjacency violation, but does not have the
status of an ECP violation. The trace t_1 is not antecedent-governed,
being separated from the matrix COMP by an S'. Hence, if lexical government requires θ-marking, t_1 is not properly governed at all, since it has no
θ-relation to the verb, *believes*, evidently an incorrect result.

    (120) is a similar example, discussed in Chomsky 1982 and then in L&S.
In this instance, the issue is proper government of the parasitic gap.

(120) someone who John expected *t* to be successful though believing *e*
        to be incompetent

The grammaticality of (120) indicates that in this example, as in (119), an
ECM verb is serving as a lexical governor. Note the sharp contrast between (120) and (121).

(121) *someone who John expected *t* would be successful though
        believing that *e* is incompetent

In (121), there is no way that the parasitic gap can satisfy the ECP by
virtue of lexical government, since there is no way that it can be governed
by *believing*.[32] How then can lexical government be formulated to accommodate these patterns? Apparently, "exceptional" lexical government
does exist but, crucially, only in instances of exceptional Case marking.
Thus, lexical government obtains when, and only when, there is a specific
relationship between the governor and the governee, namely, the relation
of either θ-role assignment or Case assignment.

    The conclusion we have arrived at places even stricter conditions on
lexical government than the standard definition in (110a) and (111). Given
the fact that the locality condition on antecedent government is relaxed in
(107), it appears that the two forms of proper government are separated
even further. Although this is not necessarily a conceptually attractive
result, the definitions of proper government that we arrived at seem to be
well motivated empirically. Hence, we will assume that there are in fact
two quite distinct forms of proper government.

    It should be noted here, however, that there are ways to unite the two
forms of proper government, at least technically. One way to achieve such
unification would be to take the definition of antecedent government as
the basic one and to revise the definition of lexical government accordingly. A possibility in this direction is suggested by Saito (1984), who
basically follows the approach proposed by Stowell (1981). Note first that
lexical government is now defined as follows:

(122) α *lexically governs* β if

    a. α governs β,

    b. α is a lexical category, X^0 ($X = [\pm N, \pm V]$), and

    c. α assigns Case or a θ-role to β.

Since Case and θ-roles are assigned under government, whenever (c) is satisfied, (a) must also be satisfied. Thus, (a) is redundant in (122). Clause (b) also seems to follow from (c) to a large extent. If we take "θ-role assignment" in (c) to be "direct θ-role assignment," as seems reasonable, then α must be an X^0 to satisfy (c). Thus, (b) reduces to the condition that α must be $[\pm N, \pm V]$; that is, α cannot be INFL. Following Huang (1982) and Pesetsky (1982), let us assume the structure in (123) for S. Then the peculiarity of INFL is that it can assign Case to the subject NP (when it is [+AGR]), even though it does not c-command this NP.

(123)   S (= I″)

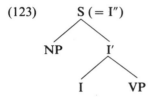

Thus, it is possible that what is important in clause (b) of (122) is not that α is not INFL, but that α c-commands β. Since all Case assigners and direct θ-role assigners c-command their assignees, with the exception of INFL, (122) can now be restated as in (124).

(124) α *lexically governs* β if

    a. α c-commands β, and

    b. α assigns Case or a θ-role to β.

As noted above, (124b) implies that α governs β. Thus, we can add the much weaker locality requirement in (107b) to (124) vacuously without affecting the definition. And if, in addition, we assume, following Stowell (1981), that θ-role assignment (and Case assignment) results in coindexation between the assigner and the assignee, then we can substitute *bind* for *c-command* in (124a) and eliminate (124b). These considerations suggest (125) as a possible redefinition of *lexical government*.

(125) α *lexically governs* β if

    a. α binds β, and

    b. there is no γ (γ an NP or S′) such that α c-commands γ and γ dominates β, unless β is the head of γ.

Now, the definitions of *antecedent government* and *lexical government* are identical. Thus, *proper government* can be defined simply as follows:

(126) α *properly governs* β if
    a. α binds β, and
    b. there is no γ (γ an NP or S′) such that α c-commands γ and
       γ dominates β, unless β is the head of γ.

If this unification of lexical government and antecedent government is correct, then "proper government" is totally independent of the notion "government." We have already proposed that "antecedent government" is independent of "government." (126) implies that, more generally, the locality requirement for "proper government" is similar to Subjacency, and is independent of "government."

We have shown one possible way to unify antecedent government and lexical government, by taking the definition of *antecedent government* in (107) as given and making the definition of lexical government similar to it. This unification still relies on a technical device at this point, and whether it can be made principled remains to be seen. Another approach might be to reintroduce a strict locality requirement on antecedent government, by reconsidering the nature of movement operations. This approach is pursued by Chomsky (1986a), who attempts a principled reunification of antecedent government and government under a strict locality condition and proposes further that the same locality is required for Subjacency. We will discuss these proposals in detail in chapter 3.

1.4 Antecedent Government and Long-Distance Movement of Adjuncts

Let us now return to the definition of *antecedent government* in (107), repeated here as (127), and examine in more detail the predictions it makes about long-distance movement of adjuncts in a variety of languages.

(127) α *antecedent-governs* β if
    a. α binds β, and
    b. there is no γ (γ an NP or S′) such that α c-commands γ and
       γ dominates β, unless β is the head of γ.

We have shown that the initial trace of an adjunct must be antecedent-governed by the nearest COMP. Thus, t_1 in (128) satisfies the ECP, but t_1 in (129) does not.

(128) a. $[_{S'}[_{COMP} \text{why}_1]_1 [_S \text{did John leave } t_1]]$
    b. $[_{S'}[_{COMP} \text{why}_1]_1 [_S \text{do you think } [_{S'}[_{COMP} t_1']_1 [_S \text{John left } t_1]]]]$

(129) $*[_{S'}[_{COMP} \text{why}_1]_1 [_S \text{do you wonder } [_{S'}[_{COMP} \text{whether}] [_S \text{John left } t_1]]]]$

The antecedent government of the initial adjunct traces in (128) is permitted by (127). But t_1 in (129) is not antecedent-governed, according to
(127), and hence violates the ECP. Further, we have shown that an intermediate trace of an adjunct must also be antecedent-governed. (91), which
shows this point, is repeated here as (130a) with its LF representation in
(130b).

(130) a. *who$_1$ [$_S$ t_1 thinks [$_{S'}$ [$_S$ Mary left why]]]
      b. *[$_{S'}$ [$_{COMP}$ why$_2$ [$_{COMP}$ who$_1$]$_1$]$_1$ [$_S$ t_1 thinks [$_{S'}$ [$_{COMP}$ t_2']$_2$
         [$_S$ Mary left t_2]]]]]

(127) correctly distinguishes between (128b) and (130b). In the former
case, antecedent government of the intermediate trace is permitted since
the embedded S' does not constitute a barrier for that trace, given head
accessibility. On the other hand, the intermediate trace in (130b) is not
antecedent-governed, since neither the matrix COMP nor *why* binds this
trace.

The configuration in (128b) also occurs in (131), taken from Huang
1982:534.

(131) [ni   renwei [ta weisheme meiyou lai]]
       you think he why   not   come
      'why do you think [he didn't come *t*]'

The LF representation of (131) is (132).

(132) [$_{S'}$ [$_{COMP}$ weisheme$_1$] [$_S$ ni renwei [$_{S'}$ [$_{COMP}$ t_1']$_1$ [$_S$ ta t_1 meiyou lai]]]]]

As usual, t_1 is antecedent-governed by the lower COMP. The trace in that
COMP, t_1', being in head position, is in turn antecedent-governed by the
matrix COMP.

Note that if t_1 in (132) is to satisfy the ECP, it is crucial that the lower
COMP have index 1, that is, that it be headed by an intermediate trace.[33]
If this COMP were not coindexed with t_1, proper government would fail,
as shown by (133), which is discussed by Huang (1982) in relation to the
ECP.

(133) ni   xiang-xhidao [Lisi weisheme mai-le sheme]
       you wonder   Lisi why   bought what

One of the WH-phrases in (133) must be in the embedded COMP at LF
because the COMP is [+WH]. A priori, it might be expected that the other
WH-phrase, either *weisheme* or *sheme*, could move to the matrix COMP in
LF. These two possibilities are presented in (134) and (135), which would
correspond to the readings indicated.

(134) $[_{S'} [_{COMP} \text{sheme}_1]_1 [_S \text{ni xiang-zhidao} [_{S'} [_{COMP} \text{weisheme}_2]_2$
$[_S \text{Lisi } t_2 \text{ mai-le } t_1]]]]$
'what is the thing x such that you wonder why Lisi bought x'

(135) $[_{S'} [_{COMP} \text{weisheme}_2]_2 [_S \text{ni xiang-zhidao} [_{S'} [_{COMP} \text{sheme}_1]_1$
$[_S \text{Lisi } t_2 \text{ mai-le } t_1]]]]$
'what is the reason x such that you wonder what Lisi bought for x,

But although (133) has the interpretation in (134), it lacks the interpretation in (135). And in fact, (134) is perfectly well formed, but (135) is ill formed. In (135), the matrix COMP cannot antecedent-govern t_2, by (127). Thus, once again we have evidence that the trace of an adjunct must be antecedent-governed. In (134), this requirement is satisfied by the lower COMP.

The contrast between (134) and (135) illustrates Huang's important observation that LF movement of adjuncts conforms, in effect, to the WH-island constraint. Such conformity is also found in the case of WH-islands headed by *whether*. (136) illustrates a simple *whether* construction, from Huang 1981/82: 387.

(136) wo xiang-zhidao [ta xi-bu-xihuan   ni]
       I   wonder   he whether-or-not-like you
       'I wonder whether he likes you or not'

Huang argues that a construction such as (136) contains an "A-not-A" operator that moves to COMP at LF, as in (137).

(137) $[_S \text{wo xiang-zhidao} [_{S'} [_{COMP} \text{"A-not-A"}_1]_1 [_S \text{ta } t_1 \text{ xihuan ni}]]]$

The "A-not-A" operator in COMP occupies the head position of COMP and is interpreted as 'whether'.

Huang points out that this "A-not-A" operator in COMP creates an island for the LF WH-movement of adjuncts. His example (1981/82: 392) is shown in (138).

(138) *ni   xiang-zhidao [ta weisheme lai-bu-lai]
       you wonder   he why   whether-or-not-come

This example is ungrammatical, and in particular, it cannot have the LF representation shown in (139).

(139) $*[_{S'} [_{COMP} \text{weisheme}_1]_1 [_S \text{ni xiang-xhidao} [_{S'} [_{COMP} \text{"A-not-A"}_2]_2$
$[_S \text{ta } t_1 t_2 \text{ lai}]]]]$

The ill-formedness of (139) is predicted, given the definition of antecedent government in (127). The matrix COMP is the only potential antecedent governor for t_1, but it cannot be an actual one since the embedded S' blocks this relation. In short, Huang's facts and his ECP account of these facts can be maintained straightforwardly under our definition of antecedent government.

Note that Huang's ECP account of (138) predicts that complement WHs do not exhibit WH-island effects in LF. This prediction is borne out by examples such as the following:

(140) ni   xiang-xhidao [$_S$ ta xi-bu-xihuan   shei]
       you wonder   he whether-or-not-like who
       Lit. 'who do you wonder [whether he likes t]'

As suggested by the translation, this sentence can have the following LF representation:

(141) [$_{S'}$[$_{COMP}$ shei$_1$]$_1$ [$_S$ ni xiang-xhidao [$_{S'}$[$_{COMP}$ "A-not-A"$_2$]$_2$
       [$_S$ ta t_2 xihuan t_1]]]]

The trace of *shei*, t_1, is lexically governed by the verb *xihuan* and hence need not be antecedent-governed. Thus, (141), in contrast with (139), is allowed by the ECP.

The theory proposed thus far, based on (127), makes a further prediction that goes beyond the data presented by Huang (1982). Consider the following configuration:

(142) [$_{S'}$ α_1 [$_S$ ... [$_{VP}$ ... [$_{S'}$[$_{COMP}$ ...] [$_S$ ... [$_{VP}$ ... [$_{S'}$[$_{COMP}$ t_1']$_1$
       [$_S$ ... t_1 ...]]]]]]]]]

Suppose that the COMP of the intermediate S' does not have index *1*, either because it has some other index, or because it has no index. Given our assumptions, t_1 is properly governed by the lowest COMP. But recall that we have argued that intermediate traces are also subject to the ECP and in fact must be antecedent-governed. We thus predict that (142) is ill formed when α_1 is an adjunct. Jim Huang (personal communication) confirms that this prediction is correct for Chinese. Consider (143a) and (144a), with their associated LF representations (143b) and (144b).

(143) a. *[$_S$ ni   xiang-xhidao [$_{S'}$ Zhangsan xiang-bu-xiangxin
              you wonder   Zhangsan whether-or-not-believe
           [$_{S'}$ Lisi weisheme mai shu]]]
              Lisi why   buy book
           Lit. 'why$_1$ do you wonder whether Zhangsan believes
           [Lisi bought books t_1]'
       b. [$_{S'}$[$_{COMP}$ weisheme$_1$]$_1$ [$_S$ ni xiang-zhidao [$_{S'}$[$_{COMP}$ "A-not-A"$_2$]$_2$
           [$_S$ zhangsan t_2 xiangxin [$_{S'}$[$_{COMP}$ t_1']$_1$ [$_S$ Lisi t_1 mai shu]]]]]]

(144) a. *[$_S$ ni   xiang-zhidao [$_{S'}$ Zhangsan xiang-bu-xiangxin

you wonder   Zhangsan whether-or-not-believe

[$_{S'}$ Lisi weisheme buneng lai]]]

Lisi why   cannot come

Lit. 'why$_1$ do you wonder whether Zhangsan believes

[Lisi cannot come t_1]'

b.   [$_{S'}$[$_{COMP}$ weisheme$_1$]$_1$ [$_S$ ni xiang-xhidao [$_{S'}$[$_{COMP}$ "A-not-A"$_2$]$_2$

[$_S$ Zhangsan t_2 xiangxin [$_{S'}$[$_{COMP}$ t_1']$_1$ [$_S$ Lisi t_1 buneng lai]]]]]]

(143) and (144) involve "long-distance" LF movement of an adjunct and contrast with examples such as the following, which involves LF movement of a complement:

(145) a.   [$_S$ ni   xiang-zhidao [$_{S'}$ Zhangsan xiang-bu-xiangxin

you wonder   Zhangsan whether-or-not-believe

[$_{S'}$ Lisi mai sheme]]]

Lisi buy what

Lit. 'what do you wonder whether Zhangsan believes

[Lisi bought t]'

b.   [$_{S'}$[$_{COMP}$ sheme$_1$]$_1$ [$_S$ ni xiang-xhidao [$_{S'}$[$_{COMP}$ "A-not-A"$_2$]$_2$

[$_S$ Zhangsan t_2 xiangxin [$_{S'}$[$_{COMP}$] [$_S$ Lisi mai t_1]]]]]]

In (143b), the LF representation of (143a), the most deeply embedded COMP is headed by t_1' and thus has index *1*. It antecedent-governs t_1. But t_1' itself is not antecedent-governed, since its nearest binder is the matrix COMP. The COMP of the intermediate S' is not eligible to antecedent-govern t_1' because it must be headed by "A-not-A." The ungrammaticality of (143a) provides strong evidence for our claims about intermediate traces. If such traces did not have to be properly governed, (143b) would not violate anything and (143a) would be incorrectly predicted to be grammatical. Further, it is evident that an intermediate trace cannot satisfy the ECP via lexical government, for if lexical government were ever to obtain for such a trace, it would be in precisely such a configuration as (143b), with t_1' lexically governed by *xiangxin*. (144) leads us to the same conclusion.

We have now shown how (143b) constitutes an ECP violation. This nearly, but not entirely, explains the ungrammaticality of (143a). This is so because there is one more possibility to consider. Suppose there were no intermediate trace in (143b). Then, patently, the intermediate trace could not violate the ECP. However, under these circumstances, the *initial* trace would fail to be properly governed. Thus, (143a) is correctly excluded under either possibility. This same issue arises mutatis mutandis with respect to (145). (145a) is grammatical, and (145b) is a well-formed LF representation. Note, however, that if there had been a trace in the lowest COMP of (145b), that trace would not have been properly governed, exactly as in the case of (143b). The crucial difference is that no intermediate trace is needed in (145b), since the initial trace, in contrast to the one in (143b), is lexically governed. Thus, the LF WH-movement of *sheme* in (145a) can be directly to the matrix COMP, thus producing no trace in the intermediate COMP.

So far, we have discussed the "WH-island effect" on the LF movement of adjuncts in Chinese and have seen that it follows from the ECP. Huang (1982) discusses another island phenomenon involving the LF movement of adjuncts and attributes it to the ECP as well. Consider the following example (Huang 1982: 52):

(146) *$[_{NP}[_S$ ta weisheme xie] de shu] zui youqu
          he why   write   book most interesting
     Lit. 'why$_1$ are [the books he wrote t_1] most interesting'

The LF representation of (146) is shown in (147).

(147) $[_{S'}[_{COMP}$ weisheme$_1]_1$ $[_S[_{NP}[_{S'}[_{COMP}$ Op$_2]_2$ $[_S$ ta t_1 t_2 xie]] de shu]
     zui youqu]]

Huang argues that relative clause formation in Chinese involves syntactic movement of an empty operator to COMP. In our terms, then, we can assume that the embedded COMP in (147) must be headed by an empty operator coindexed with the relative head. If this is the case, then the embedded COMP cannot be an antecedent governor for the trace of *weisheme*, since it cannot have the required index. Thus, the matrix COMP is the only potential antecedent governor for the trace of *weisheme*, t_1. But the relation between the matrix COMP and t_1 does not satisfy the locality requirement for antecedent government specified in (127). Both NP and S' intervene between them. Hence, (147) is ruled out by the ECP.

Our formulation of the ECP again extends to cases that the standard formulation does not account for. Just as in the case of WH-island phenomena with adjuncts, we predict that the complex NP phenomenon illustrated above is absolute. That is, we predict that a local COMP properly governing the initial trace of an adjunct cannot save a representation from the complex NP effect. Thus, the following representation is excluded by the ECP:

(148) $[_{S'}$ α_1 $[_S \cdots [_{NP} \cdots [_{S'}[_{COMP} \cdots] [_S \cdots [_{S'}[_{COMP} t_1'] [_S \cdots t_1 \cdots]]]]]]]]$

The initial trace t_1 of α is properly governed by the most deeply embedded COMP. But the intermediate trace t_1' is also subject to the ECP, and it is not properly governed in (148). The only binder for this trace is the matrix COMP, but this COMP is separated from the intermediate trace by an S' and an NP, hence is not a possible proper governor. Note that the lower S' is irrelevant in this case since t_1' is in the head position. But the intermediate S' and the NP are both relevant and hence block antecedent government.

Again, as pointed out by Jim Huang (personal communication), this prediction is borne out by the relevant Chinese examples, as seen in (149a) and (150a), with their LF representations (149b) and (150b).[34]

(149) a. *ni   zui   xihuan [$_{NP}$[$_{S'}$[$_S$ Zhangsan shuo [$_{S'}$[$_S$ Lisi weisheme
            you most like   Zhangsan said   Lisi why
            piping t_2]]]] de ren$_2$]
            criticize   man
            Lit. 'why$_1$ do you like best [the man who$_2$ Zhangsan said
            [Lisi criticized t_2 t_1]]'

      b. *[$_{S'}$[$_{COMP}$ weisheme$_1$] [$_S$ ni zui xihuan [$_{NP}$[$_{S'}$[$_{COMP}$ Op$_2$]$_2$
            [$_S$ Zhangsan shuo [$_{S'}$[$_{COMP}$ t_1']$_1$ [$_S$ Lisi t_1 piping t_2]]]] de ren]]]

(150) a. *ni   pengjian-le [$_{NP}$[$_S$ Zhangsan xiangxin [$_S$ Lisi weisheme
            you met   Zhangsan believe   Lisi why
            xihuan t_2]] de ren$_2$]
            like   man
            Lit. 'why$_1$ did you meet [the man who$_2$ Zhangsan believes
            [Lisi likes t_2 t_1]]'

      b. *[$_{S'}$[$_{COMP}$ weisheme$_1$]$_1$ [$_S$ ni pengjian-le [$_{NP}$[$_{S'}$[$_{COMP}$ Op$_2$]$_2$
            [$_S$ Zhangsan xiangxin [$_{S'}$[$_{COMP}$ t_1']$_1$ [$_S$ Lisi t_1 xihuan t_2]]]]
            de ren$_2$]]]

(149b) and (150b) exhibit the configuration in (148), with t_1 the initial trace of *weisheme* (= α_1 in (148)). t_1 is antecedent-governed by the lowest COMP, hence conforms to the proper government requirement. However, the trace in that lowest COMP, t_1', violates the ECP. Antecedent government is required for such a trace, as discussed above, but the nearest binder is the matrix COMP, which is separated from the trace in question by two barriers to antecedent government, namely, the NP and the intermediate S'.

Examples parallel to (149a) and (150a) but involving a WH-*complement* instead of a WH-*adjunct* do not violate the ECP. As expected, (151a), a complement counterpart to (149a), is well formed.

(151) a. ni   zui   xihuan [$_{NP}$[$_{S'}$[$_S$ Zhangsan shuo [$_{S'}$[$_S$ t_2 piping
            you most like   Zhangsan said   criticize

shei]]]] de ren$_2$]
who   man
Lit. 'who$_1$ do you like best [the man who$_2$ Zhangsan said
[t_2 criticized t_1]]'
   b. [$_{S'}$[$_{COMP}$ shei$_1$]$_1$ [$_S$ ni zui xihuan [$_{NP}$[$_{S'}$[$_{COMP}$ Op$_2$]$_2$ [$_S$ Zhangsan
shuo [$_{S'}$[$_{COMP}$ t_2']$_2$ [$_S$ t_2 piping t_1]]]] de ren]]]

In the LF representation (151b), t_1 is not antecedent-governed, but it need
not be, since it is lexically governed by *piping*. t_2, the initial trace of the
relative operator, is antecedent-governed by the lowest COMP, whose
head, t_2', is in turn antecedent-governed by the next higher COMP, headed
by Op$_2$.

As shown in L&S, Japanese exhibits an adjunct-complement asymmetry
with respect to LF WH-movement exactly like Chinese. The following
Japanese examples correspond to the Chinese (140) and (138):

(152) ?kimi-wa [$_{S'}$ John-ga   nani-o   katta   kadooka] siritai no
      you-top   John-nom what-acc bought whether   want-to-know
      Lit. 'what do you want to know [whether John bought t]'

(153) *kimi-wa [$_{S'}$ John-ga   naze sore-o katta   kadooka] siritai no
      you-top   John-nom why it-acc bought whether   want-to-know
      Lit. 'why do you want to know [whether John bought it t]'

These examples show an adjunct-complement asymmetry with respect to
WH-islands. Such an asymmetry is also found with respect to complex
NPs as shown in the following clear contrast between (154) and (155):

(154) kimi-wa [$_{NP}$[$_{S'}$ e_1 nani-o   katta] hito]-o   sagasite iru no
      you-top   what-acc bought person-acc looking-for
      Lit. 'what are you looking for the person [who bought t]'

(155) *kimi-wa [$_{NP}$[$_{S'}$ e_1 naze sono hon-o   katta] hito-o
      you-top   why that book-acc bought person-acc
      sagasite iru no
      looking-for
      Lit. 'why are you looking for the person [who bought that book t]'

We have established that intermediate traces are subject to the ECP and
moreover that they can satisfy this principle only by antecedent government. Some of the Chinese examples constitute strong evidence for this
conclusion, as well as for the definition of antecedent government in (127).
Each of those Chinese examples has a Japanese counterpart. (156) is the
Japanese counterpart of (131), which shows, among other things, that LF
COMP-to-COMP movement is possible.[35]

(156) kimi-wa [$_{S'}$ kare-ga naze konakatta to]   omotteru no
       you-top   he-nom why came-not COMP think
       Lit. 'why do you think [that he didn't come t]'

The ungrammaticality of Chinese examples such as (143) and (149) followed straightforwardly from the ECP and our definition of antecedent
government. Structurally similar Japanese examples are shown in (157)
and (158).

(157) *kimi-wa [$_{S'}$ John-ga   [$_{S'}$ Mary-ga   naze konakatta to]
       you-top   John-nom   Mary-nom why came-not COMP
       omotteru kadooka] siritai no
       think   whether   want-to-know
       Lit. 'why do you want to know whether John thinks
       [that Mary didn't come t]'

(158) *kimi-wa [$_{NP}$[$_{S'}$ John-ga [$_{S'}$ Mary-ga   naze e_1 Bill-ni okutta
       you-top   John-nom   Mary-nom why   Bill-to wrote
       to]   omotteru] tegami]-o yomitai no
       COMP think   letter-acc want-to-read
       Lit. 'why$_2$ do you want to read the letter which$_1$ John thinks that
       [Mary sent t_1 to Bill t_2]'

As in Chinese, complement WHs do not exhibit island effects in Japanese.
Thus, the following examples contrast with (157)–(158):[36]

(159) ??kimi-wa [$_{S'}$ John-ga [$_{S'}$ Mary-ga   nani-o   katta   to]
       you-top   John-nom   Mary-nom what-acc bought COMP
       omotteru kadooka] siritai no
       think   whether   want-to-know
       Lit. 'why do you want to know whether John thinks that
       [Mary bought t]'

(160) kimi-wa [$_{NP}$[$_{S'}$ John-ga [$_{S'}$ Mary-ga   dare-ni okutta to]
       you-top   John-nom   Mary-nom who-to sent   COMP
       omotteru tegami]-o yomitai no
       think   letter-acc want-to-read
       Lit. 'who$_2$ do you want to read the letter which$_1$ John thinks that
       [Mary sent t_1 to t_2]'

The complex NP effect on the LF movement of adjuncts is not limited to
cases where the complex NP involves a relative clause. The following examples show that "pure complex NPs" as well are islands for adjuncts but
not for complements:

(161) *kimi-wa [$_{NP}$[$_{S'}$ Taroo-ga naze sore-o te-ni ireta] koto]-o
       you-top   Taro-nom why it-acc obtained   fact-acc
       sonnani okotteru no
       so much angry
       Lit. 'why are you so angry about the fact that [Taro obtained it t]'

(162) *kimi-wa [$_{NP}$[$_{S'}$ Hanako-ga   [$_{S'}$ Taroo-ga naze sore-o te-ni ireta
       you-top   Hanako-nom   Taro-nom why it-acc obtained
       tte]   itta] koto]-o sonnani okotteru no
       COMP said fact-acc so much angry
       Lit. 'why are you so angry about the fact that Hanako said that
       [Taro obtained it t]'

(163) kimi-wa [$_{NP}$[$_{S'}$ Taroo-ga nani-o   te-ni ireta] koto]-o sonnani
       you-top   Taro-nom what-acc obtained   fact-acc so much
       okotteru no
       angry
       Lit. 'what are you so angry about the fact that [Taro obtained t]'

(164) kimi-wa [$_{NP}$[$_{S'}$ Hanako-ga   [Taroo-ga nani-o te-ni ireta tte]
       you-top   Hanako-nom Taro-nom what   obtained COMP
       itta] koto]-o sonnani okotteru no
       said fact-acc so much be angry
       Lit. 'what are you so angry about the fact that Hanako said that
       [Taro obtained t]'

   Consider LF representation (165) of example (161).

(165) *[$_{S'}$[$_S$ kimi-wa [$_{NP}$[$_{S'}$[$_S$ Taroo-ga t_1 sore-o te-ni ireta] [$_{COMP}$ t_1']$_1$]
       koto]-o sonnani okotteru] [$_{COMP}$ naze$_1$]$_1$] no

The lower COMP must be headed by an intermediate trace; otherwise, the
initial trace, t_1, will fail to be antecedent-governed. But that intermediate
trace is not antecedent-governed, since it is separated from the matrix
COMP by an NP boundary. Thus, the ECP correctly rules out (161). Note
that (163) will be allowed, since here a complement moved and no intermediate trace is required.

   Jim Huang (personal communication) points out that this adjunct-
complement asymmetry in pure complex NPs also obtains in Chinese,
just as the theory predicts. The following examples are due to Yinxia Long
(personal communication):

(166) *ni   xiangxin [$_{NP}$[$_{S'}$ Lisi weisheme lai] de shuofa]
       you believe   Lisi why   come claim
       Lit. 'why$_1$ do you believe the claim that [Lisi came t_1]'

(167)   ni   xiangxin [$_{NP}$[$_{S'}$ Lisi mai-le   sheme] de shuofa]
        you believe   Lisi bought what   claim
        Lit. 'what$_1$ do you believe the claim that [Lisi bought t_1]'

(166) is entirely parallel to the ungrammatical Japanese example (161), and (167) is parallel to the grammatical (163).

Chapter 2
Subject-Adjunct Asymmetries in WH-Movement

2.1 Subject-Adjunct Asymmetries

In the discussion of complement-noncomplement asymmetries in chapter 1, we assumed that traces in object position are lexically governed, whereas subject traces and adjunct traces are not lexically governed and hence must be antecedent-governed, given the ECP. Thus, we expected subject traces and adjunct traces to behave exactly alike, as opposed to object traces. This prediction was in fact borne out by paradigms such as the following:

(1) a. *what did you buy why
    b. why did you buy what

(2) a. *what did who buy
    b. who bought what

Essentially following Huang (1982), we argued that the LF trace of *why* in (1a) violates the ECP, since the trace of an adjunct must be antecedent-governed. Since *what* is the head of COMP, there is no possible antecedent governor for the trace of *why*. In (1b), on the other hand, *why* is the head of COMP, permitting antecedent government of the trace of *why*, whereas the LF trace of *what* is lexically governed. Precisely the same contrast obtains between (2a) and (2b).

2.1.1 Subject as a Properly Governed Position
There are, however, cases where the behavior of subjects and adjuncts diverges. In Chinese and Japanese, for example, subject traces behave like object traces and contrast with adjunct traces. This is illustrated by the following Chinese examples:

(3) ni   xiang-zhidao [$_{S'}$ Lisi weisheme mai-le sheme]
    you wonder   Lisi why   bought what

a.   what is the thing x such that you wonder why Lisi bought x

b.   *what is the reason x such that you wonder what Lisi bought for x

(4) ni   xiang-zhidao [$_{S'}$ shei mai-le sheme]
    you wonder   who bought what

a.   what is the thing x such that you wonder who bought x

b.   who is the person x such that you wonder what x bought

(3) has the reading in (a), but not the one in (b). This is expected if *sheme*, but not *weisheme*, is lexically governed. The reading in (a) requires an LF representation where *sheme* is in the matrix COMP and *weisheme* is the head of the embedded COMP. In this representation, the trace of *sheme* is lexically governed by *mai-le*, and that of *weisheme* is antecedent-governed by the embedded COMP. On the other hand, the reading in (b) requires an LF representation where *weisheme* is in the matrix COMP and *sheme* is the head of the embedded COMP. Thus, the trace of *weisheme* lacks a proper governor and hence violates the ECP.

If subject traces behave exactly like adjunct traces with respect to the ECP, we should expect that (4) also has the reading in (a) but not the one in (b). This should be so, since the reading in (b) requires the LF representation shown in (5).

(5) [$_{S'}$[$_{COMP}$ shei$_1$]$_1$ [$_S$ ni xiang-zhidao [$_{S'}$[$_{COMP}$ sheme$_2$]$_2$ [$_S$ t_1 mai-le t_2]]]]

Here, if t_1, like an adjunct trace, needs a local COMP as its antecedent governor, then (5) should be ruled out by the ECP, since the embedded COMP does not have the index of this trace. The fact that the reading (b) is possible for (4) indicates that subject traces in Chinese are like object traces in that they do not require a local COMP as an antecedent governor.

In Japanese, also, subject traces and object traces seem to behave alike, as opposed to adjunct traces, with respect to the ECP. Consider the following examples:

(6) *kimi-wa [$_{NP}$[$_{S'}$ John-ga   naze e_1 kaita] hon$_1$]-o   sagasite iru no
     you-top   John-nom why   wrote book-acc looking-for
     Lit. 'why$_2$ are you looking for the book [which$_1$ John wrote t_1 t_2]'

(7) kimi-wa [$_{NP}$[$_{S'}$ dare-ga e_1 kaita] hon$_1$]-o   sagasite iru no
     you-top   who-nom wrote book-acc looking-for
     Lit. 'who$_2$ are you looking for the book [which$_1$ t_2 wrote t_1]'

As we showed earlier, extraction of an adjunct from a complex NP results in an ECP violation, since adjunct traces need to be antecedent-governed. Thus, the LF movement of *naze* in (6) to the matrix COMP results in a violation of the ECP. On the other hand, object WHs can move freely, since their traces are lexically governed. The grammaticality of (7) shows that subject WHs are like object WHs in that they can move out of a complex NP in LF.

The example in (7) involves a complication, since the subject WH appears with an overt nominative Case marker *ga*. If we assume that *ga* can be stranded by LF WH-movement and can function as a lexical governor of the trace, then it is not surprising that subject traces of LF WH-movement need not be antecedent-governed by COMP in Japanese. Under this hypothesis, the difference between English and Japanese with respect to subject traces is attributed to the overt Case marker *ga* in the latter language. However, this hypothesis does not carry over to Chinese, and furthermore, there is evidence that the subject position in Japanese is properly governed independently of the Case marker *ga*.

We noted in section 1.2.1 that extraction out of a non-properly governed domain is prohibited in the syntax (Huang's (1982) CED). Thus, there are contrasts such as the following:

(8) a.   who$_1$ did you hear a story about t_1
    b.   ?*who$_1$ did a story about t_1 amuse you

(9) a.   ??who$_1$ do you believe the claim that Mary likes t_1
    b.   *who$_1$ does the claim that Mary likes t_1 upset Bill

The contrast in (8) illustrates the subject condition of Chomsky (1973). In (8a), a WH-phrase is extracted out of the object, which is lexically governed by the verb. In (8b), on the other hand, a WH-phrase is extracted out of the subject, which is, according to our assumptions, a non-properly governed domain. Hence, (8b) contrasts sharply with (8a). Both examples in (9) involve extraction out of a complex NP, thus violating Subjacency; hence, (9a) is marginal. (9b) is worse still, since it violates the subject condition (CED) in addition.

It is very difficult, if not impossible, to construct Japanese examples completely parallel to (8). But examples similar to (9) can be constructed in this language, and they show no subject-object asymmetry. The following examples illustrate this point:

(10) ??dono hon-o$_1$ Mary-ga   [$_{NP}$ John-ga t_1 katta   koto]-o
      which book-acc Mary-nom   John-nom   bought fact-acc
      mondai-ni siteru no
      problem-to making
      Lit. 'which book is it that Mary is calling the fact that John bought it into question'

(11) ??dono hon-o₁   Mary-ga [$_{NP}$ John-ga t_1 katta   koto]-ga
     which book-acc Mary-nom   John-nom   bought fact-nom
     mondai-da to   omotteru no
     problem-cop COMP think
     Lit. 'which book is it that Mary thinks that the fact that John
     bought it is a problem'

In both (10) and (11), an NP is preposed out of a complex NP by scrambling, an operation that left-adjoins a maximal projection to S.¹ As noted by Haig (1976) and Harada (1977), scrambling in Japanese obeys the complex NP constraint as expected. Thus, both sentences are marginal. But as far as we can tell, (11) is no worse than (10), indicating that there is no CED violation in this sentence. Recall that for the purpose of this discussion, we are assuming that the Case marker *ga* can act as a proper governor. In (11), however, *dono hon-o* has been extracted out of the entire subject *including* the Case marker. Thus, the entire subject including the Case marker must be properly governed.

The above discussion indicates that in Chinese and Japanese the subject position is properly governed, like the object position and unlike an adjunct position. In fact, the Japanese examples in (10)–(11) indicate that this is true not only in LF but also in the syntax. Huang (1982) assumes for Chinese that INFL is a proper governor for the subject position because of the lexical nature of INFL in this language. Here, we will focus the discussion on Japanese and will defer the discussion of Chinese to section 4.2.3. The hypothesis that INFL is a proper governor makes sense for Japanese, we believe, not necessarily on the basis of the lexical nature of INFL, but rather on structural grounds.

One fundamental property of Japanese phrase structure is that it is strictly head-final. And as noted in the literature, there are ways to relate this property to the fact that subject position is properly governed in this language. Suppose that the structure of sentences in English and Japanese is as in (12a) and (12b), respectively.

(12) a.

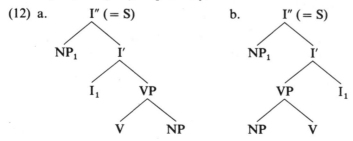

One difference between (12a) and (12b) is that the subject NP is "on the same side" as the object NP in (12b), but not in (12a). Thus, as suggested by Kayne (1983) and Travis (1984), among others, it is possible to appeal to the "directionality of (proper) government" to account for the different properties of subjects in English and Japanese. Let us suppose, for concreteness, that proper government can take place only "to the right" in English, and only "to the left" in Japanese. This allows the object NP to be properly governed by the verb in both languages. Now, suppose further that INFL fails to properly govern the subject NP in English, not because INFL is not lexical, but because proper government can only be to the right in English. Then, since the direction of proper government is to the left in Japanese, INFL will in fact properly govern the subject position in this language.

This approach refers crucially to the linear order of subject NP and INFL. An alternative hypothesis is that the hierarchical relation of these two elements differs in the two languages. We will tentatively adopt this alternative approach here, and we will discuss it in some detail in the remainder of this subsection.

As is well known, the postverbal subject in Italian and Spanish exhibits the properties of a properly governed position (see Belletti and Rizzi 1981, Jaeggli 1982). The following Spanish examples illustrate this point:

(13) a. quién dijo qué cosa
          who   said what
      b. qué cosa dijo quién
          what   said who
          '*what did who say'

Compare these examples with the English (2a–b). The following example, showing the lack of *that*-trace effects in Spanish, illustrates the same point:

(14) quién piensas   que pro vio a Juan *t*
      who (you) think that   saw Juan
      '*who do you think that saw Juan'

Since subjects in Japanese are properly governed, a possibility naturally arises that their position in the structure is similar to that of the postverbal subject in Italian and Spanish. Or more concretely, a possibility arises that the structure of Japanese sentences is as follows:[2]

(15)

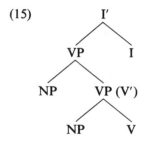

Note that given the formulation of c-command in note 28 of chapter 1, even though the subject in (15) is within VP, it still asymmetrically binds the object, as required to account for a variety of widely discussed phenomena.[3]

As far as we know, there are two possible accounts for the fact that the postverbal subject in Italian and Spanish has the properties of a properly governed position. Let us consider the structure in (16).

(16)

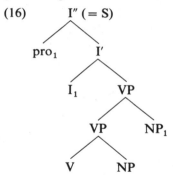

Belletti and Rizzi (1981), among others, assume that the postverbal subject NP_1 is within the projection of V and is lexically governed by V. Saito (1984), on the other hand, suggests that INFL antecedent-governs the postverbal subject in (16). Given the definition (127) in chapter 1, this antecedent government in fact obtains since INFL binds the postverbal subject and no NP or S' intervenes. The preverbal subject in (12a) fails to be antecedent-governed by INFL because INFL does not c-command this position. We will tentatively adopt the antecedent government analysis of the postverbal subject in Italian and Spanish. But under either analysis, it is predicted that the subject position in (15) is properly governed. That is, once we assume the structure in (15) for Japanese sentences, the apparently peculiar properties of the Japanese subject can be accounted for in exactly the same way as those of the postverbal subject in Italian and Spanish.

The remaining question to be addressed at this point is why the structures of sentences differ in English and Japanese, and more specifically, why English sentences cannot assume the structure in (17).[4]

(17)

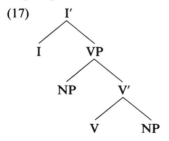

If this structure could exist, then the subject position would be incorrectly predicted to be properly governed. We tentatively suggest that (17) is ruled out because the subject NP intervenes between I and V. As argued by Chomsky (1957), Fiengo (1980), and Lasnik (1981), the inflectional element must be adjacent to V or affix hopping will be blocked. This would result in a structure violating a general morphological filter, as discussed by Lasnik (1981). Hence, the sentential structure in English is as in (12a), and the subject is not c-commanded by I in this language. Note that V and I are adjacent in (15), even though the subject NP is within the VP. This is the case exactly because Japanese is head-final. Thus, the properties of the Japanese subject are ultimately reduced to the head-final property of the language.

2.1.2   Lack of *That*-Trace Effects with Adjuncts

We have discussed a class of phenomena indicating that under certain circumstances, subject position is properly governed. In those cases, subject movement is freer than adjunct movement. There are also cases, to which we now turn, in which adjunct movement is freer than subject movement. As noted by Huang (1982), adjuncts do not display *that*-trace effects. For example, (19a) and (19b) do not contrast.[5]

(18) a.   who$_1$ [do you think [t_1' [t_1 left early]]]
      b.   *who$_1$ [do you think [that [t_1 left early]]]
(19) a.   why$_1$ [do you think [t_1' [he left early t_1]]]
      b.   why$_1$ [do you think [that [he left early t_1]]]

Given what we have said so far, the distinction between (18) and (19) is unexpected. Just as t_1 in (18b) is neither lexically governed nor antecedent-governed, so t_1 in (19b) appears not to be properly governed in either way. (19b) should be an ECP violation, yet it is fully grammatical.

Adjuncts in Japanese also seem to be immune to the *that*-trace restriction. The dialect of Japanese we have been considering, the Tokyo dialect, does not permit complementizer deletion.[6] Nonetheless, extraction of *naze* 'why' from an embedded S' (LF extraction in this case, of course) is permitted, as the grammaticality of (20) indicates.

(20) Bill-wa [$_{S'}$ John-ga   naze kubi-ni natta tte]   itta no
       Bill-top   John-nom why was fired   COMP said
       'why did Bill say [that John was fired *t*]'

Although adjuncts do not display *that*-trace effects, recall that they clearly are not exempt from ECP requirements in general. As shown in section 1.3, a wide variety of ungrammatical instances of adjunct movement (in all of the languages under consideration) are correctly excluded by the ECP, but only if the ECP applies to adjunct traces. Thus, we must assume that both subject traces and adjunct traces fall under the ECP. At the same time, we must account for the contrast between (19b) and (20) on the one hand and (18b) on the other. That is, this contrast must be attributed to an independent distinction between subject traces and adjunct traces.

Recall that the following contrast is attributed to the ECP:

(21) a. *why$_1$ do you wonder [whether John left t_1]
       b. ??what$_1$ do you wonder [whether John bought t_1]

(21b) is merely a Subjacency violation; (21a) violates the ECP in addition. The trace t_1 in (21a) needs to be antecedent-governed by the embedded COMP (see section 1.3), but this is impossible since the embedded COMP is headed by *whether* and therefore cannot have the index *1*. The grammaticality of (19b), on the other hand, indicates that the trace of *why*, t_1, is antecedent-governed by the embedded COMP, despite the fact that this COMP is headed by *that*. In the following sections, we will be concerned, in part, with exploring this phenomenon.

2.2   A Preliminary Account

2.2.1   LF Complementizer Deletion

As far as adjunct traces are concerned, it seems that a COMP headed by *that* at S-structure can serve as an antecedent governor, but a COMP headed by a noncoindexed WH-phrase cannot. Plausibly, this relates to the fact that a WH-phrase has semantic content, whereas *that* does not. Thus, one might reasonably assume that a WH-phrase, but not a pure complementizer, must be present at LF. Suppose, then, that *that* can be absent at LF, just as it can be absent at S-structure, as shown in (22).

(22) a. I think that John left early

   b. I think John left early

And if *that* can be absent in the LF representation of (19b), then it becomes possible for t_1 to satisfy the ECP at this level. Suppose that the embedded complementizer *that* in (19b) is deleted in LF. Then, assuming the simplest theory of transformations, nothing should prevent *why* from lowering to the head position of the embedded COMP and then raising back to the matrix COMP. Each of these movements is an instance of Move α, which, at least in part, characterizes the mapping from S-structure to LF. The LF representation of (19b) will then be as in (23), which is identical to (19a).

(23) why$_1$ [do you think [t_1' [he left t_1]]]

Here t_1 is antecedent-governed by the embedded COMP, which is headed by the intermediate trace t_1', and t_1' is in turn antecedent-governed by the matrix COMP. Thus, (19b) satisfies the ECP at LF. Hence, if the ECP applies only at LF, then we expect this example to be grammatical.

2.2.2 Argument-Adjunct Asymmetry

There is, however, evidence that contradicts the conclusion that the ECP applies only at LF. As we illustrated with (18), the *that*-trace effect does hold of subjects, yet the analysis we just presented of the lack of such effects with adjuncts should generalize to subjects. This would incorrectly allow (18b). In LF, the embedded complementizer can be deleted, since it lacks semantic content. Then Move α can lower and raise *who*, producing the LF representation (24), which is identical to the well-formed (18a).

(24) who$_1$ [do you think [t_1' [t_1 left early]]]

Exactly as in the case of (23), the initial trace is antecedent-governed by the embedded COMP, whose head, t_1', is antecedent-governed by the matrix COMP. This derivation must be prevented.

Evidently, an argument trace that violates the ECP at S-structure cannot be salvaged by later LF operations, but an adjunct trace can. Thus, at this point, to account for the *that*-trace contrast under discussion, we need something like (25), as a first approximation.

(25) Only argument traces are subject to the ECP at S-structure.

By (25), (18b) will be ruled out at S-structure, rendering LF operations irrelevant. Given (25), however, the superficially parallel (19b) will not be subject to the ECP at S-structure. LF operations will ultimately yield

(23), a representation conforming to the ECP, as the LF representation of (19b). For this analysis to be correct, it must be the case that any ungrammatical instance of adjunct movement that is to be ruled out by the ECP must involve a trace that fails to be properly governed at LF. Failure of proper government at S-structure alone will not suffice. And in fact, all instances of ECP violations by adjunct traces that we have seen so far do involve the failure of proper government at LF, whether or not they involve the apparent failure of proper government at S-structure.

The proposed analysis of the lack of *that*-trace effects with adjuncts directly extends to the Japanese example (26).

(26) kimi-wa [$_{S'}$ kare-ga naze konakatta to]   omotteru no
      you-top   he-nom why came-not COMP think
      'why do you think [that he didn't come t]'

Naze in (26) moves to the matrix COMP in LF. Since the embedded COMP is headed by a complementizer *to*, if this complementizer must be present at LF, then (26) should violate the ECP. The trace of *naze* must be antecedent-governed by the embedded COMP, but this will be impossible if this COMP is headed by *to*. However, given our assumption that pure complementizers can freely delete in LF, (26) is no longer problematic. The embedded complementizer in (26) can delete in LF, and then *naze* can move to the matrix COMP through the head position of the embedded COMP. The resulting LF representation will be as follows:

(27) [$_{S'}$ [$_S$ kimi-wa [$_{S'}$ [$_S$ kare-ga t_1 konakatta] [$_{COMP}$ t_1']$_1$] omotteru no]
      [$_{COMP}$ naze$_1$]$_1$]

The initial trace t_1 is antecedent-governed by the embedded COMP, and the intermediate trace t_1' is antecedent-governed by the matrix COMP. Thus, (27) satisfies the ECP. (25) is irrelevant in this case, since there is no trace at S-structure.

Our account of the lack of *that*-trace effects with adjuncts relied on LF *that*-deletion in the case of LF movement, and on (25) in addition, in the case of syntactic movement. (25) distinguishes argument traces from non-argument traces and hence predicts that intermediate traces, like adjuncts, are subject to the ECP only at LF. The following example is consistent with this prediction:

(28) who$_1$ do you believe [$_{S'}$ that [$_S$ Mary said [$_{S'}$ t_1' [$_S$ t_1 left early]]]]

The initial trace t_1 clearly satisfies the ECP by virtue of antecedent government by the most deeply embedded COMP. But, as we argued in section 1.3.2, intermediate traces are subject to the ECP and, in particular, they must be antecedent-governed. This implies that t_1' in (28) must be antecedent-governed by the COMP headed by *that*. But this is clearly impossible if *that* remains in the head position of COMP. Thus, if intermediate traces are subject to the ECP at S-structure, then (28) should be ruled out by this principle. On the other hand, if they are subject to the ECP only at LF, as stated in (25), then we correctly predict the grammaticality of this example. *That* in the middle COMP in (28) can delete in LF, and thus, *who* can lower to the head position of this COMP and then raise back to the matrix COMP in this component, exactly as in the LF derivation of (19b). The resulting LF representation of (28) will then be as follows:

(29) who$_1$ do you believe [$_{S'}$ t_1'' [$_S$ Mary said [$_{S'}$ t_1' [$_S$ t_1 left early]]]]]

Each of the three traces in (29) is antecedent-governed by the respective minimally c-commanding COMP. Thus, (28) satisfies the ECP at LF.

However, (25) does not allow us to account for the full range of examples similar to (28). As noted in L&S, a subject-adjunct asymmetry can also be observed in examples such as those in (30) with the S-structure representations in (31).

(30) a. ?*who do you believe the claim that John said saw Mary
     b. *why do you believe the claim that John said Bill left

(31) a. who$_1$ [$_S$ do you believe [$_{NP}$ the claim [$_{S'}$ that [$_S$ John said [$_{S'}$ t_1' [$_S$ t_1 saw Mary]]]]]]
     b. why$_2$ [$_S$ do you believe [$_{NP}$ the claim [$_{S'}$ that [$_S$ John said [$_{S'}$ t_2' [$_S$ Bill left t_2]]]]]]

(30b) is totally ungrammatical and has the status of an ECP violation. Thus, this example evidently violates the ECP as well as Subjacency. On the other hand, (30a) is not as bad, having merely the status of a Subjacency violation. Compare the examples of (30) with (32), where the ECP is not at issue since it is an object that has moved.

(32) ?*who$_1$ do you believe the claim that John said [Mary saw t_1]

(30a) is roughly the same as (32) in acceptability, whereas (30b) is much worse.

According to (25), t_1, the initial trace of *who* in (31a), is subject to the ECP at S-structure, and in fact, it is properly governed. The initial trace of *why* in (31b), t_2, is not subject to the ECP at S-structure. Further, neither t_1' nor t_2' is subject to that principle at that level. Consider now (33a–b), possible LF representations of (30a–b), if *that* in these examples

can undergo complementizer deletion just as it could in such examples as
(19b).

(33) a. who$_1$ [$_S$ do you believe [$_{NP}$ the claim [$_{S'}$ t_1'' [$_S$ John said
[$_{S'}$ t_1' [$_S$ t_1 saw Mary]]]]]]

 b. why$_2$ [$_S$ do you believe [$_{NP}$ the claim [$_{S'}$ t_2'' [$_S$ John said
[$_{S'}$ t_2' [$_S$ Bill left t_2]]]]]]

Recall that *all* traces are subject to the ECP at LF. In (33b), t_2 is in a
configuration of proper government, being antecedent-governed by the
COMP headed by t_2'. Further, t_2' is itself antecedent-governed by the
COMP headed by t_2''. However, t_2'' is not properly governed. Intermediate traces must be antecedent-governed, and t_2'' is too far from its nearest
binder, the matrix COMP, being separated from it by an NP boundary. (It
is also separated by an S' boundary, but since it counts as the head of this
S', this particular S' is not a barrier to antecedent government of this trace.
See section 1.3.2.) Thus, (33b) is correctly ruled out as an ECP violation
(as well as a Subjacency violation).

The problem is that (33a), which we have claimed should not be an ECP
violation, receives precisely the same analysis in relevant respects, given
the mechanisms we have developed thus far. t_1 is properly (antecedent-)
governed by the COMP headed by t_1'. This was true at S-structure, and it
is still true at LF. t_1' is antecedent-governed by the COMP headed by t_1'',
just as in (33b). Finally, t_1'' is not properly governed, again as in (33b).
Thus, (33a) should be an ECP violation just as (33b) is. The distinction
between (30a) and (30b) is not accounted for. Note that essentially the
same problem arises even if the complementizer *that* in (31a) and (31b) is
not deletable in LF.[7] In that case, the initial trace in (33a) and (33b) would
be antecedent-governed, as before. However, now the trace in the lowest
COMP would not be properly governed, since the next COMP up would
be headed by *that* and could not serve as an antecedent governor. The
nearest binder would be the matrix COMP, and it would be separated
from the trace in question, t_1' or t_2', by both an NP and a relevant S'.
Once again, we lose the distinction between adjunct movement and subject
movement, both being equally excluded by the ECP in the configuration
under consideration.

Note that what causes the LF representations in (32) to violate the ECP
is the intermediate trace t'', if it is present. This trace is required at LF only
so that the first intermediate trace t' can be properly governed. If t'' is not
present at LF, then t' will be the offending trace, and t' in turn is required
at LF so that the initial trace of WH-movement is properly governed. If t'

is not present, then t will violate the ECP at LF. Here, the only difference between (33a) and (33b) is that the initial trace in the former is a subject, and the initial trace in the latter is an adjunct. Thus, the contrast between these two examples must be attributed to this difference. In particular, if the subject trace in (33a), as opposed to the adjunct trace in (33b), is exempted from the ECP at LF, then there is no reason that the offending intermediate trace must be present at LF. We already know that adjunct traces must be subject to the ECP at LF, since they are constrained by this principle; yet, by (25), they are not subject to the ECP at S-structure. Thus, in (33b), the offending intermediate trace must be present at LF. In the following section, we propose a mechanism that in effect exempts the subject trace t_1 in (33a), but not the adjunct trace t_2 in (33b), from the ECP at LF.

2.2.3 γ-Marking

In L&S, we offered an interpretation of the ECP that makes available the necessary distinction between subject traces and adjunct traces. In effect, the ECP has two parts. First, it indicates under what circumstances proper government obtains. Second, it filters out representations containing traces for which proper government does not obtain. Notationally, the first part can be regarded as the assigment of a feature, say, $[+\gamma]$, under certain circumstances, and the assignment of $[-\gamma]$ otherwise. This is shown in (34a) ($=$ L&S's (88)). The second part is simply the γ-Filter shown in (34b) ($=$ L&S's (89)).

(34)   a. $t \rightarrow [+\gamma]$ when lexically governed or antecedent-governed.

          $t \rightarrow [-\gamma]$ otherwise.

    b. $*\ldots t \ldots$
           $_{[-\gamma]}$

Accordingly, (25) is restated as follows ($=$ L&S's (109)):

(35)   Only an argument receives a γ-feature at S-structure.

According to (35), γ-marking applies to arguments at S-structure and LF, and to nonarguments only at LF. This enables us to account for the contrast between (18b) and (19b), repeated here.

(18)   b.   *who$_1$ [do you think [that [t_1 left early]]]

(19)   b.   why$_1$ [do you think [that [he left early t_1]]]

The trace in (18b), being an argument trace, is assigned $[-\gamma]$ at S-structure. The trace in (19b), on the other hand, is not assigned a value for γ until LF. In LF, *that* can delete, and an intermediate trace can be created in the head position of the embedded COMP. Thus, the trace in (19b) is assigned $[+\gamma]$ at LF.

Given (35), we may assume here that the γ-Filter (34b) applies at both S-structure and LF. In this case, (18b) is ruled out at S-structure. Alternatively, we may assume that γ-features, once assigned, are indelible, and that the γ-Filter (34b) applies only at LF. If $[-\gamma]$ assigned to the trace in (18b) at S-structure is indelible, then it remains at LF, and consequently the trace is ruled out by the filter at LF. Here, without any evidence to the contrary, we follow L&S and adopt the latter set of assumptions. In section 2.3.4, we will show that these assumptions have certain desirable consequences.

We are now ready to reconsider examples (31a–b). γ-marking will apply to the S-structure representation (31a) to give (36).

(36) who$_1$ do you believe [$_{NP}$ the claim [$_{S'}$ that [$_S$ John said [$_{S'}$ t_1' [$_S$ t_1 saw Mary]]]]]
$\phantom{(36) who_1 do you believe [_{NP} the claim [_{S'} that [_S John said [_{S'} t_1' [_S t_1}$ $_{[+\gamma]}$

The subject trace, being an argument trace, is assigned $[+\gamma]$, since it is antecedent-governed by the COMP containing t_1'. By (35), the intermediate trace t_1' receives no γ-marking at S-structure. If this trace is still present at LF, then it is assigned $[-\gamma]$ at this level and consequently violates the γ-Filter (34b). However, given that the subject trace has already received $[+\gamma]$ at S-structure, there is no reason that the intermediate trace must be present at LF. And in fact, if the intermediate trace t_1' is not present at LF, (36) will not violate the ECP, the desired result. Here, we will adopt Stowell's (1981) proposal that intermediate traces can freely delete. Under this proposal, although deletion itself is unconstrained, the result of such deletion is ultimately constrained by general principles, for example, the ECP. That is, if an intermediate trace is needed to make a COMP a proper governor at some level, then that intermediate trace must of course be present at that level. We will provide an example of this case directly. Given the assumption that intermediate traces can freely delete, it should be clear that (36) no longer violates the ECP. Its LF representation is shown in (37).

(37) who$_1$ [$_S$ do you believe [$_{NP}$ the claim [$_{S'}$ that [$_S$ John said [$_{S'}$ [$_S$ t_1 saw Mary]]]]]]
$\phantom{(37) who_1 [_S do you believe [_{NP} the claim [_{S'} that [_S John said [_{S'} [_S t_1}$ $_{[+\gamma]}$

There is only one trace in this example, and it was marked $[+\gamma]$ at S-structure. The ECP (i.e., the γ-filter (34b)) is thus satisfied.

Note that our ECP account of (31b), whose S-structure representation is repeated here as (38), is not affected by the present considerations.

(38) why$_2$ [$_S$ do you believe [$_{NP}$ the claim [$_{S'}$ that [$_S$ John said [$_{S'}$ t_2' [$_S$ Bill left t_2]]]]]]]

Here, the initial trace t_2 is an adjunct trace and hence, by (35), is not assigned a γ-feature at S-structure. In order for it to be assigned [$+\gamma$] at LF, the intermediate trace t_2' must be present at this level, since only the COMP containing t_2' can be a proper governor of t_2. But then, t_2' is not properly governed and hence is assigned [$-\gamma$] at this level.[8] If, on the other hand, this trace is not present at LF, then the initial trace t_2 is assigned [$-\gamma$]. Thus, (38) necessarily violates the ECP at LF. Note that, crucially, γ-marking applies at the *output* of each component, and only there. If a γ-feature could be assigned at any point of the derivation, then t_2' in (38) could be used in assigning [$+\gamma$] to the initial trace t_2, and then could delete. There would then be no trace in violation of the ECP, an incorrect result.

The contrast between (39) and (40) can be accounted for similarly.

(39) ?*who$_1$ do you wonder whether John said [$_{S'}$ t_1' [$_S$ t_1 solved the problem]]

(40) *how$_1$ do you wonder whether John said [$_{S'}$ t_1' [$_S$ Mary solved the problem t_1]]

Both (39) and (40) violate Subjacency, but only the latter violates the ECP in addition. At S-structure, the initial trace t_1 in (39) is assigned [$+\gamma$] and the intermediate trace t_1' is not γ-marked at all. The intermediate trace t_1' can delete in LF, and hence (39) satisfies the γ-Filter at LF. On the other hand, (40) contains not an argument trace but an adjunct trace, and thus no trace in this example is γ-marked at S-structure, given (35). If the intermediate trace t_1' deletes in LF, then the initial trace t_1 is assigned [$-\gamma$] at LF since it is not properly governed. If, on the other hand, t_1' does not delete in LF, then this trace itself will be marked [$-\gamma$] at LF. Hence, (40) violates the γ-Filter, and the contrast between (39) and (40) is accounted for.

2.2.4 S′ as CP

Thus far, we have assumed the traditional analysis of S′ in which it is not truly part of the X′ system of phrase structure. In particular, we have assumed that S′ has a unique COMP position, which is both the position of an overt complementizer, such as *that*, and the position through which WH-movement proceeds. More recent work has questioned this view. For example, Chomsky (1986a) argues that S′ is not only is the maximal projection of COMP, which we have been assuming, but further, is a full-fledged X′ structure, as in (41).

(41)   C(OMP)P

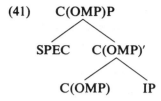

Within this CP analysis, COMP, the head, is the position for complementizers such as *that*, whereas WH-movement is to (or through) the SPEC of CP. As Chomsky (1986a) observes, this eliminates the conceptually problematic state of affairs of a maximal projection (the WH-phrase) moving into a head position (C). Our use of the older approach was largely for expository convenience. It made the discussion here consistent with our point of departure, L&S. However, since the CP hypothesis seems conceptually superior to the S' hypothesis, we will adopt it at this point, and briefly discuss the relevant issues in this section.

Beyond those discussed by Chomsky (1986a), there is one case that supports the CP hypothesis, as opposed to the S' hypothesis. As noted in L&S, Noam Chomsky points out that there are certain null operator constructions that are potentially problematic for the proposal made there that COMP has only one position. Consider the following example:

(42) I bought this book $[_{S'}$ Op$_1$ for $[_S$ John to read $t_1]]$

It seems that both an empty operator and a complementizer appear in the embedded COMP of (42). The CP hypothesis provides a straightforward solution to this problem. The empty operator can be in the SPEC position of the CP, and *for* can be in the head position.

Furthermore, the CP hypothesis basically retains the advantage of the proposal in L&S that COMP has a unique head position. Recall example (89) from chapter 1.

(43) ?kimi-wa nani-o   naze sagasiteru no
     you-top what-acc why looking-for
     'why are you looking for what'

(43) is somewhat marginal for some speakers, but it clearly does not have the status of an ECP violation. Its LF representation is shown in (44) (= (90a) of chapter 1).

(44) $[_{S'}[_S$ kimi-wa t_1 -o t_2 sagasiteru] $[_{COMP}[_{COMP}$ naze$_2]$ nani$_1]]$

As noted in chapter 1, if we assume the classic COMP-indexing mechanism of AHS, then (43) is ruled out by the ECP. Since two WH-phrases move into COMP at LF, the COMP-indexing mechanism simply fails to apply. On the other hand, if COMP has a unique head position and the index of the head percolates to the COMP node, examples such as (43) are correctly allowed. More specifically, if *naze* is in the head position of COMP and *nani* is adjoined to the COMP, then the COMP node antecedent-governs the trace of *naze* in (44). Thus, given the S' hypothesis, the assumption that COMP has a unique head position enables us to account for examples such as (43).

But the CP hypothesis, which assumes a unique SPEC of CP position, does equally well here. Suppose that the LF representation of (43) is as in (45), where the PP *naze* is in the SPEC of CP position and the NP *nani* is adjoined to this PP.

(45) $[_{CP}[_{PP}[_{NP}$ nani$]_1$ $[_{PP}$ naze$]_2]_2$ $[_{C'}[_{IP} \cdots$

Then, the PP created by adjunction antecedent-governs the trace of *naze*, since it binds, and is "close enough" to, this trace. Note that if *nani* moves to the SPEC of CP position and *naze* adjoins to this NP, then the trace of *naze* fails to be antecedent-governed, since the PP *naze* does not bind this trace. This corresponds to the case in the S' hypothesis where *nani*, and not *naze*, moved into the head position of COMP.

Once we adopt the CP hypothesis, it of course becomes necessary to reformulate the filters on COMP that we have proposed so far. To a large extent, this is straightforward. Let us first consider the filters (50)–(51) in chapter 1, repeated here as (46)–(47).

(46) A [+WH] COMP must have a [+WH] head.

(47) A [−WH] COMP must not have a [+WH] head.

These filters can be reformulated as in (48) under the CP hypothesis.[9]

(48) A COMP is [+WH] iff a [+WH] phrase is in its SPEC position.

Let us next consider the filter (53) in chapter 1, repeated here as (49).

(49) *$[\ldots \text{Head}_j \ldots]_i$, where $i \neq j$.

Recall that this filter was proposed to account for the fact that examples like (50a–b) are only two ways ambiguous, rather than three.

(50) a. who wonders where we bought what
     b. who wonders what you gave to whom

Since the ambiguity of (50b), for example, lies solely in the scope of *whom*, with *who* and *what* necessarily taking matrix and embedded scopes, respectively, the example must be prevented from having the following LF representation:

(51) $[_{CP}$ what$_1$ who$_2$ $[_{IP}$ t_2 wonders $[_{CP}$ whom$_3$ $[_{IP}$ we gave t_1 to $t_3]]]]$

With the S' system, if the index of *what* percolates up to the embedded C at S-structure, as we argued above, then (51) clearly violates the filter in (49). The embedded COMP has the index *1*, whereas its head *whom* has the index *3*.

The most straightforward reformulation of (49) within the CP system would be (52).

(52) A head and its SPEC cannot be contraindexed.

If the embedded COMP in (50b) receives the index of *what* via SPEC-head agreement at S-structure, then the filter in (52) is violated when *whom* moves into the SPEC position of this COMP at LF.

It should be noted here that the ECP analysis of (38) and (40) presented in section 2.2.3 poses an interesting problem that has certain implications for the filter in (52), or (49). In this analysis, we crucially relied on the assumption that at LF a COMP cannot legitimately retain an index assigned to it at S-structure when it no longer has a head with that index. Effects of this assumption can be seen when we examine (38) and (40) in more detail. (53) introduces some properties that were not explicit in (38).

(53) $[_{S'} [_{COMP} why_1]_1 [_S$ do you believe $[_{NP}$ the claim $[_{S'} [_{COMP}$ that$] [_S$ John said $[_{S'} [_{COMP} t_1']_1$ Bill left $t_1]]]]]]$

If the most deeply embedded COMP can retain the index *1* and properly govern t_1 after the intermediate trace t_1' is deleted in LF, then the resulting structure will incorrectly not violate the ECP.

A similar assumption is clearly necessary even if we assume the CP system. The most deeply embedded clause will have the structure in (54) after SPEC-head agreement takes place between the intermediate trace and the COMP.

(54) $[_{CP} t_1' [_{C'} C_1 [_{IP}$ Bill left $t_1]]]$

If the index on the head COMP remains legitimate at LF after the intermediate trace deletes in the LF component, the initial trace can be antecedent-governed by the COMP and (incorrectly) there will be no ECP violation. Hence, the following assumption is necessary to maintain our ECP account of examples such as (53):

(55) *C_i, where there is no SPEC with index i.

(55) states that an indexed COMP is legitimate only insofar as there is a coindexed phrase in its SPEC position. This basically means that the index of the head COMP is not only assigned, but must be licensed, through SPEC-head agreement. That is, once the head COMP is assigned an index through SPEC-head agreement, the COMP, in turn, requires a coindexed

SPEC. And if (55) is necessary on independent grounds, as we have argued, then (52) becomes redundant since it is subsumed under the more general filter in (55).

We have shown that for the class of phenomena we have investigated, there is actually very little at stake concerning the choice between the S′ and CP analyses. The one obvious exception to this generalization involves our treatment of *that*-trace effects. In chapter 1, we showed how the ungrammaticality of (56) (= (98) in chapter 1) follows as a direct consequence of the ECP, given our structural assumptions.

(56) *$[_{S′} [_{COMP}$ who$_1]_1 [_S$ do you think $[_{S′}$ that $[_S t_1$ saw John]]]]$

Subject position in English is not properly governed by anything internal to S, and the matrix COMP in (56) is too distant to serve as an antecedent governor for t_1. The only remaining possibility is the intermediate COMP. And since this position is occupied by *that*, it cannot contain an intermediate trace. Thus, t_1 is correctly assigned $[-\gamma]$.

This analysis is not available under the CP hypothesis. The relevant portion of the embedded S′ could now be as in (57).

(57)

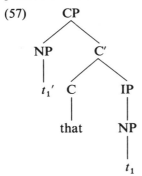

Here, $t_1′$ binds t_1, and no NP or CP intervenes between the two traces. Thus, t_1 is properly antecedent-governed by $t_1′$.

The descriptive generalization is that *that* in COMP somehow blocks antecedent government into IP. Chomsky (1986a) proposes a "minimality" constraint on antecedent government to capture this generalization; SPEC of CP cannot (antecedent-) govern into IP because COMP (*that*) is a closer governor. This account is not available to us, however, since we have argued that "antecedent government" is not, in fact, an instance of government. For the moment, we will simply assume the correctness of the descriptive generalization, postponing until section 5.5 consideration of what it follows from.

2.3 Properties of the Transformational Mapping

2.3.1 Toward Affect α

In the ECP analysis of some of the examples discussed above, we relied
on the assumption that the complementizer *that*, and, following Stowell
(1981), an intermediate trace in COMP, can delete in LF. The former case
arises with respect to examples such as (58).

(58) why$_1$ do you think [$_{CP}$ t_1' [$_{C'}$ that [$_{IP}$ John left t_1]]]

The trace t_1, being an adjunct trace, is subject to γ-marking at LF. If this
trace is to receive $[+\gamma]$ at this level, the LF representation of (58) must
be as in (59), since, as noted earlier, *that* in COMP blocks antecedent
government.

(59) why$_1$ do you think [$_{CP}$ t_1' [$_{C'}$[$_{IP}$ John left t_1]]]

According to our analysis, the mapping from (58) to (59) is achieved by the
deletion of *that* and, if the intermediate trace was not already present at
S-structure, the movement of *why*, first to the embedded COMP and then
back to the matrix COMP, in LF.

The deletion of an intermediate trace is relevant for examples such as the
following:

(60) ?*who$_1$ do you wonder [$_{CP}$ whether [$_{IP}$ Mary thinks [$_{CP}$ t_1' [$_{IP}$ t_1 left]]]]

(60), unlike (61), has the status of a simple Subjacency violation and hence
should not be an ECP violation.

(61) *why$_1$ do you wonder [$_{CP}$ whether [$_{IP}$ Mary thinks [$_{CP}$ t_1' [$_{IP}$ John
       left t_1]]]]

In (60), t_1, being an argument trace, is assigned $[+\gamma]$ at S-structure, by
virtue of the intermediate trace t_1'. But this intermediate trace will be
assigned $[-\gamma]$ at LF, if it is present at this level. Thus, the intermediate
trace t_1' must be deleted in the mapping from S-structure to LF. This is
possible if traces in COMP can freely delete in LF. Note that if this operation applies to the intermediate trace in (61), the resulting structure still
violates the ECP at LF, as desired. The initial trace in (61), being an adjunct trace, is γ-marked only at LF and hence requires a proper governor
at this level.

Along with Stowell (1981), we assume that the deletion of trace in
COMP is a special case of a more general operation proposed by Chomsky
and Lasnik (1977), which can be stated roughly as follows:[10]

(62) Delete anything in COMP.

Although (62) was proposed, in part, to allow the deletion of *that* in COMP in the syntax, it also subsumes the LF deletion of *that* discussed above. Like all other operations, (62) is constrained by recoverability. Thus, a pure complementizer *that* and intermediate traces can be deleted, but WH-phrases, which clearly have semantic content, cannot.

Given that deletion is constrained by recoverability, there is no clear reason to stipulate as in (62) that only items in COMP are subject to deletion. Consider the following examples:

(63) a. John tried [[PRO to solve the problem]]
     b. John was arrested *t*
     c. what did John read *t*

In these examples, however recoverability is to be formulated, it will surely prohibit the deletion of any of the lexically realized categories. Note that (63a–c) all have empty categories—PRO, NP-trace, or WH-trace—as well as lexically realized categories. In none of these examples can the empty category be deleted, either; but this follows entirely from independent principles. In both (63b) and (63c), the Projection Principle (ultimately the θ-Criterion) demands the presence of the trace. Further, the prohibition against vacuous quantification also requires that the trace in (63c) be present, at least at LF. Finally, the "extended" part of the Extended Projection Principle forces the presence of PRO in (63a).

These examples seem quite representative. Given the many independent conditions guaranteeing the presence of categories in the course of a derivation, (62) can be generalized to (64).

(64) Delete anything anywhere.

(64) might be restated as (65), parallel to Chomsky's (66).

(65) Delete α.

(66) Move α.

Thus, in either syntactic component (the one culminating in S-structure or the one culminating in LF), anything can be moved anywhere and anything can be deleted (both operations, or their outputs, subject to general conditions). That is, anything can be done to anything. We combine (65) and (66) into (67).

(67) Affect α.

2.3.2 Toward an Account of the Argument-Adjunct Asymmetry

As we have shown, our account of (68) relies on the deletion of *that* in the LF component.

(68) why$_1$ do you think [$_{CP}$ t_1' [$_{C'}$ that [$_{IP}$ John left t_1]]]

This allows this example to have the LF representation shown in (69).

(69) why$_1$ do you think [$_{CP}$ t_1' [$_{C'}$[$_{IP}$ John left t_1]]]

Our account of (68) also relies on (35), repeated here as (70).

(70) Only an argument receives a γ-feature at S-structure.

(70) was necessary to distinguish (68) and (71).

(71) *who$_1$ do you think [$_{CP}$ t_1' [$_{C'}$ that [$_{IP}$ t_1 left]]]

Since t_1 in (71) is an argument trace, given (70), it receives a γ-feature at S-structure. Thus, deletion of *that* in LF cannot save this trace from the ECP, because it is assigned $[-\gamma]$ at S-structure. On the other hand, t_1 in (68), being an adjunct trace, is assigned a γ-feature only at LF, according to (70), and it can receive $[+\gamma]$ at this level by virtue of *that*-deletion.

However, as it is stated, (70) is still a stipulation, and we would therefore hope that it follows from a general principle, or from the interaction of general principles. As noted in L&S (p. 269), (70) should in some way be related to the Extended Projection Principle, which requires, among other things, that arguments be present at every level of syntactic representation, in particular, at S-structure. In fact, since the Extended Projection Principle requires the trace of an argument, but not the trace of an adjunct, it appears that (70) follows straightforwardly from this principle. An argument trace is assigned a γ-feature at S-structure because it is present at this level. An adjunct trace is assigned a γ-feature at LF because it is required to be present only at this level. If this hypothesis can provide an account for all cases of subject-adjunct asymmetries that we attributed to (70), then we can dispense with (70) and simply assume that at both S-structure and LF, all traces that are present and not yet γ-marked receive γ-features.

This hypothesis clearly provides an account for the contrast between (68) and (71). The trace t_1 in (71) is marked $[-\gamma]$ at S-structure, since it must be present at this level because of the Extended Projection Principle, and it is not properly governed at this level. On the other hand, the Extended Projection Principle does not require the trace of *why* to be present at S-structure; hence, we can simply assume that there is no trace in the S-structure representation (68).[11] At LF, t_1 in (69) will presumably be required, to satisfy the constraint against vacuous quantification, which we may plausibly assume as a constraint on LF representations. Then, in LF, after *that*-deletion, *why* can lower to the position of t_1 and then move back to its S-structure position through the SPEC of CP position. According to this hypothesis, both t_1 and t_1' in (69) are created in LF. Hence, they are both assigned γ-features only at LF and are both marked $[+\gamma]$ at this level. Thus, the contrast between (68) and (71) can be accounted for without the stipulation in (70).

2.3.3   A Note on WH-Lowering

The LF lowering needed in the derivation of (69) evidently conforms to all constraints on LF Move α. Here, a comment on such lowering may be in order. Lowering is allowed by Move α in the absence of a stipulation to the contrary. Move α specifies the relations between D-structure and S-structure, and S-structure and LF, and does not by itself say anything about the representations at each syntactic level. S-structure representations such as the following, produced by lowering, are certainly ill formed:

(72)   *Bill asked t_1 [$_{CP}$ who$_1$ [$_{IP}$ Mary left]]

However, this example is ruled out quite independently of how it is derived. In particular, it violates the constraint against vacuous quantification and the Proper Binding Condition. The former constraint is independently motivated by examples such as the following:

(73)   *who does Mary like Bill

In (73), *who* does not bind a variable, and hence, this example is ruled out by the constraint in question.

As we will discuss in chapter 4, the following example, pointed out to us by Anthony Kroch (who credits it to Mark Baltin), rather clearly shows the effects of the Proper Binding Condition:

(74)   *[$_{AP}$ how likely [$_{IP}$ t_1 to be a riot]]$_2$ [$_{IP}$ is there$_1$ t_2]

The trace t_1 is not bound by *there*, in violation of the Proper Binding Condition. Since there is evidently no vacuous quantification involved, it is this condition that accounts for the ungrammaticality of (74).[12]

Thus, assuming that (72) represents the general case, a specific prohibition against lowering would be an unnecessary, hence mistaken, complication of the theory. And this, in effect, has been assumed in the development of generative syntax, especially since the early 1970s. (See, in particular, Fiengo 1974, 1977 and Chomsky 1976, 1981.) Consequently, where the results of lowering do not violate independent principles, lowering will be allowed. This is exactly what we have illustrated with (69). Thus, there is both conceptual and empirical motivation for allowing Move α to operate freely, unconstrained by a lowering prohibition.[13]

2.3.4 Extending the Extended Projection Principle

As noted in L&S (p. 269), the proposed account of (68) and (71) does not generalize to contrasts such as that between (39) and (40). (39) and (40) are repeated here as (75) and (76) (but now assuming the CP hypothesis).

(75) ?*who$_1$ do you wonder whether John said [$_{CP}$ t_1' [$_{C'}$ [$_{IP}$ t_1 solved the problem]]]

(76) *how$_1$ do you wonder whether John said [$_{CP}$ t_1' [$_{C'}$ [$_{IP}$ Mary solved the problem t_1]]]

As noted earlier, (75) has the status of a Subjacency violation, and (76) is worse, having the status of an ECP violation. However, if we assume that (70) is reduced to the Extended Projection Principle, then (76) should not violate the ECP. Note that the Extended Projection Principle entails that adjunct traces *need not* be present at S-structure. Thus, it does not prevent t_1' and t_1 in (76) from being present at this level. And if they are present at this level, then t_1 can be assigned [$+\gamma$] at this level, and t_1' can delete in LF. Consequently, (76) should merely violate Subjacency, exactly like (75). Thus, the consequence of the Extended Projection Principle that adjunct traces *need not* be present at S-structure is not sufficient. The contrast between (75) and (76) indicates that adjunct traces *cannot* be present at this level. If t_1 in (76) is not present at S-structure, then it cannot be assigned [$+\gamma$] at this level. Thus, it must be assigned this feature at LF. But this implies that t_1' must also be present at this level. Since this trace can receive [$+\gamma$] neither at S-structure nor at LF, (76) will violate the ECP.

This consideration led to the tentative conclusion in L&S that (70) is at least in part independent of the Extended Projection Principle and hence must remain a principle. Here, we continue to accept the former conclusion, but we will call the latter into question. In the remainder of this section, we will examine both. First, we will consider the Extended Projection Principle itself and discuss an implication of our analysis so far for the status of this principle. Second, we will speculate on the kind of principle that interacts with the Extended Projection Principle to produce the effects of (70). We will tentatively propose a constraint on chains that has this property.

Let us take the following statement of the Extended Projection Principle (EPP) as the point of departure:

(77) a. Representations at each syntactic level (D-structure, S-structure, and LF) are projected from the lexicon, in that they observe the subcategorization properties of lexical items. (Chomsky 1981: 29)
   b. Every clause must have a subject.

As a constraint on D-structure, S-structure, and LF, (77) requires that every argument be present at all these levels. In addition, the mapping between the syntactic levels is characterized by Move α or, more generally, Affect α. Thus, we have the model of syntax shown in (78).

(78)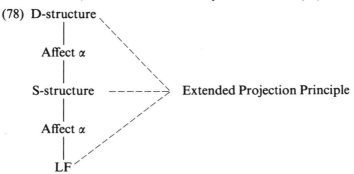

In (78), there is a clear division of labor. Affect α specifies how the D-structure and the S-structure representations, or the S-structure and LF representations, of a sentence can differ. On the other hand, the EPP specifies, in part, what must remain constant in the three representations. Recoverability works in concert with the EPP toward this goal.[14] Thus, given the D-structure representation in (79), the former states that its S-structure representation cannot be the one in (80), and the latter that it cannot be the one in (81).

(79) John solved this problem

(80) a.   Mary solved this problem
     b.   John likes this problem
     c.   *John this problem

(81) a.   *this problem, John solved   (with no object empty category)
     b.   *this problem was solved by John   (with no object empty category)

From (80a), the lexical content of the subject in (79) is not recoverable. Similarly, in (80b–c), some lexical content is lost. In (81a–b), no lexical content is lost, but the subcategorization properties of the verb are not categorially represented. There is no [NP, VP] in either (81a) or (81b). Another constraint similar to recoverability is that no lexical item with semantic content can be inserted at S-structure or at LF (*inverse recoverability*).[15] Thus, (82a–b) cannot be the S-structure representation of (79).

(82) a.   John solved this trivial problem
     b.   John solved this problem easily

If insertion, or Insert α, is a subcase of Affect α, as seems reasonable, then inverse recoverability, too, must be a constraint on the application, or output, of Affect α.

The above three conditions constrain the application of Affect α, or its output. In particular, as noted in the discussion of Affect α in section 2.3.1, Delete α is constrained by recoverability. Given the conception outlined above, Affect α, with the constraints, characterizes the possible mapping between levels. The EPP and recoverability can be construed as constraints on Affect α itself, specifying what has to be mapped. Given this conception of these two principles, they can in fact be considered two facets of a deeper requirement, say, *Conservation*.

If we adopt the reasonable assumption that Conservation is a constraint on Affect α rather than on syntactic levels, then the standard *that*-trace violation in (83) can be given a more precise analysis.

(83) *who$_1$ do you think [$_{CP}$ t_1' [$_{C'}$ that [$_{IP}$ t_1 left]]]

The trace t_1 is assigned $[-\gamma]$ at S-structure and hence violates the γ-Filter at LF. However, note that if Conservation (EPP) were merely a constraint on levels, then nothing would prevent the deletion of t_1 $[-\gamma]$ in LF, as long as a new trace were generated in the same position in the LF component. That is, under this assumption, the following operations must be possible in LF.

(84)

who$_1$ do you think [$_{CP}$ t_1' [$_{C'}$ that   [$_{IP}$ $t_1 \atop [-\gamma]$ left]]]

Delete α Delete α

The complementizer *that* and the trace t_1 with $[-\gamma]$ can be deleted. Further, a new "initial" trace can be created by the back-and-forth movement of *who* in the LF derivation of (83). The resulting LF representation of (83) would be as follows:

(85) who$_1$ [$_{IP}$ do you think [$_{CP}$ $t_1 \atop [+\gamma]$ [$_{C'}$ [$_{IP}$ $t_1 \atop [+\gamma]$ left]]]]

Hence, we predict incorrectly that (83) is grammatical, since Conservation (EPP) is satisfied at each level. On the other hand, if the EPP is taken to be a constraint on Affect α itself, then the LF deletion of the subject trace t_1 in (84) is impossible, since this trace is required by the EPP. Hence, the derivation in (84) is disallowed, and we correctly predict the ungrammaticality of (83).[16]

By constraining Affect α, Conservation specifies what must be mapped in the derivation from one level to another. As far as we know, most constraints on mapping that have been proposed in the literature are of this nature. However, as we noted in the case of "inverse recoverability," there are also constraints on what Affect α may add to a structure. Here, we will speculate on another constraint that has a similar effect.

Recall that contrasts such as the one between (75) and (76) can be accounted for without the stipulation in (70) if traces of adjuncts cannot be present at S-structure. (70) and (75)–(76) are repeated here as (86) and (87)–(88), respectively.

(86) Only an argument receives a γ-feature at S-structure.

(87) ?*who$_1$ do you wonder whether John said [$_{CP}$ t_1' [$_{C'}$[$_{IP}$ t_1 solved the problem]]]

(88) *how$_1$ do you wonder whether John said [$_{CP}$ t_1' [$_{C'}$[$_{IP}$ Mary solved the problem t_1]]]

However, as noted earlier, Conservation (EPP) entails only that the trace t_1 in (88) need not be present at S-structure, and not that it must not be present at this level. This suggests, then, that there is an additional constraint prohibiting the presence of t_1 in (88) at S-structure. The effect of this constraint must be complementary to that of the EPP. Loosely speaking, the EPP specifies where traces must be present, and this constraint specifies where traces must not be present. We will tentatively propose a formulation of this constraint as a constraint on chains.

It has been widely assumed that Move α results in the formation of a chain, both at S-structure and at LF.[17] Consider, for example, (89)–(91).

(89) this problem$_1$ was solved t_1

(90) what$_1$ did you buy t_1

(91) what$_1$ did you think [$_{CP}$ t_1' [$_{C'}$[$_{IP}$ Mary bought t_1]]]

In (89), *this problem* and t_1 constitute an A-chain, where the head *this problem* is in an A-position. In (90), *what* and t_1 make up an Ā-chain, and in (91), the Ā-chain consists of *what*, t_1', and t_1. In each of these chains, the tail of the chain, t_1, is required by the EPP both at S-structure and at LF.[18] The trace t_1 in (90) and (91) is required in addition by the constraint against vacuous quantification at LF. We can then say that these traces are not only required but also licensed by those conditions. Their presence is in effect guaranteed by the conditions mentioned above. This fact suggests the following condition on chains:

(92) a. Every trace must be a member of a chain.

   b. Every chain must have as its tail an empty category that is
      licensed.

We assume that certain conditions can license an empty category by requiring its presence. We will tentatively assume that Conservation (EPP)
can license empty categories at S-structure and LF, and that the constraint
against vacuous quantification can do so at LF.

   The constraints in (92) have the effect of (86) and hence make it possible
to do away with (86) and maintain that all traces, unless already γ-marked,
are subject to γ-marking at S-structure and at LF. They ensure that traces
are only present when they are required by the EPP or by the constraint
against vacuous quantification. In particular, they imply that the trace t_1
in (88) cannot be present at S-structure. Suppose that (88) is a possible
S-structure representation of the example. Then, there will be a chain consisting of *how*, t_1', and t_1. But this chain violates the constraint in (92),
since t_1 is licensed at S-structure neither by the EPP nor by the constraint
against vacuous quantification. This implies that t_1 cannot be present in
the S-structure representation of this example. Suppose, then, that the
S-structure representation of the example is as in (93).[19]

(93) how$_1$ do you wonder whether John said [$_{CP}$ t_1' [$_{C'}$ [$_{IP}$ Mary solved
     the problem]]]

In this case, there will be a chain consisting only of *how* and t_1'. But this
chain is also ruled out by (92), since t_1' is licensed neither by the EPP nor
by the constraint against vacuous quantification.

   Finally, suppose that the S-structure representation of the example is as
in (94).

(94) how$_1$ do you wonder whether John said [$_{CP}$[$_{IP}$ Mary solved the
     problem]]

Since (94) does not contain any chain whose tail is a trace, (92) is irrelevant. But the LF representation of (94) must contain a trace of *how*, for
otherwise the constraint against vacuous quantification will be violated. In
fact, the LF representation must contain a trace of *how* in the most deeply
embedded IP for the sentence to receive the intended interpretation. Thus,
how in (94) must move back and forth to yield the LF representation
shown in (95).

(95) how$_1$ do you wonder whether John said [$_{CP}$ t_1' [$_{C'}$ [$_{IP}$ Mary solved
     the problem t_1]]]

But this LF representation clearly violates the ECP. If the intermediate
trace t_1' is not present, then t_1 is assigned [$-\gamma$], and (95) is ruled out by the

γ-Filter. If t_1' is present, then t_1 is assigned $[+\gamma]$. But then, t_1' is assigned $[-\gamma]$, and again, (95) is ruled out. Thus, the constraints in (92) correctly force (88) to be analyzed as an ECP violation.

On the other hand, (87) can be analyzed essentially as before. It has a chain consisting of WH, t_1', and t_1 at S-structure, and this chain satisfies the constraint in (92) because t_1 is licensed by the EPP. In addition, the trace t_1 is required by the EPP to be present at S-structure. Thus, t_1 is assigned $[+\gamma]$ at S-structure, and t_1', although it is assigned $[-\gamma]$ at this level, can delete in LF. Hence, this example does not violate the ECP.

Note here that in our analysis of (87), the intermediate trace is assigned $[-\gamma]$ at S-structure, but it does not violate the γ-Filter since it is deleted in LF. This account implies that the γ-Filter applies only at LF, and not at S-structure. If the filter applied at S-structure, then (87) would be ruled out as an ECP violation at that level. The same argument can be constructed on the basis of the following similar, but perfectly grammatical, example:

(96) who$_1$ do you believe [$_{CP}$ t_1'' [$_{C'}$ that [$_{IP}$ Mary said [$_{CP}$ t_1' [$_{C'}$[$_{IP}$ t_1 left early]]]]]]

In S-structure representation (96), modified from (28), t_1 is licensed by Conservation (EPP), and t_1' is licensed by (92a), as part of the chain of t_1. Thus, at S-structure, t_1 can be marked $[+\gamma]$ by t_1'. However, now that we have eliminated (86) as a principle, t_1' will itself be subject to γ-marking at S-structure and will in fact be marked $[-\gamma]$. If the γ-Filter applied at S-structure, (96) would have just the status of a *that*-trace violation. The fact that the example is fully acceptable argues strongly that the filter applies only at LF.

We have seen that given our model of grammar, a constraint such as (92) can be naturally assumed, and further that, given this constraint, the stipulation in (86) can be dispensed with. Our discussion here has been speculative, and it remains to be seen whether (92) can be maintained. But since (92) is more principled than (86), and since we know of no evidence against it, we will provisionally assume it to be correct.[20]

Chapter 3
Topicalization

In this chapter, we will examine Chomsky's (1986a) modification of the theory of proper government. In the course of this examination, we will explore a range of topicalization phenomena in some detail. These phenomena turn out to provide a crucial test case for theories of bounding and proper government. Our investigation of them will lead us to certain revisions of Chomsky's (1986a) model.

3.1 Barriers

The approach to ECP phenomena presented thus far is based on Chomsky 1981, AHS, and Huang 1982, as developed in L&S. Chomsky (1986a) argues for a modification of this approach, to which we now turn. His concern is to develop a theory that, among other things, (1) explains why certain configurations are islands and gives a unified account of these, (2) relates Subjacency and antecedent government, and (3) unifies antecedent government and government. Central to the first of these concerns is the goal of bringing the CED, which prohibits movement out of a subject or adjunct, under Subjacency. More generally, Chomsky explores the question of whether there is a reasonable notion of "barrier" that has the property that the same categories in the same configurations constitute barriers to government and to movement. We will briefly outline Chomsky's proposals in this section, to the extent that they are relevant to the present investigation, and will then, in the light of certain data not considered by Chomsky, suggest revisions. Our goal will be to formulate a theory that accounts for the range of facts investigated in L&S and in chapters 1 and 2 of this monograph while addressing, to the extent possible, Chomsky's above-mentioned concerns.

3.1.1 Subjacency

Chomsky (1986a) proposes the following formulation of Subjacency:

(1) (= Chomsky's (59))

β is *n-subjacent* to α iff there are fewer than $n + 1$ barriers for β that exclude α.

(2) is Chomsky's proposed constraint (p.30).[1]

(2) In a well-formed chain with a link (α_i, α_{i+1}), α_{i+1} must be 1-subjacent to α_i.

Exclusion is defined as in (3).

(3) (= Chomsky's (17))

α *excludes* β if no segment of α dominates β.

With respect to the notion "segment" in (3), following May (1985), Chomsky proposes the following (p. 7):

[I]n a structure of the form [4], a typical adjunction structure with α adjoined to β, α is not dominated by the category β; rather, β consists of two "segments," and a category is dominated by β only if it is dominated by both of these segments.

(4) (= Chomsky's (11))

$[_\beta \alpha [_\beta \ldots]]$

We will mainly be concerned with the question of what constitutes a barrier for the purposes of definition (1). Chomsky introduces the concept *blocking category* (BC), and then defines *barrier* in terms of BC.

(5) (= Chomsky's (25))

γ is a *BC* for β iff γ is not L-marked and γ dominates β.

(6) a. (= Chomsky's (28))

α *L-marks* β iff α is a lexical category that θ-governs β.

b. (= Chomsky's (27))

α θ-*governs* β iff α is a zero-level category that θ-marks β, and α, β are sisters.

c. (= Chomsky's (12))

α *is dominated by* β only if it is dominated by every segment of β.

(7) (= Chomsky's (26))

γ is a *barrier* for β iff (a) or (b):

a. γ immediately dominates δ, δ a BC for β;

b. γ is a BC for β, $\gamma \neq$ IP.

Immediate domination in (7) is a relation between maximal projections. γ immediately dominates δ if there is no intervening maximal projection, that is, no maximal projection that dominates δ and is dominated by γ.

The Subjacency Condition as defined in (2) unifies the classical cases of Subjacency violations (complex NP constraint, WH-island constraint) with those subsumed under Huang's (1982) CED (subject condition, adjunct condition). Let us briefly consider some examples:

(8) a. *where$_2$ did you see [$_{NP}$ the book$_1$ [$_{CP}$ which$_1$ [$_{IP}$ John put t_1 t_2]]]
    b. ?*who$_1$ [$_{IP}$ did [$_{NP}$ pictures of t_1] please you]

The movement of *where* in (8a) clearly crosses two barriers. The embedded CP is a BC since it is not θ-marked by any lexical category. Thus, it is a barrier, and it also makes the NP dominating it a barrier. Similarly, in (8b), the subject NP is a BC. Thus, it is itself a barrier and makes the IP another barrier. Therefore, the movement of *who$_1$* from the position of t_1 to SPEC of CP crosses two barriers, and hence, (8b) violates Subjacency.

Let us next consider some grammatical examples:

(9) a. what$_1$ [did you [see t_1]]
    b. what$_1$ [did you [think [[John [saw t_1]]]]]

Chomsky (1986a) assumes that VP is not L-marked. Thus, if the movement of *what* in (9a) takes place in one step from the position of t_1 to SPEC of CP, then it violates Subjacency, since it crosses VP and IP, both barriers. VP is a barrier since, by hypothesis, it is a BC (and is not IP). IP is a barrier since it immediately dominates a BC, VP. This implies that *what* in (9a) moves to SPEC of CP in two steps. Chomsky (1986a) therefore proposes that *what* in (9a) first adjoins to VP and then moves to SPEC of CP, as shown in (10).

(10) [$_{CP}$ what$_1$ [$_{IP}$ did you [$_{VP}$ [$_{VP}$ see t_1]]]]

The VP is a BC—and hence, a barrier—for t_1. However, since this node does not exclude the landing site of the first movement, it does not count for the purpose of Subjacency (see (1)). Thus, t_1 is 0-subjacent to the position adjoined to VP. The position adjoined to VP is also 0-subjacent to SPEC of CP. The VP is not a BC, thus not a barrier for this movement, since it does not dominate the position adjoined to VP. IP is a BC for this movement, but is not a barrier since IP, by definition, is a barrier only when it immediately dominates a BC. Thus, (10) does not violate Subjacency.

The hypothesis that WH-movement can proceed through adjunction also saves (9b) from violating Subjacency. The movement can proceed as follows:

(11) [$_{CP}$ what$_1$ [$_{IP}$ did you [$_{VP}$ [$_{VP}$ think [$_{CP}$ [$_{IP}$ John [$_{VP}$ [$_{VP}$ saw t_1]]]]]]]]]

Movement 1 is allowed just like the first movement in (10). Movements 2 and 4 are just like the second movement in (10). For movement 3, neither the CP nor the VP is a barrier for Subjacency. CP is not a BC, and hence, not a barrier, since it is L-marked by the verb *think*. The VP of the matrix clause is a potential barrier, but it is irrelevant for this movement, because it does not exclude the landing site. Thus, (9b) is allowed.

However, if WH-movement can adjoin phrases to all maximal projections, then the definition of Subjacency becomes too permissive. Consider (12).

(12) ??what$_1$ did you wonder whether John bought t_1

As Chomsky (1986a) points out, if IP-adjunction is allowed for WH-movement, then (12) will, incorrectly, not violate Subjacency, as shown in (13).

(13) [$_{CP}$ what$_1$ [$_{IP}$ did you [$_{VP}$ [$_{VP}$ wonder [$_{CP}$ whether [$_{IP}$ [$_{IP}$ John [$_{VP}$

[$_{VP}$ bought t_1]]]]]]]]]

In (13), there are *no* barriers. CP, the likeliest candidate, is not, since it is not a BC, nor is the IP that it immediately dominates a BC for IP-adjoined position. This is so because IP does not dominate this position (see definition (5)). To eliminate this difficulty, Chomsky (1986a: 5, 32) thus proposes (14).

(14) A WH-phrase may not adjoin to IP.

Derivation (13) is excluded by (14). Now, as illustrated in (15), the embedded IP will be a BC for the position adjoined to the embedded VP, and CP will thus be a barrier for movement 2.

(15) [$_{CP}$ what$_1$ [$_{IP}$ did you [$_{VP}$ [$_{VP}$ wonder [$_{CP}$ whether [$_{IP}$ John [$_{VP}$

[$_{VP}$ bought t_1]]]]]]]]

Since each link still conforms to 1-subjacency, Chomsky suggests that 0-subjacency is required for full grammaticality. The marginality of the example is then a consequence of the fact that link 2 does not conform to 0-subjacency.

Before we can conclude that the marginal status of (12) is accounted for, there is one more derivation that must be considered. Even if IP is not an available adjunction site, nothing we have said so far prevents adjunction to the complement CP. But such an operation makes a derivation available in which 0-subjacency is satisfied everywhere:

(16) [$_{CP}$ what$_1$ [$_{IP}$ did you [$_{VP}$ [$_{VP}$ wonder [$_{CP}$ [$_{CP}$ whether [$_{IP}$ John [$_{VP}$

[$_{VP}$ bought t_1]]]]]]]]]]

The crucial link is created by step 2 of the derivation. Note that VP is not a BC in this case; hence, IP is not a barrier. Further, although IP is a BC, it is not a barrier, by the second clause in (7b). The movement must not be allowed to proceed as in (16), then; instead, it must be as in (15). Chomsky ensures this by principle (17).[2]

(17) (= Chomsky's (6))
Adjunction is possible only to a maximal projection (hence, X″) that is a nonargument [thus generally not NP or CP].

Given the restrictions on adjunction sites stated in (14) and (17), Subjacency correctly rules out complex NP constraint violations and subject condition violations, even on the sorts of successive adjunction derivations just examined. Consider the examples in (8) again, repeated here in (18).

(18) a. *where$_2$ did you see [$_{NP}$ the book$_1$ [$_{CP}$ which$_1$ [$_{IP}$ John put t_1 t_2]]]
b. ?*who$_1$ [$_{IP}$ did [$_{NP}$ pictures of t_1] please you]

If IPs and NPs were possible adjunction sites for WH-movement, then these examples would not violate Subjacency at all, as shown in (19).

(19) a. [$_{CP}$ where$_2$ [$_{IP}$ did you [$_{VP}$ [$_{VP}$ see [$_{NP}$ [$_{NP}$ the book$_1$ [$_{CP}$

[$_{CP}$ that [$_{IP}$ John [$_{VP}$ [$_{VP}$ put t_1 t_2]]]]]]]]]]]]

b. [$_{CP}$ who$_1$ [$_{IP}$ did [$_{NP}$ [$_{NP}$ pictures of t_1]] please you]]

Given (17), the steps 2, 3, and 4 in (19a) must be combined, and this movement crosses two barriers, CP and NP. Similarly, steps 1 and 2 in (19b) must be combined, and this movement also crosses two barriers, NP and IP. Note that each step in the derivations in (19) crosses no barrier for Subjacency. Thus, without (17), we would incorrectly predict that the examples in (18) are perfect.

3.1.2 Antecedent Government
The concepts discussed in the preceding section are relevant not just to Subjacency but to antecedent government as well. Chomsky (1986a:17) suggests the following formulation of antecedent government:

(20) Antecedent government holds of a link (α, β) of a chain, where α governs β.

In this formulation, antecedent government is an instance of government. *Govern* is defined in (21).

(21) (= Chomsky's (18))

α *governs* β iff α m-commands β and there is no γ, γ a barrier for β, such that γ excludes α.

The notion "barrier" here is the same one developed above for Subjacency. Finally, *m-command* is defined in (22) (Chomsky 1986a: 8).

(22) α *m-commands* β iff α does not dominate β and every maximal projection that dominates α dominates β.

Now consider (23).

(23) $[_{CP}$ who$_1$ $[_{IP}$ do you $[_{VP}$ t_1' $[_{VP}$ wonder $[_{CP}$ why$_2$ $[_{IP}$ t_1 won the race $t_2]]]]]]$

Here, t_1 is not antecedent-governed: t_1' does not govern t_1, since the lower CP is a barrier for t_1, by "inheritance" from the IP that it immediately dominates. Similarly, *who*$_1$ does not govern t_1. Since t_1 is not antecedent-governed, and since it clearly is not lexically governed, it is not properly governed at all, the desired result in this case.[3]

The treatment of adjuncts is now also straightforward. Recall from chapters 1 and 2 that LF is the only relevant level for the traces of non-arguments. Recall further that in the LF component, *that* can be deleted as an instance of Affect α. Thus, we need not consider a representation with *that*. With this in mind, consider (25), the LF representation of both (24a) and (24b), under the assumptions of the preceding section.[4]

(24) a. how do you think $[_{CP}$ that John fixed the car $t]$
     b. how do you think $[_{CP}$ John fixed the car $t]$

(25) $[_{CP}$ how$_1$ $[_{IP}$ do you $[_{VP}$ t_1'' $[_{VP}$ think $[_{CP}$ t_1' $[_{IP}$ John fixed the car $t_1]]]]]]$

Here, t_1' governs t_1, since IP is "defective," that is, never an inherent barrier; t_1'' governs t_1', since CP, being L-marked, is not a barrier; and finally, *how* governs t_1''. In both (24a) and (24b), then, antecedent government holds, and extraction of the adjunct is correctly permitted.

We now turn to a configuration where antecedent government fails. Consider (26).

(26) $[_{CP}$ how$_1$ $[_{IP}$ did Bill $[_{VP}$ t_1''' $[_{VP}$ wonder $[_{CP}$ who$_2$ $[_{IP}$ t_2 $[_{VP}$ t_1'' $[_{VP}$ wanted $[_{CP}$ t_1' $[_{IP}$ PRO to fix the car $t_1]]]]]]]]]]]$

As in (25), t_1' governs t_1. Further, t_1' is governed by t_1'', CP being L-marked and hence not a barrier. However, t_1'' violates the ECP. t_1''' is too distant to govern it, since the intervening CP inherits barrierhood from the intermediate IP. Recall that the BC effect of this IP cannot be evaded by adjunction to it, given (14). t_1'' is thus an offending trace. Note that t_1'' need not have been created, but if it were not present, t_1' would be an offending trace. Similarly, t_1' need not have been created, but then t_1 itself would be the offending trace. Correctly, then, extraction of an adjunct from an island always results in an ECP violation.[5]

In the following sections, we will examine a further range of data in the light of this theory, and based on that examination, we will suggest certain revisions.

3.2 Analyses of Topicalization

3.2.1 The Standard Analysis

Chomsky (1977a) presents a detailed analysis of topicalization in English. He notes first that the construction with a gap, shown in (27), seems in some respects to parallel the so-called left dislocation (LD) construction, shown in (28), which lacks a gap.[6]

(27) John, I like t

(28) John, I like him

This parallelism suggests a common structure. Chomsky proposes that in both constructions, the "topic" is base-generated in Topic position under S'':

(29)
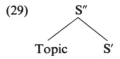

The difference between (27) and (28) does not involve the position of *John* at any level, then. Rather, the difference is that (27) involves movement of a WH-operator (later deleted) to COMP, whereas (28) involves no such movement, in fact involves no movement at all.

This analysis of (28) straightforwardly explains Ross's (1967) original observation that LD freely violates island constraints. For example, the relationship between *this book* and *it* in (30) crosses the boundary of a complex NP, yet the example is well formed:

(30) this book, I accept the argument that John should read it

Topicalization, on the other hand, conforms to island constraints. The topicalized analogue of (30) is substantially worse.

(31) ??this book, I accept the argument that John should read t

This difference is predicted by the interaction between Chomsky's theory of island constraints—namely, Subjacency as a constraint on movement—

and his accounts of the two constructions. Since (27) involves movement, in fact WH-movement, topicalization conforms to Subjacency in just the same way as relativization or WH-question movement:

(32) ??the book which I accept the argument that John should read *t*

(33) ??which book do you accept the argument that John should read *t*

Another argument that could be offered for Chomsky's proposal is based on *that*-trace effects. Topicalization in (34) is just as bad as WH-question movement in (35).

(34) *John, I think that *t* won the race

(35) *who do you think that *t* won the race

LD in (36), however, is fine.

(36) John, I think that he won the race

Assuming, as in Chomsky and Lasnik 1977 or Chomsky 1981, that the phenomenon illustrated in (34) and (35) involves a constraint on traces, the similarity between (34) and (35), and the difference between these two examples and (36), is accounted for. In particular, in the framework of Chomsky 1981, both (34) and (35) are straightforwardly ruled out by the ECP.

3.2.2 A Revised Analysis

Chomsky's analysis predicts that under certain circumstances where LD is available, topicalization should be unavailable, for example, where Subjacency or the ECP would be violated. On the other hand, wherever topicalization is possible, LD should always be possible. This is so because the structures are identical except that topicalization involves movement. The former prediction is strongly confirmed, as Chomsky demonstrates. We will argue in this section that the latter prediction is incorrect.

It is known that topicalization is possible, although marginal for some speakers, in an embedded clause. Some examples are given in (37).

(37) a. I believe that this book, you should read *t*
      b. I believe that the books, I gave *t* away to some friends

In (37a–b), the topic follows the COMP of the embedded clause. To account for such examples, Chomsky (1977a) proposes the PS rule in (38a), which can be restated as in (38b) under his (1986a) framework.

(38) a. S′ → COMP S″
      b. C′ → COMP TP, where TP = Topic Phrase

According to this analysis, (37a), for example, has the following structure:

(39) a. [$_S$ I believe [$_{S'}$ that [$_{S''}$ this book [$_{S'}$ (WH) [$_S$ you should read t]]]]]

   b. [$_{IP}$ I believe [$_{CP}$ that [$_{TP}$ this book [$_{CP}$ (WH) [$_{IP}$ you should read t]]]]]

Given this analysis, since S″ (TP) can be generated within an embedded clause, LD should also be possible in embedded clauses. Further, as noted above, we should expect that embedded LD is possible *whenever* embedded topicalization is possible.

However, as Baltin (1982) has pointed out, there are cases where embedded topicalization is possible but embedded LD is not. He cites contrasts such as the following:

(40) (= Baltin's (69))
   the man to whom liberty, we could never grant

(41) (= Baltin's (86))
   *the man to whom liberty, we could never grant it

In order to account for this contrast, Baltin proposes that LD involves a base-generated topic (and hence, S″), whereas topicalization involves adjunction to S, and, further, that S″ is a bounding node. According to him, it is the relativization in (41) that is illicit. Relativization violates Subjacency in (41), but in (40) it does not. Such an analysis of the contrast between (40) and (41) is impossible if we assume that embedded LD and embedded topicalization have identical structures, as proposed by Chomsky (1977a).

Note that although Baltin (1982) and Chomsky (1977a) disagree on the nature of topicalization—for Baltin, it involves adjunction to S rather than base generation of a topic and WH-movement of an operator—they agree on the recursive character of S″. However, there is reason to believe that S″ (TP) is only possible for the matrix in the variety of English under consideration. Consider the LD analogue of (37a):[7]

(42) *I believe that this book, you should read it

In (43)–(44), also, topicalization is possible but LD is quite bad.

(43) that this solution, I proposed last year is widely known

(44) *that this solution, I proposed it last year is widely known

Neither (42) nor (44) involves movement, and hence, neither can be ruled out by Subjacency (or any other constraint on movement). Thus, the ungrammaticality of these sentences shows that (41) must be ruled out independently of Subjacency and suggests, more generally, that in English S″ (TP) can occur only in matrix clauses. And if S″ (TP) can occur only in matrix clauses, then embedded topicalization cannot involve a base-generated topic. This indicates that S(IP)-adjunction must be an option for topicalization, as argued by Baltin (1982). Here, we propose that embedded topicalization necessarily involves IP-adjunction, and that matrix topicalization can involve either movement to SPEC of CP (as in Chomsky's analysis) or IP-adjunction. In what follows, we will explore the consequences of this hypothesis.

The most straightforward way to prevent embedded S″ (TP) in a language is to preclude this category from appearing on the right-hand side of any PS rule, or, in a rule-free system, to disallow S″ (TP) as the complement of COMP. This would have the further consequence that multiple S″s (TPs), hence multiple Topic (Top) positions, are excluded even from the matrix. To begin to test this prediction, consider the following example:

(45) John, Mary, he likes *t*

(45) seems reasonably acceptable, and in fact either our proposal or Chomsky's would allow it. For Chomsky, the structure of (45) would be essentially that given in (46).

(46)

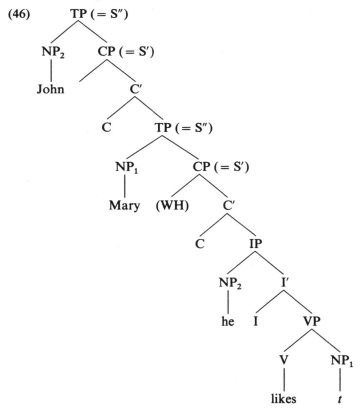

But now notice that the ill-formed (47) will also be generated. Structure (48) is clearly available, since it is parallel to (46) except that it involves no movement.

(47) *John, Mary, he likes her

(48)

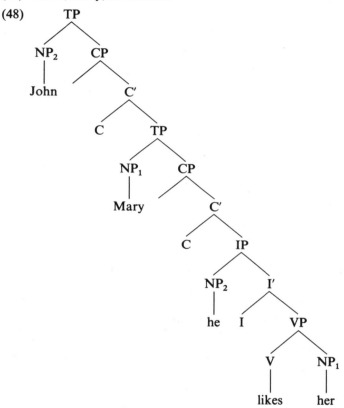

This problem does not arise under our proposal. If TP is not recursive in English, such a structure as (48) can never be generated. There can be at most one base-generated Top position in a sentence. Example (45), then, will not involve multiple Top positions. Rather, as (49) illustrates, only *John* will be in Top, and *Mary* will be adjoined to IP.

(49)

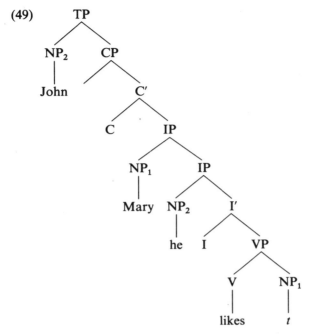

It is possible to have a base-generated topic and a topic adjoined to IP simultaneously in a single clause. This is so because, according to our hypothesis, two distinct types of "topicalization" are allowed in matrix clauses: by base generation of a topic under TP, and by adjunction of a topic to IP. We will reserve the term *topicalization* for the latter type.[8]

Once we accept the possibility of IP-adjunction for the topic construction, we must reexamine the Subjacency effects on this construction. Recall that Chomsky's (1977a) S″ analysis of topicalization was motivated in part by the interaction of topicalization and Subjacency. Thus, it is crucial that we consider the consequences of the IP-adjunction hypothesis in this domain.

Let us first consider the following example of "long-distance" movement:

(50) this book, I think that you should read *t*

Here, if this example is an instance of topicalization, (i.e., IP-adjunction), a question may arise concerning its derivation. However, given that the TP analysis is possible for the matrix, there is no need to assume that (50) must involve movement of *this book*. This example can be derived straightforwardly by WH-movement as proposed by Chomsky (1977a).

More interesting are those cases of "long-distance" movement that *must* be derived by topicalization. Two such cases are shown in (51) and (52).

(51) John said that this book, he thought you would like *t*

(52) John, this book, he thought you would like *t*

In (51), *this book* must be adjoined to IP, since embedded topics cannot be base-generated under TP. Similarly, *this book* in (52) must be preposed by topicalization, since, as we have shown (see (47)), an English sentence cannot have more than one base-generated topic. Thus, both (51) and (52) clearly involve "long-distance" topicalization by adjunction.

There are several possibilities to consider for the derivation of examples such as (51) and (52). Given that IP-adjunction is available, one possibility might be successive cyclic adjunction to IP. That is, in (51), *this book* would first adjoin to the deepest complement IP and would then move again, adjoining to the next IP up. However, if this derivation is possible, it is difficult to see how we can explain the fact that topicalization conforms to the WH-island constraint, as illustrated in (53).

(53) ??that book, I wonder where John put *t t*

Compare (54).

(54) ??which book do you wonder where John put *t t*

If *this book* in (51), for example, can be preposed successive-cyclically through IP-adjunction without moving into the most deeply embedded SPEC of CP, then the same derivation should be available for (53). The derivations of (51) and (53) through successive-cyclic IP-adjunction are illustrated in (55) and (56), respectively.

Thus, clearly, the derivation of (51) cannot be as in (55).

(55) ... [this book$_1$] [$_{IP}$ he thought [$_{CP}$[$_{IP}$ [$_{IP}$ you would like t_1]]]]

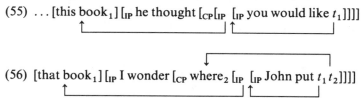

(56) [that book$_1$] [$_{IP}$ I wonder [$_{CP}$ where$_2$ [$_{IP}$ [$_{IP}$ John put $t_1 t_2$]]]]

Thus, clearly, the derivation of (51) cannot be as in (55).

The crucial difference between (55) and (56) is surely that in (56), the embedded SPEC of CP is occupied by a WH-phrase, whereas in (55), it is not. Hence, it must be the WH in SPEC of CP that blocks the preposing of *that book* in (56). In fact, it is because of contrasts such as the one between (51) and (53) that Chomsky (1977a) proposed that topicalization involves

movement to COMP (SPEC of CP). In our terms, this contrast implies
that successive-cyclic IP-adjunction should be prohibited by Subjacency,
and that the most deeply embedded SPEC of CP must be crucially utilized
in the derivation of (51). Here, note that what we established in the earlier
discussion is not that embedded topicalization cannot utilize SPEC of CP,
but rather, that the ultimate S-structure position of embedded topics must
be the position adjoined to IP. Thus, nothing we have said prevents
the movement of *this book* through the embedded SPEC of CP in (55),
whether or not it first adjoins to the embedded IP. This derivation is
illustrated in (57).

(57) ... [this book$_1$] [$_{IP}$ he thought [$_{CP}$ [$_{IP}$ [$_{IP}$ you would like t_1]]]]

This option is not available in the case of (54); hence, that example violates
Subjacency, again assuming that successive-cyclic IP-adjunction can be
prevented.

Consideration of *that*-trace effects with topicalization leads to the same
conclusion, that is, that long-distance topicalization does not take place
via successive-cyclic IP-adjunction. Consider first a well-formed instance
of long topicalization of subject, as in (58).

(58) John, I think t won the race

Suppose the derivation of (58) were as in (59).

(59) [$_{IP}$ John$_1$ [$_{IP}$ I think [$_{CP}$ [$_{IP}$ t_1'[$_{IP}$ t_1 won the race]]]]]

Since this derivation does not involve the embedded SPEC of CP at all,
nothing should prevent the identical derivation where the embedded
COMP is filled, as in (60).

(60) [$_{IP}$ John$_1$ [$_{IP}$ I think [$_{CP}$ that [$_{IP}$ t_1'[$_{IP}$ t_1 won the race]]]]]

However, (61), the result of the derivation in (60), is completely out.

(61) *John, I think that t won the race

Our Subjacency account of (53) might superficially appear to carry over
to this case as well, but in fact it does not. This is so for two reasons. First,
that in COMP, unlike a WH-phrase in SPEC of CP, does not cause
Subjacency violations, as is evident from considering (62), where
the presence or absence of *that* has no effect on grammaticality.

(62) that race, I think (that) John won t

Second, (61) is substantially worse than a mere Subjacency violation, contrasting sharply with (53), for example. We conclude that (61) should be treated as an ECP violation. We will return to consequences of this conclusion after examining formulations of Subjacency and of antecedent government.

3.3 Subjacency and Antecedent Government

We have shown that our analysis of topicalization has consequences for the formulation of Subjacency. In particular, we concluded that successive-cyclic IP-adjunction, as schematized in (63), must be prohibited by that condition.

(63) $[_{IP} [_{IP} \cdots [_{VP} \cdots [_{IP} [_{IP} \cdots$

In section 3.3.1, we will attempt to extend the proposals of Chomsky (1986a), presented in section 3.1, in light of the problematic facts of topicalization.

3.3.1 Topicalization and Subjacency

As noted above, Chomsky (1986a) crucially relies on the assumption that WH cannot adjoin to IP, in order to rule out WH-island violations (see (14)). He shows that descriptively speaking, topicalization conforms to the WH-island constraint exactly as WH-question movement does. But clearly, (14) will not help in the case of topicalization, if the latter is to be analyzed as a case of adjunction to IP. The derivation illustrated in (64) will be permitted, since *this book* is not a WH-phrase. But then, as we have shown, every link will satisfy 0-subjacency.

(64) $[_{IP}$ this book$_1$ $[_{IP}$ Mary $[_{VP}$ $[_{VP}$ wonders $[_{CP}$ whether $[_{IP}$ $[_{IP}$ John $[_{VP}$
$[_{VP}$ bought t_1]]]]]]]]]] (cf. (13))

Step 2 would be ruled out for a WH-phrase by (14). But clearly, no constraint prevents the adjunction of *this book* to IP. In fact, we argued in the preceding section that topicalization can, and sometimes must, involve precisely adjunction to IP. Given that (14) does not apply to topicalization, (65a) can have the derivation shown in (65b).

(65) a. this book, John thinks Mary read t

b. $[_{IP}$ this book$_1$ $[_{IP}$ John $[_{VP}$ $[_{VP}$ thinks $[_{CP}$ $[_{IP}$ $[_{IP}$ Mary $[_{VP}$

   ↑_____5_____| ↑___4___| ↑3|↑__2__|

$[_{VP}$ read t_1]]]]]]]]]

  ↑___1___|

But if (65b) is a possible derivation for (65a), (64) should be possible for (66).

(66) ??[this book$_1$, Mary wonders whether John bought t_1

We made essentially this same point in section 3.2 in the context of a more traditional version of movement constraints. Since (66), but not (65a), violates Subjacency, it must be step 3 in (64) that violates this constraint. However, given the definition of Subjacency proposed in Chomsky 1986a, step 3 satisfies 0-subjacency, and constraint (14) cannot be appealed to in the present case. A reformulation seems to be required.

Suppose first, contrary to Chomsky's proposal, that for the purposes of Subjacency, adjunction creates an additional category. The adjoined item is dominated by this "new" node, but is not dominated by the original node to which it adjoined. That is, in (67), even though β does not dominate α, β' does, where β' is the "new" occurrence of β created by adjoining α to β.

(67) $[_\beta, \alpha [_\beta \ldots]]$

Given this, let us focus on step 3 of derivation (64):

(68) ... [$[_{VP}$ wonders $[_{CP}$ whether $[_{IP}$ $[_{IP}$ ...

   ↑_____|

Movement is from within an IP to a position outside this IP (and outside CP and VP). Thus, this IP node is a BC, and it makes the CP a barrier. In addition, the movement is to a position outside the VP. Consequently, the VP node is a BC and hence is also a barrier. Thus, the movement in (68) crosses two barriers, violating Subjacency.

Although this account of (68) gives the correct result, there is evidence that it cannot be maintained as such. First consider the following example:

(69) a. what did you see t

b. $[_{CP}$ what$_1$ $[_{IP}$ did you $[_{VP}$ $[_{VP}$ see t_1]]]]

   ↑___2___| ↑_1_|

Step 2 in (69b) crosses VP and IP. According to our hypothesis, this step moves *what* from a position inside the upper VP to a position outside it. Thus, if VP is a BC and a barrier, as we have been assuming so far, then step 2 in (69b) crosses two barriers, VP and IP, the latter a barrier by "inheritance," and hence, (69a) is incorrectly assigned the status of a WH-island violation by Subjacency. This is so because, given our assumption on adjunction structures, an adjunction site can never function as an escape hatch for movement. If an item to be moved is within a barrier, adjunction to that barrier simply creates a higher occurrence of that very barrier. We therefore conclude that VP is not a barrier. Given the definitions in section 3.1.1, this requires that VP be L-marked.[9] Thus, VP must be a complement. Further, it must be a complement of a lexical category. The former requirement is relatively straightforward: VP is the complement of INFL. Chomsky (1986a:79) takes this to constitute a relevant form of complementation. The latter requirement is more problematic. At this point, we will simply stipulate, contra Chomsky (1986a:79), that INFL is suitably lexical, but we will return to this issue in section 5.5. Given that VP is not a barrier, the movement in (64) crosses only one barrier, namely, CP. This is in complete accordance with Chomsky's assumption that movement out of a WH-island crosses only one barrier and hence constitutes a weak Subjacency violation.

Summarizing, on the basis of the WH-island effects involving topicalization, we arrive at the following two working hypotheses:

(70) a. In an adjunction structure, $[_\beta \alpha [_\beta \ldots$, where β is a maximal projection, the two instances of β count as separate maximal projections for the purpose of Subjacency.

    b. VP is not a barrier.

Before we leave this section, let us examine some further consequences of (70a).

Consider again Baltin's (1982) example (69), which we cited earlier in (40):

(71) the man to whom liberty, we could never grant

Baltin, assuming that topicalization is IP-adjunction, states that (71) is a Subjacency violation for those speakers who have IP as a bounding node, but not for those who have CP as a bounding node:[10]

(72) $[_{NP}$ the man $[_{CP}$ to whom$_1$ $[_{IP}$ liberty$_2$ $[_{IP}$ we could never grant t_2 t_1]]]]

This is so because the movement of *to whom* crosses two IPs and no CPs. Note that under our proposal, the movement of *to whom* crosses one barrier. Since the two IPs count as separate maximal projections, the higher IP constitutes a barrier for this movement, inheriting its barrierhood from the lower IP. Thus, (71) should have the status of a WH-island violation such as (66), repeated here as (73).

(73) ??[this book]$_1$ Mary wonders whether John bought t_1

(71) actually seems to us somewhat better than (73), but other examples of the same basic structure as (71) seem comparable to (73) in grammaticality:

(74) ??the man [to whom]$_1$ [that book]$_2$, I gave t_2 t_1

(75) ??the place where$_1$ [that book]$_2$ John put t_2 t_1

Another construction with the same properties is double topicalization, as in (76).

(76) ??[on the table]$_2$, [this book]$_1$ John put t_1 t_2

If *on the table* is base-generated under TP, the structure of (76) will be as follows:

(77) [$_{TP}$ on the table$_2$ [$_{CP}$ WH$_2$ [$_{IP}$ this book$_1$ [$_{IP}$ John put t_1 t_2]]]]

Here, the movement of the WH topic operator crosses two IPs, of which the higher one is a barrier. If, on the other hand, (76) is a result of multiple adjunction to IP, its structure will be as in (78).

(78) [$_{IP}$ on the table$_2$ [$_{IP}$ this book$_1$ [$_{IP}$ John put t_1 t_2]]]

In this case also, one of the movements, that of *on the table*, crosses two IPs. Thus, (76) will violate Subjacency.

Note that the examples discussed above, (72) and (74)–(76), involve extractions out of a structure created by adjunction. Descriptively, they indicate that the movement schematized in (79) violates Subjacency.

(79) [$_{IP}$ α [$_{IP}$ ... t

This represents a special case of a proposal made by Ross (1974). (Also see Wexler and Culicover 1977.) Ross argues that the configuration in (80) is always an island.

(80)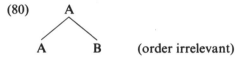
     A   B   (order irrelevant)

We showed above that the case where A = IP, and the extraction is out of the lower A, can be subsumed under Subjacency.

3.3.2 Subjacency and the Revised *Barriers* Model

In the preceding section, we arrived at the following conclusions:

(81) a. VP is not a barrier.

     b. Adjunction creates a separate maximal projection.

Chomsky (1986a) uses the notion BC to define barriers for two reasons. One is to incorporate the defective character of IP into the theory. According to Chomsky, a BC is a barrier if it is not IP. Second, he assumes that barriers are best defined through the mediation of the notion BC. Barriers are either BCs or maximal projections immediately dominating BCs. In the first case, the notion BC is not crucial, except for IP. But in the second, the mediation of BC plays a crucial role in defining barriers.

The question naturally arises whether it is possible to define barriers without relying on the notion BC. The first reason for relying on BC disappears if we can make IP nondefective and treat it like any other maximal projection. The second reason can be eliminated if the "mediation" of BC can be expressed in another way. We now explore these possibilities.

Consider the configuration in (82).

(82) $\alpha \ldots [_y \ldots [_z \ldots \beta \ldots$, where y, z are maximal projections.

Suppose that z is a BC for β. Then, given that there are no defective categories, z is also a barrier for β. Here, z, as a BC, performs another function. That is, it makes y a barrier for β also, even if y is not a BC for β. Thus, movement from β to α constitutes a strong Subjacency violation since it crosses two barriers. We can state this property of the analysis in a different way. Suppose that z is a BC for β. Then, β is not subjacent to α if α is outside the maximal projection immediately dominating z. Substituting the term *barrier* for *BC*, we can state this definition more precisely as follows:

(83) γ is a *barrier* for β if

     a. γ is a maximal projection,

     b. γ is not L-marked, and

     c. γ dominates β.

     (Cf. Chomsky's definition of BC in (5).)

(84) β is *subjacent* to α if for every γ, γ a barrier for β, the maximal projection immediately dominating γ dominates α.

The definitions given in (83)–(84) differ from Chomsky's in that they do not use the notion BC, and consequently, IP is not—in fact, cannot be—treated as a defective category. The system embodying (83)–(84) is to a large extent a notational variant of Chomsky's, but as we will show, it makes certain different predictions, especially with respect to weak versus strong Subjacency violations. In the remainder of this section, we will discuss how the concepts defined in (83) and (84), together with our proposals in the preceding section, apply to standard cases of island violations.

Let us first consider extraction out of relative clauses. Example (8a) is repeated here as (85).

(85) *where$_2$ [$_{IP}$ did you see [$_{NP}$ the book$_1$ [$_{CP}$ which$_1$ [$_{IP}$ John put t_1 t_2]]]]

The movement in (85) clearly violates Subjacency. The embedded IP is a barrier for t_2 according to (83), since (1) it is a maximal projection, (2) it is not L-marked, and (3) it dominates t_2. Thus, Subjacency requires that *where$_2$* be dominated by the embedded CP, the maximal projection immediately dominating the IP; but this is not the case in (85). Note also that the embedded CP is also a barrier for t_2. Thus, Subjacency requires *where$_2$* to be dominated not only by the embedded CP but also by the NP. Hence, Subjacency is in fact doubly violated in (85), yielding a strong violation. This accords with the status of the example.[11] Note that we need not consider derivations involving successive adjunction, since, under the theory developed in section 3.3.1, adjunction to a barrier does not provide an escape route. It merely creates another instance of the original barrier.

Consider next the case of WH-island violations. Example (12) is repeated here as (86).

(86) ??what$_1$ did you wonder [$_{CP}$ whether [$_{IP}$ John bought t_1]]

Here again, the embedded IP is a barrier for t_1. Hence, unless the movement of *what* out of the embedded IP is to a position dominated by the embedded CP, Subjacency is violated. Since no such position is possible, (86) violates Subjacency. In this case, the embedded IP is the only relevant barrier, and Subjacency is violated only once. Thus, we expect WH-island violations to be in general weaker than Subjacency effects with relative clauses. Although there are unclear cases, this prediction seems to be borne out in general, as pointed out by Chomsky (1986a). Even a very bad WH-island violation seems somewhat better than the corresponding relative clause extraction. For example, compare (87) with (85).[12]

(87) ?*where$_2$ did you wonder [$_{CP}$ what$_1$ [$_{IP}$ John put t_1 t_2]]

Now consider movement out of a nonrelative complex NP:

(88) ??which book$_1$ [$_{IP}$ did you study [$_{NP}$ the evidence [$_{CP}$

[$_{C'}$ that [$_{IP}$ Harry stole t_1]]]]]

Assuming that movement into the lower SPEC of CP is allowed in this configuration, (88) will incorrectly not violate Subjacency, given the theory outlined thus far. The lower IP will be a barrier for the original trace, but movement 1 will still not violate Subjacency since it is not out of the maximal projection immediately dominating that IP. For movement 2, neither CP nor NP is a barrier since both are L-marked complements to lexical heads: *evidence* in the former case, *study* in the latter. The matrix IP will be a barrier, but movement to the matrix SPEC of CP will not escape the maximal projection immediately dominating this IP, so once again, Subjacency is satisfied. A suggestion by Chomsky (1986a: 36) may provide a way out of this dilemma: "It may be that nouns assign oblique Case and that this imposes an inherent barrier to government."[13] Under this assumption, the lower CP in (88) will be a barrier, and movement 2 will violate Subjacency since it crosses NP, which is the maximal projection immediately dominating the CP.[14]

We have shown that the classical cases of Subjacency violations can be accommodated under the new formulation of Subjacency. Let us now turn to cases that were subsumed under Huang's (1982) CED, that is, subject condition and adjunct condition violations. Consider again (8b), repeated here as (89).

(89) ?*[$_{CP}$ who$_1$ [$_{IP}$ did [$_{NP}$ pictures of t_1] [$_{VP}$ please you]]]

The movement in (89) violates Subjacency, since the subject NP containing t_1 is a barrier for t_1, and who$_1$ is not contained in the maximal projection immediately dominating this NP, namely, the IP. However, certain questions arise with respect to this example.

The first one, noted by Barss (1986), concerns its derivation. Suppose that the example in question is derived, not as in (89), but as in (90).

(90) [$_{CP}$ who$_1$ [$_{IP}$ did [$_{NP}$ pictures of t_1] [$_{VP}$ [$_{VP}$ please you]]]]

Here, the first step is adjunction to VP. The derivation in (90) does not violate Subjacency. The subject NP is a barrier for t_1, but movement 1 does not violate Subjacency, since this movement does not move the WH out of IP, the maximal projection immediately dominating the NP. Movement 2 is also licit since the only barrier it crosses is IP, and the movement is to a position contained within the CP, the first maximal projection dominating the IP. Thus, we seem to have found one situation where adjunction does create an escape route. There is, however, one significant difference between this case and the ones we discussed earlier. In those cases, the adjunction was to a containing maximal projection, a process that did not eliminate a barrier, since a new barrier of the same type was invariably created. But in the present case, the adjunction is not to a containing category, and this allows an escape route, incorrectly it appears. Thus, it seems that adjunction to a noncontaining maximal projection should be prohibited. The configuration created by such adjunction is shown in (91).

(91)

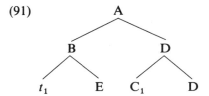

Fiengo (1977) notes that such a configuration is ill formed at S-structure and proposes the Proper Binding Condition to rule it out.[15] However, Fiengo's condition does not rule out the derivation in (90), since it is a condition on S-structure representation, and at S-structure, the trace t_1 is bound by who_1. Thus, what this example suggests is that the configuration in (91) is prohibited not only at S-structure, but in general. We propose to extend Fiengo's condition as follows:

(92) *The Generalized Proper Binding Condition*
      Traces must be bound throughout a derivation.

Given (92), the derivation in (90) is ruled out, since after movement 1, the example has the following structure:

(93) $[_{CP}[_{IP}$ did $[_{NP}$ pictures of $t_1]$ $[_{VP}$ who$_1$ $[_{VP}$ please you]]]]

In fact, for movements that must leave a trace, (92) in general limits the adjunction site of movement to a containing category, exactly the result required to distinguish (90) from other cases of adjunction discussed above.[16]

The other problem that arises with respect to (89) is that this sentence is somewhat less acceptable than, for example, (88). This is puzzling since both (88) and (89) contain only one barrier relevant for Subjacency. Although we do not have a clear account of the difference between (88) and (89), we suspect that it is related to the internal constituent effect noted by Kuno (1973). He points out that extraction out of "internal constituents" is prohibited in general.[17] For example:

(94) a.   who$_1$ did you see pictures of t_1
     b. ??who$_1$ did you give pictures of t_1 to John

(95) a.   who$_1$ did you meet friends of t_1
     b. ??who$_1$ did you tell friends of t_1 to be there

The effect exhibited in (94) and (95) could well be active in subject condition cases, as Kuno notes. If this is so, the lessened acceptability of (89) relative to (88) does not bear on the formulation of Subjacency.

Finally, let us consider adjunct condition violations, as in (96).

(96) ??[which linguist]$_1$ [$_{IP}$ did you [$_{VP}$ write your thesis] [after you consulted t_1]]

This case is ruled out in basically the same way as the above-mentioned subject condition violation. Because the adjunct clause is a barrier, Subjacency requires that movement out of the adjunct clause can be only to positions inside the matrix IP. But possible landing sites outside the adjunct clause for such movement are all outside the matrix IP, because of the Generalized Proper Binding Condition. Hence, (96) violates Subjacency. Note that (96) has the status of a weak Subjacency violation, and consequently, we expect the adjunct clause to be the only relevant barrier in this case. If there were another relevant barrier, then Subjacency would be doubly violated, and we would expect (96) to be as bad as (85), which it is not. Here, we will tentatively assume, following Huang (1982), that the adjunct clause in (96) has the structure shown in (97).[18]

(97) [$_{CP}$[$_{C'}$ after [$_{IP}$ you consulted t]]]

Then, if *after* in COMP, as opposed to the complementizer *that*, functions as an L-marker for the embedded IP—that is, if the IP is a complement to the lexical head *after*—then the IP in (97) is not a barrier. Thus, the WH-movement in (96) crosses only one barrier (the adjunct clause), whether or not it proceeds through the SPEC of the adjunct CP.

As noted earlier, our formulations of *barrier* and *Subjacency* in (83) and (84) account for the island effects basically in the same way as Chomsky (1986a). To account for the "pure complex NP" constraint, we tentatively adopted Chomsky's (1986a) assumption that X^{max} with inherent Case constitutes a barrier. Our assumption that the Proper Binding Condition applies to every step of a derivation, or something equivalent, seems to be needed independently of our reformation of barriers and Subjacency.

In the remainder of this section, we will consider how our formulation of Subjacency affects the derivations of a class of grammatical sentences.

Let us first consider the simple case of successive-cyclic WH-movement:

(98) what$_1$ did you think John bought t_1

This sentence can be derived exactly as proposed by Chomsky (1973):

(99) $[_{CP}$ what$_1$ $[_{IP}$ did you $[_{VP}$ think $[_{CP}$ $[_{IP}$ John $[_{VP}$ bought t_1]]]]]]]

Since the VPs and the embedded CP in (99) are L-marked, the only potential barriers are the embedded IP and the matrix IP. The embedded IP is a barrier for movement 1, but this movement is to a position contained within the embedded CP. Thus, it conforms to Subjacency. Similarly, the matrix IP is a barrier for movement 2, but the movement is to a position within the matrix CP. Hence, the derivation in (99) is licit.

Let us next consider successive-cyclic topicalization, as in (51), repeated here as (100).

(100) John said that [this book]$_1$, he thought you would like t_1

Suppose that (100) is derived by successive-cyclic adjunction to IP, as shown in (101).

(101) John said that $[_{IP}$ this book$_1$ $[_{IP}$ he thought $[_{CP}[_{IP}$

$[_{IP}$ you would like t_1]]]]]

Then, movement 2 violates Subjacency, since the IP created by the first adjunction is a barrier. In fact, the discussion of the impossibility of a derivation such as the one in (64) carries over unchanged. There, we concluded that long-distance topicalization could not be successive adjunction to IP, but rather, must crucially involve SPEC of CP. This means that (102) is available as a derivation.

(102) ... $[_{IP}$ this book$_1$ $[_{IP}$ he thought $[_{CP}$ $[_{IP}$ you would like t_1]]]]

Both movement 1 and movement 2 clearly conform to Subjacency. CP is not a barrier, since it is L-marked. The intermediate IP is a barrier, but the moved item is contained in the next maximal projection up, that is, the "new" IP. Recall that topicalization exhibits WH-island effects. This follows from our account, since we have shown that a derivation like (101) is unavailable in general, and one like (102) will be unavailable when the intermediate SPEC of CP is occupied by a WH.

As a derivation, (102) has two noteworthy properties. First, it crucially involves movement of a non-WH-phrase, *this book*, through SPEC of CP. Second, it involves movement from SPEC of CP to a non–SPEC of CP position. Since it is often assumed that such derivations are not allowed, we must examine the potential ramifications of permitting them.

Chomsky (1973) explicitly precluded movement with the second property. Movement from COMP (SPEC of CP) had to be to another COMP (SPEC of CP). "Improper movement" of the type illustrated in (103) was thus prevented.

(103) John is believed [$_{CP}$ [$_{C'}$ (that) [$_{IP}$ Mary likes t]]]

May (1981) accepted the claim that improper movement is not permitted, but argued that this follows from independent principles and hence need not be stipulated. Essentially, May claimed that movement to SPEC of CP leaves behind a name-like element (an R-expression, in current parlance). Movement from SPEC of CP to an A-position thus results in an illicit A-bound R-expression.[19] Notice that May's improper movement constraint is actually slightly narrower in scope than that of Chomsky (1973), in a way directly relevant to the present investigation. The heart of May's proposal is that the trace of improper movement is A-bound, thus violating the binding theory. Hence, the movement in (103) is prevented. But now notice that the movement in (102), which May did not consider, *is* permitted, since the landing site of the moved NP is not an A-position.

Even May's (1981) assumption that the trace of movement to an Ā-position is obligatorily an R-expression may not be necessary to rule out cases of improper movement. In (103), *John* and *t* must form an A-chain so that *John* can receive the θ-role assigned by *like*. Then, following standard assumptions about A-chains, *t* must be an anaphor. But if it is an anaphor, it violates Condition A of the binding theory. If there is an intermediate trace in COMP in (103), the S-structure representation violates an additional condition. As stated by Chomsky (1981) and argued for by Rizzi (1986a) and Lasnik (1985), each link of an A-chain must be related to the next through local A-binding. That is, in an A-chain of the form shown in (104),

(104) $(\alpha_1, \ldots, \alpha_i, \alpha_{i+1}, \ldots, \alpha_n)$

α_i must locally A-bind α_{i+1}.[20] But if the representation of (103) is as in (105), then the chain between *John* and *t* violates this condition.

(105) John$_1$ is believed [$_{CP}$ t_1' [$_{IP}$ Mary likes t_1]]

The constraint on A-chains discussed above rules out another case of improper movement. Consider the following example:

(106) John$_1$ is believed [$_{CP}$ (that) [$_{IP}$ it$_2$ is likely [$_{IP}$ t_1 to win]$_2$]]

In L&S, we argued that this example is ruled out by the ECP. (See chapter 1.) But that account assumed that the movement in (106) cannot take place through the embedded SPEC of CP, leaving a trace there. Thus, the question arises why the following configuration is not allowed:

(107) John$_1$ is believed [$_{CP}$ t_1' [$_{IP}$ it is likely [$_{IP}$ t_1 to win]]]

(107) violates neither the ECP nor Condition A (under the formulation in Chomsky 1981). (See L&S and chapter 1.) Given the present formulation of Subjacency, it does not violate this condition, either. Movement 1 crosses one barrier, namely, the intermediate IP, but it is to a position contained within the maximal projection immediately dominating this node. Movement 2 crosses no barrier at all. Here again, May's (1981) assumption that the trace of movement to an Ā-position is an R-expression accounts for the example. Given this assumption, the initial trace in (107) must be an R-expression. However, it is A-bound and therefore violates Condition C of the binding theory. Independently of this account, though, (107) violates the constraint on A-chains discussed above. *John* and t_1 must form an A-chain so that *John* receives a θ-role. But the former does not locally A-bind the latter. Hence, (107) is straightforwardly ruled out.

3.3.3 The ECP and the Revised *Barriers* Model

In this section, we apply the revised model we have developed thus far to ECP phenomena. Following Chomsky (1986a), we take it as the null hypothesis that barriers are defined the same way for both Subjacency and antecedent government.[21] In particular, we propose the following definition of antecedent government, where "subjacent to" is exactly as in (84):

(108) α *antecedent-governs* β if
    a. α binds β, and
    b. β is subjacent to α.

Consider now the ECP phenomena presented in section 3.1.2. (109), repeated from (23), represents the standard COMP-trace case. Here, we have eliminated the trace adjoined to VP in line with our conclusions of the preceding section.

(109) $[_{CP}$ who$_1$ $[_{IP}$ do you wonder $[_{CP}$ why$_2$ $[_{IP}$ t_1 won the race t_2]]]]

The lower IP is a barrier for t_1, and the nearest binder for t_1 is outside the maximal projection immediately dominating that barrier (i.e., the embedded CP). Thus, t_1 is not subjacent to any binder, hence is not antecedent-governed, the correct result. With an intermediate trace in place of *why*, antecedent government does obtain, as in S-structure representation (110).

(110) $[_{CP}$ who$_1$ $[_{IP}$ do you think $[_{CP}$ $t_1{'}$ $[_{IP}$ t_1 won the race]]]]

The intermediate trace binds t_1 and is contained in the maximal projection immediately dominating IP, the only barrier separating them. Hence, t_1 is antecedent-governed. $t_1{'}$ is in a configuration of antecedent government as well (though that is of no consequence in the present case, given that it can serve to license t_1 at S-structure and delete at LF). CP is not a barrier for $t_1{'}$, since CP is L-marked, being the complement of *think*. VP is the complement of INFL, hence not a barrier. The matrix IP is a barrier, but the immediately dominating maximal projection, CP, contains a binder for $t_1{'}$.

Although antecedent government of the intermediate trace is not relevant in the case of an argument WH, it is crucial in the case of an adjunct WH. Consider, then, LF representation (25), repeated here as (111), again with the trace adjoined to VP eliminated.

(111) $[_{CP}$ how$_1$ $[_{IP}$ do you think $[_{CP}$ $t_1{'}$ $[_{IP}$ John fixed the car t_1]]]]

Exactly as in (110), the initial trace t_1 is antecedent-governed by the intermediate trace $t_1{'}$. Further, again as in (110), that intermediate trace is antecedent-governed by the WH-phrase itself. The relevance of this last fact is that the intermediate trace must be present at LF in this case. This is so because, as argued in chapters 1 and 2, γ-marking of nonargument traces takes place only at LF. Thus, in contrast to what happens in (110), $t_1{'}$ cannot be used in (111) to license t_1 at S-structure and then itself delete. (26), adapted as (112), crucially receives its account in these terms.

(112) *$[_{CP}$ how$_1$ $[_{IP}$ did Bill wonder $[_{CP}$ who$_2$ $[_{IP}$ t_2 wanted $[_{CP}$ $t_1{'}$ $[_{IP}$ PRO to fix the car t_1]]]]]]

As usual, the initial trace of *how* is antecedent-governed by the intermediate trace $t_1{'}$. However, $t_1{'}$ is not itself antecedent-governed. The intermediate IP is a barrier for this trace, and the nearest binder is not contained in the CP immediately dominating that IP. Note that a trace adjoined to the VP headed by *want* would be of no help, since, although it would salvage $t_1{'}$, it would itself become the offending trace, just as in the earlier discussion. Finally, note once again that t_1 must not be permitted to be γ-marked at S-structure, since if it were, $t_1{}'$ could delete in the LF component, and, incorrectly, there would then be no offending trace.

Given that IP can be a barrier, and given that adjunction to a maximal projection creates an additional maximal projection, a configuration of topicalization should block antecedent government from outside that configuration. (Recall from section 3.3.1 that such a configuration does create a barrier for Subjacency.) In this light, consider example (113), with S-structure representation (114).

(113) *John, this book, t likes t

(114) $[_{IP}$ John$_1$ $[_{IP}$ this book$_2$ $[_{IP}$ t_1 likes t_2]]]

(114) is now directly excluded. t_1 is not antecedent-governed since it is not subjacent to its binder: the "original" IP is a barrier, and there is no binder for t_1 in the maximal projection immediately dominating that IP, namely, the intermediate IP.[22] This conclusion carries over to an alternative representation available for (113) as a matrix:

(115) $[_{TP}$ John$_1$ $[_{CP}$ WH$_1$ $[_{IP}$ this book$_2$ $[_{IP}$ t_1 likes t_2]]]]

Here, the nearest binder of t_1 is WH$_1$, but once again, that binder is not contained in the maximal projection immediately dominating the lowest IP, which is a barrier for t_1. On either available representation, then, (113) is correctly ruled out as an ECP violation.

As expected, WH-question movement displays the same behavior, whether the movement is "short," as in (116), or "long," as in (117).

(116) *I wonder who this book t likes t

(117) *who do you think this book t likes t

The S-structure representations of (116) and (117) are as in (118) and (119), respectively.

(118) I wonder $[_{CP}$ who$_1$ $[_{IP}$ this book$_2$ $[_{IP}$ t_1 likes t_2]]]

(119) $[_{CP}$ who$_1$ $[_{IP}$ do you think $[_{CP}$ $t_1{}'$ $[_{IP}$ this book$_2$ $[_{IP}$ t_1 likes t_2]]]]]

Just as in (115), t_1 in (118) and (119) is not antecedent-governed. In both cases, the lowest IP is a barrier, and the maximal projection immediately dominating that IP is the IP created by topicalization of *this book*. The latter IP does not contain a binder for t_1.[23]

The behavior of adjuncts in a configuration such as (119) now comes as something of a surprise. (120) has merely the status of a Subjacency violation, rather than that of an ECP violation such as (112).

(120) ??how do you think (that) this problem, John solved t t

If the LF representation of (120) is as in (121), the initial trace of *how* should not be antecedent-governed any more than the initial trace of *who* is in (119).

(121) $[_{CP}$ how$_1$ $[_{IP}$ do you think $[_{CP}$ t_1' $[_{IP}$ this problem$_2$ $[_{IP}$ John solved t_2 t_1]]]]]

However, it is not clear that (121) is the appropriate LF representation for (120). Recall from chapters 1 and 2 that at S-structure, the initial trace of an adjunct need not, perhaps even must not, be present. Then, in the LF component, an "initial" trace is created, possibly by adjunction to IP. For (120), this leaves open the question of whether the adjunction should be to the original embedded IP or to the "super" IP created by topicalization of *this problem*. If the former is chosen, the result is indistinguishable from (121):

(122) ... $[_{CP}$ t_1' $[_{IP_3}$ this problem$_2$ $[_{IP_2}[_{IP_1}$ John solved t_2 t_1]]]

Here IP_2 is a barrier for t_1, and, again, IP_3 is the maximal projection immediately dominating that barrier. Since IP_3 does not contain a binder for t_1, antecedent government fails. However, now suppose that when a trace of *how* is created in the LF component, it is adjoined, not to the original lowest IP, but to the IP that was created by topicalization. This gives the configuration in (123).

(123) ... $[_{CP}$ t_1' $[_{IP_3}[_{IP_2}$ this problem$_2$ $[_{IP_1}$ John solved t_2 t_1]]

In (123), t_1, the "initial" trace of *how*, clearly is antecedent-governed. Although IP_3 is a barrier for t_1, the maximal projection immediately dominating that barrier contains a binder for t_1, namely, the intermediate trace t_1'. t_2 is antecedent-governed as well, but that is of no import, since it is lexically governed by *solved*. Finally, as usual, the trace in SPEC of CP, t_1', will be antecedent-governed by the WH-phrase in the matrix SPEC of CP.[24]

It is possible to block such antecedent government of a trace in SPEC of CP. For example, topicalization in the next clause up will create an intervening maximal projection. The prediction, then, is that the resulting configuration, in contrast with (123), should violate the ECP. This prediction seems to be confirmed. Consider (124).

(124) *how do you think that Mary, Bill told *t* that $[_{IP}$ John solved the problem *t*]

This is substantially worse than movement of an adjunct across a topicalized clause-mate NP, as in (120). It is also much worse than long movement of an adjunct without intervening topicalization, as in (125), or with a topicalized clause-mate, as in (126).

(125)   how do you think that Bill told Mary that [$_{IP}$ John solved the problem t]

(126)   ??how do you think that Bill told Mary that [$_{IP}$ the problem, John solved t]

Finally, it is much worse than extraction of a complement:

(127)   ??which problem do you think that Mary, Bill told t that John solved t

Thus, we are presumably dealing with an ECP effect in (124).
    Consider (128), the LF representation of (124).

(128)   [$_{CP}$ how$_1$ [$_{IP}$ do you think [$_{CP}$ t_1'' [$_{IP}$ Mary$_2$ [$_{IP}$ Bill told t_2 [$_{CP}$ t_1' [$_{IP}$ John solved the problem t_1]]]]]]]]

t_1 is antecedent-governed by the lower intermediate trace t_1'. But t_1' is not antecedent-governed, because of the extra maximal projection created by the topicalization of *Mary*. Further, if the adjunct variable is to be understood in the lowest clause, the option of creating that variable higher than the topicalized NP is not available, as it was in the case of (120) (or (126)). This is so because if the variable is higher than *Mary*, it is outside the lowest clause entirely. And there is no possibility of eliminating the offending trace, t_1', since that would merely make t_1 the offending trace. Thus, (124) is correctly excluded by the ECP, in striking confirmation of the analysis developed thus far.

3.4   Related Issues

3.4.1   Parasitic Gaps
Another phenomenon bearing on the formulation of Subjacency is the parasitic gap construction. Chomsky (1986a) argues that this construction must obey Subjacency in two ways. First, he shows that the parasitic gap (PG) is actually a trace, and the movement (of an empty operator) creating this trace obeys island constraints. The distinction between (129) and (130) seems parallel to that found in classic island paradigms.

(129)   ?*who did you hire t after talking to the man who recommended PG

(130)   ?who did you hire t after finding out that Mary said that Bill recommended PG

    Second, he argues that the empty "parasitic" operator must be subjacent to a "real" trace. In his terms, this is a requirement on chain composition, an operation creating a sort of unified chain out of the separate real and parasitic chains. Thus, the following contrast is accounted for by Subjacency on chain composition:[25]

(131)   ?which linguist$_1$ did you write to t_1 [$_{CP}$ Op$_1$ [$_{C'}$ after [$_{IP}$ you consulted t_1]]]

(132)   ?*which linguist$_1$ did you write to t_1 [$_{CP}$ in order to get an offprint [$_{CP}$ Op$_1$ [$_{C'}$ after [$_{IP}$ you consulted t_1']]]]

In (132), the empty operator is not subjacent to the trace t_1, and hence, the composition of the two chains, (which linguist$_1$, t_1) and (Op$_1$, t_1'), is blocked by Subjacency. In our terms, the most deeply embedded CP is a barrier, and trace t_1 is not contained in the maximal projection immediately dominating this node. Thus, Op$_1$ is not subjacent to t_1. Recall that the IP immediately dominating Op$_1$ is not a barrier for Op$_1$ since it is the complement of *after*. Note also that Op$_1$ cannot move to a position subjacent to t_1 without violating Subjacency, since it must move out of the adjunct headed by *after* to do so.

The derivation of the acceptable parasitic construction in (131) raises no such difficulty. The IP is not a barrier for the movement of Op$_1$ since it is the complement of *after*. The entire adjunct CP is a barrier for Op$_1$, but this does not block chain composition since the maximal projection immediately dominating this barrier also dominates the trace of *which linguist*. This result obtains regardless of whether an adjunct is taken to be a constituent of IP as in Chomsky 1982 or a constituent of VP as in Chomsky 1986a. This is so because the real trace is dominated by IP and is also dominated by VP.[26] (See our definition (84).)

Let us consider another parasitic gap construction, exemplified in (133).

(133)   ?who$_1$ do close friends of e_1 admire t_1

This sentence can have the following structure prior to chain composition:

(134)   [$_{CP}$ who$_1$ [$_{IP}$ do [$_{NP}$ close friends [$_{PP}$ Op$_1$ [$_{PP}$ of t_1']]] [$_{VP}$ admire t_1]]]

Here again, Op$_1$ is subjacent to t_1. The PP immediately dominating Op$_1$ is not a barrier since it is a complement of *friends*. The subject NP is a barrier for Op$_1$, but t_1 is contained within the node immediately dominating this NP, namely, the matrix IP. Thus, (133) is allowed by our definition of Subjacency.

Note that as desired, our account of (133) does not extend to ungrammatical extraction out of subject, as in (135).

(135) $[_{CP}$ who$_1$ $[_{IP}$ do $[_{NP}$ close friends of $t_1]$ $[_{VP}$ admire Bill]]]]

In (135), the subject NP is a barrier for t_1, and the movement is not to a position contained within the IP. Thus, (135) violates Subjacency. Recall that (135) is ruled out even if the movement proceeds via adjunction to IP, as in (136).

(136) $[_{CP}$ who$_1$ $[_{IP}$ $[_{IP}$ do $[_{NP}$ close friends of $t_1]$ $[_{VP}$ admire Bill]]]]]

This is so because, as usual, the two IPs in (136) are separate maximal projections, and movement 1 is to a position outside the lower IP. Recall also that the example cannot be derived via adjunction to VP, as in (137).

(137) $[_{CP}$ who$_1$ $[_{IP}$ do $[_{NP}$ close friends of $t_1]$ $[_{VP}$ $[_{VP}$ admire Bill]]]]]

(137) does not violate Subjacency. However, movement 1 violates the Generalized Proper Binding Condition (GPBC), which requires that traces be bound throughout the derivation. Hence, (137) is not a possible derivation, entirely apart from Subjacency considerations.

The acceptable (134) is superficially rather similar to (137). In both cases, a Subjacency violation is avoided because of a trace in VP.[27] The crucial difference is that this trace is created by movement out of the subject in (137), but not in (134). The consequence of this is that the creation of the VP-internal trace will result in a GPBC violation at an intermediate point in the derivation in (137), but not in (134). Thus, (134) and (137) are correctly distinguished.

3.4.2 Extraction out of Constituents in $\bar{\text{A}}$-Positions

The formulation of Subjacency presented above also has implications for cases of extraction out of constituents in $\bar{\text{A}}$-positions. Consider the following examples illustrating extraction out of an extraposed constituent:

(138) $[_{IP}[_{NP}$ a man] $[_{VP}$ walked in] $[_{CP}$ who$_1$ $[_{IP}$ t_1 was from California]]]

(139) *$[_{CP}$ what state$_2$ $[_{IP}$ did a man walk in $[_{CP}$ who$_1$ $[_{IP}$ t_1 was from $t_2]]]]$

We provisionally assume that (138) involves extraposition of the relative clause from within the subject. Thus, the extraposed constituent is not L-marked, and hence, as Baltin (1984) points out, we expect it to be an island for extraction. In our terms, the movement of *what state* in (139) crosses two relevant barriers and therefore doubly violates Subjacency. The first barrier is the IP in the relative clause. Since *what state* is not dominated by the relative clause CP, Subjacency is violated. The second barrier is the relative clause CP itself, and Subjacency is violated again, since *what state* is not dominated by the maximal projection immediately dominating this CP. The third barrier, which is the matrix IP, is not relevant here, since *what state* is contained within the matrix CP.

Let us next consider the following sentence, which illustrates topicalization out of a topicalized constituent:

(140) a. I think that [$_{IP}$ you should read [$_{NP}$ articles about vowel harmony] carefully]

      b. I think that [$_{IP}$[$_{NP}$ articles about vowel harmony], [$_{IP}$ you should read *t* carefully]]

      c. ??vowel harmony, I think that [$_{IP}$[$_{NP}$ articles about *t*], [$_{IP}$ you should read *t* carefully]]

In (140b), *articles about vowel harmony* has been topicalized from its base position in (140a). In (140c), further movement has taken place, topicalizing *vowel harmony* out of the larger NP. (140c) is marginal, and this is what we expect given our definition of Subjacency. When an NP is topicalized out of a topicalized NP, the latter is a barrier for this movement. Consequently, Subjacency requires that *vowel harmony* in (140) not move out of the IP created by embedded topicalization. Hence, (140c) violates Subjacency. But if *vowel harmony* moves through the embedded SPEC of CP, Subjacency is violated only once in this example. Thus, we also expect (140c) to be a weak Subjacency violation.

Although our formulation of Subjacency gives the correct result for (140c), there is reason to doubt the validity of the account. Note first that examples like (140c) are better than subject condition violations, as shown in (141).

(141) a. ?*who$_1$ do you think that [pictures of t_1] are on sale

      b. ??who$_1$ do you think that [pictures of t_1]$_2$, John wanted t_2

We speculated above that extraction out of a subject is strongly ungrammatical because it falls under Kuno's (1973) internal constituent effect in addition to violating Subjacency. That is, the WH-movement in (141a) violates Subjacency and at the same time involves movement out of a constituent that is not the rightmost branch. If this speculation is correct, and if (141b) does violate Subjacency, then we expect this example to have the ungrammatical status of subject condition violations, because it also involves movement out of a non–rightmost branch constituent. But this prediction is incorrect, since (141b) is clearly better than (141a). Hence, we conclude that (141b) does not violate Subjacency, and that its marginality is due to the internal constituent effect, as in the case of (142).

(142) ??who$_1$ did you give pictures of t_1 to Bill

But this raises the question of why (141b) does not violate Subjacency. In both (141a) and (141b), *pictures of t_1* is not L-marked. But in the latter, and not in the former, this phrase Ā-binds a trace. The contrast between (141a) and (141b) might be attributed to this difference. We propose that the fact that *pictures of t_1* in (141b) is an Ā-binder makes it a nonbarrier. Formally, we propose to revise the definition of *barrier* as follows:

(143) γ is a *barrier* for β if
   a. γ is a maximal projection,
   b. γ is not an Ā-binder,
   c. γ is not L-marked, and
   d. γ dominates β.

Since the embedded topic in (141b) is an Ā-binder, it is not a barrier for WH-movement.[28] Hence, (141b) does not violate Subjacency.

The formulation of *barrier* in (143) correctly accounts for the examples in (144).

(144) a. ??who$_1$ do you wonder [which picture of t_1]$_2$ Mary bought t_2
   b. ??who$_1$ do you wonder [which picture of t_1]$_2$ t_2 is on sale
   c. ??who$_1$ do you think that [pictures of t_1]$_2$, Mary believes t_2 are on sale

Chomsky (1986a) discusses examples similar to (144a–b), which he attributes to Esther Torrego. These examples involve WH-movement out of a WH-phrase in SPEC of CP. In (144c), a WH-phrase is extracted out of an embedded topic, as in (141b). We expect all of these examples to exhibit the internal constituent effect, independently of Subjacency. Hence, the fact that they are only marginal, and are better than subject condition violations such as (141a), indicates that they do not violate Subjacency. This is predicted by the formulation of *barrier* in (143). The embedded WH-phrases in (144a–b) and the embedded topic in (144c) are Ā-binders and hence are not barriers for further extraction.[29]

As we have shown, the fact that (141b) and (144a–c) are only marginal indicates that movement out of a phrase in Ā-position is in principle possible and does not violate Subjacency. This conclusion implies that we must provide an account independent of Subjacency for those clearly ungrammatical examples that involve movement out of a moved constituent. Let us first consider the following example:

(145) ?*what$_1$ did you give t_2 to John [$_{NP}$ a book about t_1]$_2$

Given the Principle of the Strict Cycle, this example is derived as follows: First, the D-structure object, *a book about what*, is adjoined to VP, and then *what* is moved to SPEC of CP. The second movement involves extraction out of an adjoined phrase, and hence, Ross (1974) subsumed this example under his generalization that adjunction structures are islands for movement. However, unlike the ungrammaticality of (74)–(76), the ungrammaticality of (145) does not follow from Subjacency. The VP-adjoined object is an Ā-binder and hence is not a barrier for further extraction. In addition, we do not expect this example to show the internal constituent effect because the VP-adjoined phrase is on the right branch. We tentatively assume that the ungrammaticality of (145) is due to the crossing effect, discussed by Baker (1977), Kuno and Robinson (1972), and Pesetsky (1982).[30]

Let us next consider examples such as (146), which are discussed in detail by Postal (1972).

(146) *who$_1$ do you think that [$_{PP}$ to t_1]$_2$, John gave a book t_2

This example, too, does not violate Subjacency, since the embedded topic is an Ā-binder and hence not a barrier. Yet it is far worse than the examples in (147).

(147) a. ?*who$_1$ do you think that [$_{PP}$ to friends of t_1]$_2$, John gave a
         book t_2
      b. ??who$_1$ do you think that [$_{NP}$ friends of t_1]$_2$, John gave a book
         to t_2

Apparently, the relevant difference between (146) and (147) is that in the former, the embedded topic consists only of a preposition and a trace. Noting this fact, we propose that topics must have a feature [+top], which parallels [+WH] for WH-phrases, and we make the following assumptions:

(148) a. If α is a topic (i.e., [+top]), then it must dominate a constituent
         with the feature [+top].
      b. P cannot be [+top].
      c. A trace cannot be [+top].

Given (148), (146) is ruled out, since the embedded topic cannot satisfy the requirements of a topic. For it to be a topic, it must dominate a constituent with the feature [+top]. But it only dominates P and a trace, neither of which can be [+top]. Hence, the sentence is ruled out.[31,32]

(148) extends to the contrast between (149a) and (149b) as well.

(149) a.   Mary thinks that [to John]$_1$, Bill should send the book t_1
      b.   *who$_2$ t_2 thinks that [to who]$_1$, Bill should send the book t_1

Who in the embedded topic in (149b) must move to the matrix SPEC of CP in LF to be properly interpreted. Then, the embedded topic contains only P and a trace at LF. Thus, if (148) applies at LF, (149b) is ruled out. Note that (150b), like (147a–b), is consistent with (148).

(150) a.   Mary thinks that [books about John]$_1$, Bill should read t_1
      b.   ?who$_2$ t_2 thinks that [books about who]$_1$, Bill should read t_1

After LF WH-movement, the embedded topic in (150b) contains N in addition to P and a trace. Hence, it can have the feature [+ top].

Before we end this section, let us return to (139), repeated here as (151), and briefly consider the implications of (143) for this example.

(151) *[$_{CP}$ what state$_2$ [$_{IP}$ did a man walk in [$_{CP}$ who$_1$ [$_{IP}$ t_1 was from t_2]]]]

We analyzed this sentence above as a double Subjacency violation. The movement of *what state* crosses the embedded IP and CP, both barriers, and the WH-phrase is not dominated by the maximal projections immediately dominating these barriers. However, we argued that Ā-binders are not barriers. Thus, if the relative clause is extraposed from within the matrix subject and is adjoined to the matrix IP, leaving behind a trace, then the extraposed relative itself can no longer be considered as a barrier. Then, the WH-movement in (151) crosses only one relevant barrier (the embedded IP), and we should expect this example to be only a weak Subjacency violation. This is clearly contrary to the facts. Hence, our analysis implies that the extraposed CP in (151) is not an Ā-binder adjoined to IP. We suggest then that the relative clause in (151) is base-generated in place, its relationship to the head established not by movement but by some sort of predication.

We should note that the theory developed so far leads us to the base-generation analysis of "extraposed relative clauses" on independent grounds. Consider again the grammatical (138), repeated here as (152).

(152) [$_{IP}$[$_{NP}$ a man] [$_{VP}$ walked in] [$_{CP}$ who$_1$ [$_{IP}$ t_1 was from California]]]

Suppose first that the CP moves out of the subject NP, leaving a trace. If the CP does not bind its trace, then the structure is clearly excluded by the Proper Binding Condition. On the other hand, if the CP does bind its trace, it must be adjoined to IP. But then, the extraposition itself straightforwardly violates Subjacency, the subject NP serving as barrier and the original IP as the minimal maximal projection dominating the barrier.

Suppose next that the CP in (152) moves out of the subject NP without leaving a trace. Then, the movement need not be adjunction to IP, since the Proper Binding Condition is irrelevant. It can be adjunction to a lower node (e.g., VP), thus obeying Subjacency. However, some mechanism other than Ā-chain formation will be needed to establish the required relationship between the relative clause and the head. But this is then essentially equivalent to the base-generation approach. Thus, we are led again to the base-generation analysis of "extraposed" relative clauses.[33]

Chapter 4

A Constraint on Antecedent Governors for Traces of A- and Ā-Movement

In the preceding chapter, we argued for the following definition of *barrier*:

(1) γ is a barrier for β if
   a. γ is a maximal projection,
   b. γ is not an Ā-binder,
   c. γ is not L-marked, and
   d. γ dominates β.

Further, we proposed the following locality relation for both Subjacency and antecedent government.

(2) β is *subjacent* to α if for every γ, γ a barrier for β, the maximal projection immediately dominating γ dominates α.

(3) *Subjacency Condition*
   X can move from position α to position β only if α is subjacent to β.

(4) α *antecedent-governs* β if
   a. α binds β, and
   b. β is subjacent to α.

More specifically, we have departed from the *Barriers* theory in the following respects:

(5) a. Adjunction creates an additional maximal projection, rather than a "segmented" single maximal projection.
   b. VP can be L-marked by INFL, and hence, when it is, it is not a barrier.
   c. IP is not a "defective category"; in other words, like other categories, it becomes a barrier when not L-marked.
   d. All barriers are "inherent" barriers in the terminology of Chomsky (1986a); that is, there is no inheritance of barrierhood.[1]

(2)–(5) correctly account for examples such as the following:

(6) a. ??the place [$_{CP}$ where$_1$ [$_{IP}$ that book$_2$ [$_{IP}$ John put t_2 t_1]]]
   b. *the man [$_{CP}$ who$_1$ [$_{IP}$ that book$_2$ [$_{IP}$ t_1 read t_2]]]

The most deeply embedded IP is a barrier for both t_1 and t_2 in (6a–b). Given that adjunction creates an additional maximal projection, as argued in chapter 3, the movement of *where* and *who* to SPEC of CP in (6a–b) violates Subjacency. (6b) violates the ECP, in addition, since t_1 is neither lexically governed nor antecedent-governed. In particular, it is not antecedent-governed since it is not subjacent to *who*$_1$. Thus, the grammatical status of (6a–b) is correctly accounted for.

In this chapter, we turn from the locality requirement on antecedent government to the question of what can be an antecedent governor. More specifically, in section 4.1, we argue that only X^0 categories can be proper governors. Then, in sections 4.2 and 4.3, we discuss some phenomena that are potentially problematic for this hypothesis. In section 4.2, we are concerned with quantifier raising of quantified NPs in subject position and, more generally, with the LF movement of subject NPs. In section 4.3, we examine a range of NP-movement phenomena and show that the formulation of the ECP motivated earlier can directly account for a wide range of cases. Certain other cases, however, are found to be outside the domain of the ECP. For them, we argue that an extension of the Uniformity Condition of Chomsky (1986b) is the appropriate mechanism. Given this, we will briefly reconsider the role of the ECP, among other conditions, in constraining NP-movement.

4.1 A Condition on Possible Antecedent Governors

4.1.1 Topicalization of Subject NPs

Let us consider once again standard *that*-trace violations arising from topicalization, as in (7).[2]

(7) *[$_{IP}$ John$_1$ [$_{IP}$ you think [$_{CP}$ that [$_{IP}$ t_1 left]]]]

In (7), *John* is clearly too far from its trace to serve as its antecedent governor. In particular, the IP of the complement is a barrier for t_1. Thus, (7) is apparently straightforwardly excluded in just the same way as (8) is generally taken to be.

(8) [$_{CP}$ who$_1$ [$_{IP}$ do you think [$_{CP}$ that [$_{IP}$ t_1 left]]]]

Further, we continue to assume, as in chapter 2, that *that* in COMP prevents an intermediate trace in SPEC of CP from serving as an antecedent governor. Thus, these structures are indeed excluded.

But there are other structures that must be considered, given that topicalization can involve adjunction, as shown in chapter 3. For example, suppose that long-distance topicalization of a subject involves an initial adjunction to the lowest IP. Then, in place of (7), we might have an S-structure representation such as (9).

(9) $[_{IP}$ John$_1$ $[_{IP}$ you think $[_{CP}$ that $[_{IP}$ t_1' $[_{IP}$ t_1 left]]]]]

Here, t_1' would seem to antecedent-govern t_1. Then, t_1 would be marked $[+\gamma]$ at S-structure. At LF, if there are no further applications of Affect α, t_1' will be an offending trace, since it is too far from its nearest binder to be antecedent-governed. However, nothing prevents the deletion of this intermediate trace. Thus, the only trace remaining at LF will be t_1, marked $[+\gamma]$, as shown in (10).

(10) $[_{IP}$ John$_1$ $[_{IP}$ you think $[_{CP}$ (that) $[_{IP}$ t_1 left]]]]
$[+\gamma]$

This is obviously an incorrect result, since (11) is clearly a *that*-trace violation.

(11) *John, you think that left

The derivation leading to this incorrect result is quite reminiscent of those involved in grammatical examples such as (12), discussed in L&S and also in chapter 2.

(12) who$_1$ $[_{IP}$ do you believe $[_{CP}$ that $[_{CP}$ Mary said $[_{CP}$ t_1' $[_{IP}$ t_1 left early]]]]]

Here too there is a trace, t_1', which serves as an antecedent governor at S-structure but which would not itself be antecedent-governed at that level. However, at LF, this potentially offending trace can be deleted. It will be crucial to somehow distinguish the ill-formed (9) from the well-formed (12).

The derivation incorrectly generating (11) is even more reminiscent of another analysis discussed in L&S. One of our major concerns there was to answer a question posed by Huang (1982): Why are there no *that*-trace effects with adjuncts? In L&S, we considered a number of possible analyses for this phenomenon. The one most directly relevant to the present discussion involved escape from an embedded clause via adjunction to IP. Under such an analysis, (13) could have (14) as its S-structure representation.

(13) why do you think that he left

(14) $[_{CP}$ why$_1$ $[_{IP}$ do you think $[_{CP}$ that $[_{IP}$ t_1' $[_{IP}$ he left t_1]]]]]

In (14), t_1' is in a position to antecedent-govern t_1. If t_1 is marked $[+\gamma]$ at

S-structure, and t_1' deletes in the LF component, there will be no offending trace at the level of LF, just as in the analysis of (12).

However, we argued that such an analysis of (13) could not be maintained in general, because it failed to entirely distinguish the grammatical (13) from completely impossible long movement out of islands as in (15), with S-structure representation (16).

(15) *why do you wonder whether he left

(16) $[_{CP}$ why$_1$ $[_{IP}$ do you wonder $[_{CP}$ whether $[_{IP}$ t_1' $[_{IP}$ he left t_1]]]]]

Exactly as in (14), t_1' apparently can antecedent-govern t_1 at S-structure, then delete in LF. On the basis of this fact, and on the basis of certain other phenomena as well, we concluded that only arguments are γ-marked at S-structure.[3] Then, in (16), t_1, being an adjunct trace, can be γ-marked only at LF, and hence, for this trace to be marked $[+\gamma]$, t_1' must be present at this level. Thus, either t_1 or t_1' will necessarily violate the γ-Filter at LF, correctly excluding (15). But now note that this line of reasoning does not carry over to the superficially quite similar (9). In that example, the initial trace is in fact an argument and hence can (indeed must) be γ-marked at S-structure. At this point, our theory incorrectly predicts that (11), with the S-structure representation in (9), does not violate the ECP, exactly as (12) does not.

The task here is to make the ECP rule out the S-structure representation (9), while still allowing (12).

(9) $[_{IP}$ John$_1$ $[_{IP}$ you think $[_{CP}$ that $[_{IP}$ t_1' $[_{IP}$ t_1 left]]]]]

(12) $[_{CP}$ who$_1$ $[_{IP}$ do you believe $[_{CP}$ that $[_{IP}$ Mary said $[_{CP}$ t_1' $[_{IP}$ t_1 left early]]]]]]

One clear difference between these two examples lies in the position of the intermediate trace. It is adjoined to IP in (9), whereas in (12), it is in the SPEC of CP. In fact, what antecedent-governs the initial trace in (12) need not be the intermediate trace t_1', but can be the COMP node coindexed with it by SPEC-head agreement (see chapter 2). Hence, if we assume that COMP, but not an intermediate trace, is eligible to be an antecedent governor, the contrast between (9) and (12) is accounted for. The subject trace t_1 in (9) will be neither lexically governed nor antecedent-governed and thus will be marked $[-\gamma]$ at S-structure. The assumption follows from the more general hypothesis (17), which is argued for on independent grounds by Stowell (1981) and Rizzi (1986b).[4]

(17) Only X^0 categories can be proper governors.

(17) allows COMP, but not a trace of the category NP, to be an antecedent governor.

(17) makes further predictions concerning topicalization of a subject. First, it predicts correctly that "long" topicalization of a subject is possible. (18a), for example, can have the S-structure representation in (18b).

(18) a. John, I think left
     b. $[_{IP}$ John$_1$ $[_{IP}$ I think $[_{CP}$ t_1' $[_{C'}$ C$_1$ $[_{IP}$ t_1 left]]]]]

The COMP coindexed with the intermediate trace, being an X^0 category, assigns $[+\gamma]$ to the initial trace at S-structure, and the intermediate trace can itself delete in LF. Hence, (17) does not affect the analysis of examples such as (18) offered in Chapter 3. On the other hand, we expect that "short" topicalization of a subject by adjunction is impossible, since the resulting structure will be as follows:

(19) $[_{IP}$ John$_1$ $[_{IP}$ t_1 left]]

The trace t_1 in (19) is not lexically governed, and there is no X^0 category that can serve as an antecedent governor for this trace. Hence, (19) violates the ECP. On the face of it, it might seem difficult, or even impossible, to test this claim. Since the movement producing (19) is string vacuous, how can (19) be distinguished from the obviously grammatical (20)?

(20) $[_{IP}$ John left]

Surprisingly, however, there is evidence that distinguishes these two structures and supports our claim that structures such as (19) are to be excluded. Consider first the effects of topicalization on anaphor binding:

(21) a. *John thinks that Mary likes himself
     b.   John thinks that himself, Mary likes t

(21a) represents a standard Condition A violation, with *himself* free in its governing category, the lower IP. (21b) illustrates that topicalizing *himself* releases it from this governing category and allows it to find its antecedent in the next clause up. Notice that a topicalized anaphor is not freed from all binding requirements, as (22a) shows, or even from locality requirements, as (22b) shows.

(22) a. *himself, Mary likes t
     b. *John thinks that Mary said that himself, Susan likes t

Rather, the anaphor, by virtue of being topicalized, is given a more inclusive governing category.[5,6]

Consider now potential subject topicalization parallel to the object topicalization in (20):

(23) a. *John thinks that himself likes Mary

    b. *John thinks that himself, t likes Mary

(23a) is excluded in the usual way. That is, *himself* is free in its governing category, namely, the embedded IP. (23b) is potentially more problematic, however. The relationship between *John* and *himself* cannot be the source of the ill-formedness, since the relationship is identical in the well-formed (21b). Evidently, the offending element is the trace.[7] But that is exactly what (17) claims. The trace in (23b) is not properly governed because, unlike the trace in (21b), it is not lexically governed; nor is it antecedent-governed, since its nearest binder, *himself*, is not an X^0. Thus, in addition to preventing certain *that*-trace violations, (17) also serves to close a Condition A loophole made available by topicalization.[8]

Another argument for the ill-formedness of the structure in (19) can be constructed on the basis of the following paradigm:[9,10]

(24) a. ?which athletes do you wonder which pictures of Mary bought

    b. ??which athletes do you think that pictures of, Mary bought

(25) a. ?which athletes do you wonder which pictures of are on sale

    b. ?*which athletes do you think that pictures of, are on sale

As we discussed in chapter 3, extraction out of NPs in $\bar{\text{A}}$-position is reasonably acceptable. Thus, (24a) and (25a), in which a WH-phrase is extracted out of a WH-phrase in embedded SPEC of CP, are no worse than marginal. (25a), in particular, contrasts with subject condition violations such as (26).

(26) ?*who do you think that pictures of are on sale

This indicates that subject condition violations can be ameliorated by moving the subject to an $\bar{\text{A}}$-position. In (24b), a WH-phrase is extracted out of an embedded NP topic instead of a WH-phrase in embedded SPEC of CP. The result is again no worse than marginal, and it conforms to the generalization that extraction out of NPs in $\bar{\text{A}}$-position is marginally allowed.[11]

What is surprising is the ungrammaticality of (25b). In this example, the embedded subject is topicalized and a WH-phrase is extracted out of it. It seems that there is nothing wrong with the WH-movement itself, since the same movement is allowed, at least marginally, in (24b). Hence, what is wrong with this example must be the embedded topicalization. And such topicalization is prohibited, given our hypothesis that the configuration in (19) violates the ECP.

4.1.2 More Arguments for the X^0 Hypothesis

In this section, we will present further arguments for the hypothesis that only X^0 categories can be antecedent governors, and we will discuss further implications of this proposal.

4.1.2.1 Heavy NP Shift Rizzi (1986b) points out that one striking restriction on heavy NP shift (henceforth HNPS) follows immediately from the hypothesis that only X^0 categories can be antecedent governors.

As is well known, an NP object of a verb can generally move rightward if it is "heavy" enough.[12] The following examples illustrate this operation:

(27) I gave t_1 to John [all of my books on vowel harmony]$_1$
(28) Mary put t_1 on the desk [the mail that had been accumulating for two weeks]$_1$

As is also well known, the subject in an exceptional Case marking environment is also eligible to undergo HNPS:

(29) we believe t_1 to have good judgment [everyone who took the time to analyze this phenomenon]$_1$

Assuming that the trace in these cases, like all other traces we have considered, is subject to the ECP, the question of proper government of the trace immediately arises. In these particular examples, lexical government obtains. In (27), the trace is lexically governed by *gave*, in (28), by *put*, and in (29), by *believe*. Note that in all these cases, in addition to being lexically governed, the trace is bound. In particular, the trace is bound by the shifted heavy NP, which we assume is adjoined to VP in (27) and (28), and to IP or the higher VP in (29).[13] We have argued that such binding does not, in general, create a configuration of antecedent government. That is, if what is adjoined is not a head, as it is not here, it will not be eligible to antecedent-govern. That fact is of no import in (27), (28), and (29), since lexical government obtains.

Let us then consider an example of the same basic structure as (29) but in which lexical government does not obtain:

(30) *we believe t_1 has good judgment [everyone who took the time to analyze this phenomenon]$_1$

The subject position of a finite clause is not lexically governed. If, as we have argued, binding by an adjoined NP does not constitute antecedent government, then t_1 in (30) will not be properly governed at all, straightforwardly accounting for the unacceptability of the example.[14]

As mentioned above, this analysis of the preceding HNPS examples is suggested by Rizzi (1986b: fn. 30). Rizzi proposes the following account for the contrast between (31) (his (ii)) and (32) (his (iv)):

(31) I consider EC to be desirable the perspective that IP

(32) *I consider that EC is desirable the perspective that IP

The impossibility of [(32)] and the contrast with [(31)] naturally suggests an account in terms of the ECP; but this implies that the rightward-moved subject cannot count for antecedent government. This result can be achieved if it is assumed that antecedent government (in fact, government in general) can only take place from a head position. Therefore, a WH-element or trace in COMP (a head position) can antecedent-govern a trace in subject position, but an NP right-adjoined to S [IP] or S' [CP] (a nonhead position) cannot antecedent-govern; hence, [(32)] is ruled out by the ECP.[15]

4.1.2.2 Parasitic Gaps Now consider the following ungrammatical parasitic gap example, pointed out to us by Juan Uriagereka:

(33) *who$_1$ did you telephone t_1 after e_1 arrived

This example seems to have the status of a *that*-trace violation. (See Chomsky 1982 for discussion of ECP effects with parasitic gaps.) The structure of the *after* clause is not entirely clear. There is some reason to believe that the structure is as in (34) (as proposed in Huang 1982 and assumed in chapter 3) rather than (35).

(34) $[_{CP}[_C$ after$]$ $[_{IP} \ldots]]$

(35) $[_{PP}$ after $[_{CP} \ldots]]$

If structure (35) were correct, there would be no reason to expect that *after* cannot cooccur with a complementizer. But in fact, it cannot, as shown by (36).

(36) I left after (*that) John arrived

Structure (34) gives this result directly: there is one head position, and it is filled by *after*. There is thus no position for *that*.

Huang (1982) provides another piece of evidence for the structure in (34). He points out contrasts such as the following and proposes an ECP analysis for them on the basis of (34):

(37) a. ??who$_1$ did you leave for London after you visited t_1

     b. *Who$_1$ did you leave for London after t_1 visited you

A similar contrast can be observed with topicalization, as shown in (38).

(38) a. ??John$_1$, Mary left for London after she visited t_1

     b. *John$_1$, Mary left for London after t_1 visited her

The ECP analysis for *that*-trace effects with topicalization discussed above carries over to (38b), if we assume the structure in (34). Then, the S-structure representation of (38b) is as in (39).

(39) $[_{IP}$ John$_1$ $[_{IP}$ Mary left for London $[_{CP}$ after $[_{IP}$ (t_1') $[_{IP}$ t_1 visited her]]]]]

The intermediate trace t_1', even if it is present, cannot antecedent-govern t_1, since it is not X^0. Hence, (38b) violates the ECP, whereas (38a) violates only Subjacency. On the other hand, if (35) is correct, then the structure of (38b) can be as in (40).

(40) $[_{IP}$ John$_1$ $[_{IP}$ Mary left for London $[_{PP}$ after $[_{CP}$ t_1' $[_{C'}$ C_1 $[_{IP}$ t_1 visited her]]]]]]

The COMP coindexed with t_1' assigns $[+\gamma]$ to t_1, and if t_1' deletes in LF, there will be no ECP violation. Hence, we predict incorrectly that both (38a) and (38b) are mere Subjacency violations. There is, then, good reason to believe that (34), and not (35), is the correct structure.

Our ECP analysis of (38b) crucially relies on the hypothesis that only X^0 categories can be antecedent governors, since, as we argued above, topicalization can involve adjunction. If it could not, then the intermediate trace in (39) could not exist. But we can construct an argument for the X^0 category hypothesis that is independent of our adjunction analysis of topicalization.

Let us return to (33), repeated here as (41).

(41) *who$_1$ did you telephone t_1 after e_1 arrived

If we assume with Chomsky (1986a) that parasitic gap constructions involve a null parasitic operator, then (41) raises the question why the parasitic operator cannot antecedent-govern e_1. There are two cases to consider. Either the operator is in an adjoined position, or it is in the SPEC of the adjunct CP. The adjunct in (42), then, might have structure (43a) or (43b), with Op adjoined to CP or IP, respectively, or structure (44), with Op in SPEC of CP.[16]

(42) ?who$_1$ did you telephone t_1 after John mentioned e_1

(43) a. $[_{CP}$ Op$_1$ $[_{CP}[_{C'}$ after $[_{IP}$ John mentioned e_1]]]]
     b. $[_{CP}[_{C'}$ after $[_{IP}$ Op$_1$ $[_{IP}$ John mentioned e_1]]]]]

(44) $[_{CP}$ Op$_1$ $[_{C'}$ after $[_{IP}$ [John mentioned e_1]]]]

Note that in none of these structures is Op$_1$ an eligible antecedent governor, since it is an XP rather than an X^0. Further, as we will show in detail in chapter 5, SPEC-head agreement should be blocked by a lexical head of

CP; otherwise, *that*-trace violations are incorrectly allowed. And this implies that the head COMP in (44) cannot antecedent-govern the parasitic gap. Thus, antecedent government will be entirely excluded. That is of no consequence in the case of (42), since the parasitic gap is lexically governed by *mentioned*.

The parasitic gap is not lexically governed in (41), however. (45) shows the structure of the adjunct in (41), assuming now, for concreteness, that the parasitic operator is adjoined to IP (as in (43b)).

(45) $[_{CP} [_{C'}$ after $[_{IP} Op_1 [_{IP} e_1$ arrived]]]]

As we indicated above, not only is this not a configuration of lexical government, it is also not a configuration of antecedent government, since Op_1 is not a head. Thus, (45), like other possible structures for the adjunct in (41), is ruled out by the ECP. Note that our account of (41) is essentially identical to our account of *that*-trace effects with topicalization. Although successive-cyclic topicalization via adjunction could potentially create a configuration of binding by a superjacent antecedent (an intermediate trace), that binding would not constitute antecedent government, since the binder would not be a head. Similarly, an empty parasitic operator in an adjoined position may bind a parasitic gap, but it does not qualify as an antecedent governor since it is not a head. Thus, the ungrammaticality of (41) constitutes additional evidence that only X^0 categories can be antecedent governors.[17]

Parasitic operators and topics behave alike in other respects as well. For example, both can be moved "long distance" from an embedded subject position if the embedded COMP is empty. Thus, the following examples are acceptable and contrast with (41):

(46) ?who$_1$ did you telephone t_1 after Mary said e_1 arrived

(47) (I think that) this book$_1$, Mary said t_1 is interesting

Recall that (47) is grammatical because the trace t_1 can be antecedent-governed by the embedded COMP, as shown in (48).

(48) $[_{IP}$ this book$_1$ $[_{IP}$ Mary said $[_{CP} t_1' [_{C'} C_1 [_{IP} t_1$ is interesting]]]]]

The licitness of the parasitic gap in (46) can be accounted for in exactly the same way. The structure of the adjunct clause in (46) can be as in (49).

(49) $[_{CP}$ after $[_{IP} Op_1 [_{IP}$ Mary said $[_{CP} t_1' [_{C'} C_1 [_{IP} t_1$ arrived]]]]]]

The initial trace t_1 in (49) is antecedent-governed by the embedded COMP. Thus, just as in the case of topicalization by adjunction, subject parasitic operators can move "long distance" but not "short distance."

4.2   LF Movement of Subjects Revisited

We argued above that only X^0 categories can be antecedent governors and hence, given our other assumptions, that the following configuration violates the ECP:

(50) $[_{IP} NP_1' [_{IP} t_1 [_{I'} INFL VP]]]$

A further example that seems directly relevant to this hypothesis is (51).

(51) everyone left

Under standard assumptions, quantifier raising (QR) adjoins *everyone* to IP in the LF component, and the LF representation of (51) is as in (52).

(52) $[_{IP} everyone_1 [_{IP} t_1 left]]$

(52) has just the configuration in (50), and hence, it seems that it should violate the ECP. Yet (51) is completely grammatical.

There are two plausible approaches to this problem. One is to hypothesize that QR does not apply in the LF component. There are, in turn, two ways to instantiate this hypothesis. QR might not exist at all, in which case, quantifier scope is read off S-structure as proposed by Kroch (1974), for example. Alternatively, QR might exist, but apply to the output of the LF component, rendering the ECP irrelevant. The second plausible approach to the problem is to exploit the distinction between the levels of S-structure and LF. In section 4.1, we considered only cases of syntactic movement, arguing that the configuration in (50) is ill formed. There might be some independent property of LF that serves to salvage a subject trace left by QR. In this section, we will reexamine LF movement of subjects in general and, by doing so, explore the second approach to the problem.

4.2.1   LF INFL Raising

Recall the following contrast from chapter 2:

(53) a. *who$_1$ do you think that t_1 left
       b. ?who$_1$ t_1 thinks that who$_2$ left

Who$_2$ in (53b) moves to the SPEC of the matrix CP in LF, but the example is far better than (53a). Thus, it seems that long syntactic WH-movement of subject, like "short" topicalization of subject, violates the ECP, but structurally parallel cases in LF do not violate this principle.

Let us first discuss the contrast in (53), and then consider whether the contrast between "short" topicalization and QR can be accounted for in a similar way. In L&S, we proposed that the trace of LF movement in (53b) is properly governed by virtue of the application of a further LF movement process. In particular, we argued that following LF deletion of *that*, INFL can raise to COMP, giving (54) for the complement clause in (53b).

(54) ... $[_{S'(=CP)}[_{COMP_2}$ INFL$_2$] $[_{IP}$ t_2 leave]]

Note that the head position is available for INFL, *that* having been deleted by Affect α in the LF component. Assuming that subject and INFL are coindexed and furthermore that this coindexation is relevant for the ECP, we proposed that the index of the head percolates to COMP, which is then an appropriate antecedent governor for t_2. No such LF process can salvage the ill-formed (53a), since there the subject trace is created in the syntactic component and obligatorily marked $[-\gamma]$ at the level of S-structure.

A type of example discussed by May (1985) falls under the same analysis. May points out that (55) has the same status as (53b).

(55) ?who wonders whether who left

(55) posed a problem for the account of (53b) in L&S, since *whether*, unlike *that*, cannot be deleted in LF, and hence, in (55), the embedded INFL cannot be in COMP at this level. But the CP analysis provides a natural solution to this problem. Assuming, as suggested in chapter 2, that *whether* is in SPEC of CP, the embedded COMP is available for INFL. The LF trace of the WH-moved subject of the lower clause can then be antecedent-governed by that INFL.

Though INFL movement to COMP provides a means for satisfying the ECP in (53b) and (55), it still does not seem to provide an account for the problematic (51), repeated here as (56).

(56) everyone left

Consider then the LF representation in (57).

(57) $[_{CP}[_{C'}$ INFL$_1$ $[_{IP}$ everyone$_1$ $[_{IP}$ t_1 leave]]]]

Here INFL$_1$ binds t_1, but the latter is not subjacent to the former, so antecedent government fails. We thus propose that, at least as one option, INFL may adjoin to IP. For (56), this can produce (58).

(58) $[_{IP}$ everyone $[_{IP}$ INFL$_1$ $[_{IP}$ t_1 leave]]]

And in this configuration, INFL$_1$ *does* antecedent-govern t_1.

A further problem arises with respect to (59).

(59) why did everyone leave

If we adopt the analysis of Chomsky (1986a), INFL is already in COMP at S-structure in (59). The LF representation of (59) is then seemingly as in (60) or (61), depending on where the LF trace of *why* is created.

(60) $[_{CP} \text{why}_1 [_{C'} \text{did}_2 [_{IP} \text{everyone}_2 [_{IP} t_2 \text{ leave } t_1]]]]$

(61) $[_{CP} \text{why}_1 [_{C'} \text{did}_2 [_{IP}[_{IP} \text{everyone}_2 [_{IP} t_2 \text{ leave}]] t_1]]]$

But in neither case is t_1 properly governed: there is no X^0 to bind it. Further, antecedent government of t_2 fails because of the subjacency requirement. We thus propose that here, too, INFL adjoins to IP, lowering from COMP (if, in fact, it was in COMP at S-structure). The empty COMP is then free to agree with *why*, giving the LF representation (62).

(62) $[_{CP} \text{why}_1 [_{C'} C_1 [_{IP}[_{IP} \text{everyone}_2 [_{IP} \text{INFL}_2 [_{IP} t_2 \text{ leave}]]] t_1]]]$

In (62), t_2 is antecedent-governed by INFL_2 and t_1 is antecedent-governed by COMP_1.[18]

It is important to note that antecedent government of a subject trace by INFL will be impossible without INFL movement, since prior to movement, INFL in English does not c-command the subject position. In effect, the raising of INFL gives English an LF structure equivalent in relevant respects to S-structure in Japanese, as discussed in chapter 2.

4.2.2 Superiority Effects

The INFL movement analysis presented here correctly accounts for the S-structure–LF asymmetry with respect to IP-adjunction of subject and the *that*-trace effect, but at the same time has a consequence that may seem curious, given the history of the ECP. As noted in chapter 1, one of the original arguments for this principle was based on the contrast in (63).

(63) a. $\text{who}_1 \ t_1$ bought what$_2$
     b. *what$_2$ did who$_1$ buy t_2

According to the analysis developed so far, the LF representation of (63b) is as in (64).

(64) $[_{CP}[\text{who}_1 [\text{what}_2]]_2 [_{C'} C_2 [_{IP} t_1 \text{ bought } t_2]]]$

Here, t_1 is neither lexically governed nor antecedent-governed. Hence, it violates the ECP. However, given the INFL movement hypothesis, the LF representation of (63b) can now be as in (65).

(65) $[_{CP} \ldots [_{IP} \text{INFL}_1 [_{IP} t_1 \text{ buy } t_2]]]$

In (65), t_1 is antecedent-governed by INFL, exactly as in (58) and (62). Hence, (63b) does not violate the ECP.

We suggest that although this conclusion is somewhat surprising, it is nonetheless correct. First consider the following example:

(66) who$_1$ t_1 wonders what$_2$ who$_3$ bought t_2

As one might expect, (66) is ungrammatical with *who*$_3$ interpreted in the lower SPEC of CP along with *what*$_2$. In fact, with such a reading, it has exactly the status of (67), which in turn has the status of (63b).

(67) *Bill wonders what$_1$ who$_2$ bought t_1

However, (66) is dramatically improved on the reading where *who*$_3$ takes matrix scope, that is, where (66) is a matrix double question on *who*$_1$ and *who*$_3$. This fact suggests that an LF representation like (68) is well formed.

(68) $[_{CP}$[who$_3$ [who$_1$]]$_1$ $[_{C'}$ C$_1$ $[_{IP}$ t_1 wonders $[_{CP}$ what$_2$ $[_{C'}$ C$_2$ $[_{IP}$ t_3 bought t_2]]]]]]

It would seem that t_3 in (68) is no more properly governed than t_1 in (64), strongly suggesting that neither (63b) nor (67) should be treated as an ECP violation. As we have noted, under the INFL-raising proposal, t_1 in (65) (the LF representation of (63b)) will be antecedent-governed by INFL$_1$. Similarly, t_3 in (69) (the LF representation of (66)) will be antecedent-governed by INFL$_3$.

(69) ... $[_{CP}$ what$_2$ $[_{C'}$ C$_2$ $[_{IP}$ INFL$_3$ $[_{IP}$ t_3 buy t_2]]]]

If, as we have argued, the ECP is not the appropriate mechanism for excluding (63b), (67), and the embedded double question reading of (66), the question immediately arises what the appropriate mechanism might be for handling such examples. Those examples had been analyzed by Chomsky (1973) as violations of the Superiority Condition, a condition that was later subsumed under the ECP.[19] Chomsky's (1973:246) formulation of the Superiority Condition is shown in (70).

(70) a. No rule can involve X, Y in the structure
    ...X...$[_{\alpha}$...Z...-W Y V...]...
    where the rule applies ambiguously to Z and Y and Z is superior to Y.

  b. "... the category A is 'superior' to the category B in the phrase marker if every major category dominating A dominates B as well but not conversely."

Under our analysis, (63b), (67), and the embedded double question reading of (66) must be considered as cases of Superiority violations that do not fall under the ECP.

As is well known, there are other superiority effects that clearly do not fall under the ECP, as shown by Hendrick and Rochemont (1982). (See also Pesetsky 1982 for extensive discussion, and L&S, fn. 10.) (71) and (72) illustrate such a "pure" superiority contrast.

(71) a. who did you tell to read what
   b. $[_{CP}$[what$_2$ [who$_1$]]$_1$ $[_{C'}$ C$_1$ $[_{IP}$ you told t_1 $[_{CP}[_{IP}$ PRO$_1$ to read t_2]]]]]]

(72) a. ?*what did you tell who to read

b. $[_{CP}[\text{who}_1 \ [\text{what}_2]]_2 \ [_{C'} \ C_2 \ [_{IP} \ \text{you told} \ t_1 \ [_{CP}[_{IP} \ \text{PRO}_1 \ \text{to read}$
$t_2]]]]]$

In (71b), the LF representation of the grammatical (71a), both traces are lexically governed, t_1 by *told* and t_2 by *read*. But in (72b), the LF representation of the much less acceptable (72a), the lexical government relations are identical. Thus, the ECP clearly fails to distinguish (71a) from (72a). Similarly, the following contrast is predicted by the Superiority Condition, but is not accounted for by the ECP, since the traces of all the WHs are lexically governed both at S-structure and at LF.

(73)   what$_1$ did you give t_1 to who$_2$

(74)   ?*who$_2$ did you give what$_1$ to t_2

Given the status of (66) and of the examples in (71)–(74), the Superiority Condition must be maintained independently of the ECP. At the same time, we must make sure that this condition rules out (63b), (67), and the embedded double question reading of (66), while allowing the matrix double question reading of (66). It is not clear that even Chomsky's (1973) formulation of Superiority has the latter property.[20] Let us consider (66) again, whose D-structure and S-structure representations are shown in (75a) and (75b), respectively.

(75) a. $[_{CP}[_{IP} \ \text{who wonders} \ [_{CP}[_{IP} \ \text{who bought what}]]]]$

b. $[_{CP} \ \text{who}_1 \ [_{IP} \ t_1 \ \text{wonders} \ [_{CP} \ \text{what}_2 \ [_{IP} \ \text{who}_3 \ \text{bought} \ t_2]]]]$

If the Superiority Condition is a condition on transformations, as Chomsky (1973) assumes, then (75b) is evidently ruled out regardless of its interpretation. The embedded *who* and *what* in (75a) are both apparently available for movement to the embedded SPEC of CP; hence, the former must move, since it is superior to the latter.

Since *who*$_3$ in (75b) can move to the matrix SPEC of CP but not to the embedded SPEC of CP in LF, as indicated by the possible interpretation of the sentence, it then seems that the Superiority Condition should choose between two WH-phrases only when they are to wind up in the same SPEC of CP at LF. In particular, when *who*$_3$ in (75b) is to move into the matrix SPEC of CP in LF, this condition should not prevent *what*$_2$ from moving into the embedded SPEC of CP in syntax. Given this fact, we can describe the superiority effects more accurately as follows:

(76) a. A WH-phrase X in SPEC of CP is Op-disjoint (operator-disjoint) from a WH-phrase Y if the assignment of the index of X to Y would result in the local $\bar{A}$-binding of Y by X. (S-structure)

    b. If two WH-phrases X and Y are Op-disjoint, then they cannot undergo absorption.

(76a) will apply to S-structure representation (75b) and will mark $what_2$ and who_3 Op-disjoint, since assignment of the index of *what* to *who* will result in the local $\bar{\text{A}}$-binding of *who* by *what*. Then, if who_3 moves into the lower SPEC of CP in LF, absorption will fail, given (76b), and the resulting LF representation will have no interpretation. On the other hand, who_3 and who_1 will not be marked Op-disjoint. Because of the intervening trace, t_1, assignment of index *1* to who_3 would not result in local $\bar{\text{A}}$-binding of the latter. Thus, absorption of who_1, who_3 will ultimately be possible, correctly allowing the desired reading.

Note that just the same effects obtain in the case of "pure" Superiority violations, and these effects are correctly accounted for in the same way. Consider (77), which is essentially (72a) embedded under *wonder*, and its S-structure representation (78).

(77) who wonders what you told who to read

(78) who_1 [$_{IP}$ t_1 wonders [$_{CP}$ $what_2$ [$_{IP}$ you told who_3 [$_{IP}$ PRO to read t_2]]]]

This example, like (66), has only the matrix double question reading. By (76a), who_3 and $what_2$ are marked Op-disjoint. At LF, who_3 will then not be able to be in the embedded SPEC of CP, since by (76b), absorption will fail. However, nothing will prevent who_3 from winding up in the matrix SPEC of CP, since (76a) will not apply between who_1 and who_3. This is so because who_3, even if it were assigned the index of who_1, would not be locally $\bar{\text{A}}$-bound by it. Rather, it would be locally A-bound by t_1. Thus, it is correctly predicted that (77) is well formed as a matrix double question on who_1 and who_3 but ill formed as an embedded double question on $what_2$ and who_3.[21]

We have now eliminated one major potential problem for our claim that INFL in English serves as a proper governor for a subject trace at LF. That is, the superiority effect that was handled via the ECP can no longer be handled in that way. But we have shown that that consequence is a positive one since the ECP has proved to be both too weak in its application to superiority phenomena, as originally observed by Hendrick and Rochemont, and too strong, as shown by examples such as (75b).

4.2.3 Subjects in Chinese

To reiterate, our INFL movement analysis entails that in English, there is no subject-object asymmetry in LF with respect to the ECP. As we have shown, this consequence is largely confirmed. Now, it is well known that there is no subject-object asymmetry in languages such as Chinese and Japanese, and hence, it has been widely assumed that those languages are distinct from English in that the subject position of a finite clause is properly governed. However, since we have argued that nominative subject position is properly governed at LF in English also, this hypothesized distinction between English, on the one hand, and Chinese ant Japanese, on the other, becomes much less clear.

Recall from chapter 2 that examples such as the following provide evidence that subject position is properly governed in Chinese and Japanese.

Chinese

(79) ni   xiang-zhidao [shei mai-le sheme]
     you wonder   who bought what
     a. 'who is the x such that you wonder what x bought'
     b. 'what is the x such that you wonder who bought x'

(80) [[shei xie]   de shu] zui   youqu
     who wrote DE book most interesting
     'books that who wrote are the most interesting'

Japanese

(81) kimi-wa [$_{CP}$ dare-ga   dono hon-o   tosyokan-kara karidasita
     you top   who-nom which book-acc library-from   checked-out
     ka] siritai no
     Q want-to-know
     ??'who is the x such that you want to know which book x checked out from the library'

(82) [$_{NP}$[$_{IP}$ dare-ga   kaita] hon]-ga   itiban omosiroi no
             who-nom wrote book-nom most interesting
     'books that who wrote are the most interesting'

As indicated in (79) and (81), a subject WH, *shei* in (79) and *dare* in (81), can move out of a WH-island in LF in Chinese and Japanese.[22] One possible LF representation of (79), which corresponds to the reading in (79a), is roughly as in (83).

(83) [$_{CP}$ shei$_1$ [$_{IP}$ ni xiang-zhidao [$_{CP}$ sheme$_2$ [$_{IP}$ t_1 mai-le t_2]]]]

Similarly, (80) and (82) indicate that a subject WH can move out of a complex NP in LF in those languages. The LF representation of (80) is roughly as in (84).

(84) [$_{CP}$ shei$_1$ [$_{IP}$[$_{NP}$[$_{IP}$ t_1 xie t_2] de shu$_2$] zui youqu]]

The English sentences "corresponding to" the LF representations of (83)–

(84) violate the ECP and are completely ungrammatical, as shown in (85)–(86).

(85) *who$_1$ do you wonder what$_2$ t_1 bought t_2

(86) *who$_1$ are the books (that) t_1 wrote most interesting

It has been widely assumed, on the basis of these examples, that Chinese and Japanese differ from English in that the subject position of a finite clause is lexically governed in those languages. If t_1 in (83)–(84) is lexically governed, then it need not be antecedent-governed, and hence, (83)–(84) are well formed.

However, given our discussion of LF subject traces in English, the difference illustrated in the preceding paragraph may be not a difference among languages but rather a difference between S-structure and LF. As we showed earlier, in (69), one possible LF representation for (66), a trace in the position of t_1 in (85) does not yield ECP violation status when it is produced in LF. (66) is repeated here as (87).

(87) ?who$_1$ t_1 wonders what$_2$ who$_3$ bought t_2

LF

Similarly, a trace in the position of t_1 in (86) does not yield ECP violation status when it is produced in LF, as shown in (88).

(88) ??who$_1$ t_1 thinks that books that who$_2$ wrote are the most interesting

This is predicted under the INFL movement analysis, since the LF trace of *who$_2$* will be antecedent-governed by the moved INFL of the relative clause at that level. And this analysis extends to the examples from Chinese and Japanese in (79)–(82). The LF traces in the subject position of a finite clause are all antecedent-governed by the moved INFL in these languages also, and hence, (79)–(82), with the relevant interpretations, may be acceptable for the same reason that the English examples in (87)–(88) are. According to this hypothesis, Chinese and Japanese are exactly like English with respect to the proper government of a nominative subject.

There is evidence that this hypothesis is correct for Chinese. The data in Huang 1982 indicate that there are subject condition effects on syntactic movement in Chinese. The relevant examples are shown in (89)–(90) (where RM = relative marker).

(89) ??[$_{IP}$[$_{IP}$ Lisi da-le t_1 shi   wo hen bugaoing] de   ren$_1$ lai-le
          Lisi hit-asp   make I   very unhappy   RM man come-asp
     Lit. 'the man who that Lisi hit t made us very unhappy has come'

(90)   [$_{IP}$ ni renwei [$_{IP}$ dajia   dou bu xihuan t_1]] de ren$_1$ lai-le
       you believe   everyone all not like   RM man come-asp
       'the man who you believe that nobody likes t has come'

(89) involves relative clause formation, which Huang argues to be a syntactic movement process. This process is constrained by the sentential subject condition, which is one subcase of the subject condition, ultimately Subjacency. Note that in (90), movement out of a sentential complement is completely grammatical. As discussed in chapter 3, subject condition effects follow from the barrierhood of the subject, if the subject is not L-marked. Thus, we have evidence that the subject position in Chinese is not L-marked. But the grammatical "long" LF movement of subject in (79) and (80) provides evidence that subject position is properly governed. This state of affairs is, of course, familiar: it is exactly the state of affairs that obtains in English. Further, the proposal we made for English carries over essentially unchanged. At S-structure, the subjects in the relevant cases are not lexically governed and hence not L-marked. Thus, they constitute barriers for syntactic movement. This gives the desired result for such cases as (89). On the other hand, at LF, the raised INFL will be in a position to antecedent-govern a subject trace, thus allowing the long LF movement seen in (79a) and (80), as noted above. The LF representation of (79a) will be (91).

(91) [$_{CP}$ shei$_1$ [$_{IP}$ ni xiang-zhidao [$_{CP}$ sheme$_2$ [$_{IP}$ INFL$_1$ [$_{IP}$ t_1 mai-le t_2]]]]]

This discussion indicates that contrary to what is often claimed, there are no differences between English and Chinese with respect to the proper government of the subject. The situation is somewhat different in Japanese. As we showed in chapter 2, there do not seem to be any subject condition effects on syntactic movement in this language over and above complex NP constraint effects. The relevant examples, (10) and (11) of chapter 2, are repeated in (92) and (93), respectively.

(92) ??dono hon-o$_1$ Mary-ga [$_{NP}$ John-ga t_1 katta   koto]-o
     which book-acc Mary-nom   John-nom   bought fact-acc
     mondai-ni siteru no
     problem-to making
     Lit. 'which book is it that Mary is calling the fact that John
     bought it into question'

(93) ??dono hon-o$_1$ Mary-go [$_{NP}$ John-ga t_1 katta   koto]-ga
     which book-arc Mary-nom   John-nom   bought fact-nom
     mondai-da to   omotteru no
     problem-cop COMP think

>   Lit. 'which book is it that Mary thinks that the fact that John
>   bought it is a problem'

In both (92) and (93), an NP is scrambled out of a complex NP, and hence,
these sentences are both marginal. But there is no clear contrast between
(92) and (93), despite the fact that the complex NP is in object position in
(92) but in subject position in (93). This lack of subject-object asymmetry,
in contrast with the Chinese (89)–(90), indicates that there is no proper
government distinction between subject and object, not only at LF, but
also at S-structure, in Japanese.

We proposed in chapter 2, partially on the basis of examples such as
(92)–(93), that sentences in Japanese, which is a strictly head-final language, have the S-structure configuration shown in (94).[23]

(94)

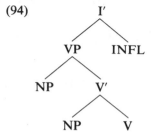

There, assuming Huang's (1982) CED, we suggested that INFL antecedent-
governs and hence properly governs the subject NP in the configuration in (94). But given the discussion on Subjacency above, we must now
assume that INFL in fact L-marks the subject NP in this configuration.
We tentatively suggest here that in (94), INFL can assign Case to the subject NP, when it is [+tense], and further, that INFL, as a Case assigner,
L-marks the Case assignee when it c-commands the NP.[24] But whatever
the exact mechanism of L-marking in (94) may be, the relevant difference
now is not between English on the one hand and Chinese and Japanese on
the other, but rather, between English and Chinese on the one hand and
Japanese on the other. And the relevant distinction seems to come from
the D-structure position of INFL, which we believe ultimately follows
from the strict head-final property of Japanese, in contrast with English
and Chinese.

4.2.4 Some Remaining Questions
Let us now return to the hypothesis that only X^0 categories can be antecedent governors. We were led to this hypothesis by the analysis of topi-

calization in chapter 3, and in turn, it led us to the hypothesis that Superiority is a condition independent of the ECP. Despite the desirable properties of this analysis, certain questions still remain.

First of all, we have stated the Superiority Condition in (76), but it still remains to be seen what the most principled formulation of this condition is, and whether it can be made to follow from a more general principle.[25] Second, although we correctly account for the fact that neither (95) nor (96) has the status of an ECP violation, it remains a mystery why (95) is somewhat marginal whereas (96) is perfect.

(95) ?who$_1$ t_1 said that who$_2$ left

(96) everyone left

The trace of *who$_2$* in (95) produced by LF WH-movement, and the trace of *everyone* in (96) produced by QR, will both be antecedent-governed by the raised INFL at LF. Thus, there is no ECP violation in (95) or (96). Consequently, the marginality of (95) must be attributed to a constraint independent of the ECP.

Another, and possibly related, problem is posed by a contrast in French and Italian discussed by Kayne (1981a) and Rizzi (1982). (The following French examples are from Kayne 1981a.)

(97) je n'ai exigé   qu'ils   arrêtent personne
      I did not demand that they arrest   anyone
      'for no x, I demanded that they arrest x'

(98) *je n'ai exigé   que personne soit arrêté
      I did not demand that anyone   be arrested
      'for no x, I demanded that x be arrested'

Kayne points out that (97)–(98) present the sort of subject-object asymmetry that might be attributed to the ECP.[26] *Personne* can move to the matrix in LF when in embedded object position, as shown in (97), but not when in embedded subject position, as shown in (98). But under the INFL movement analysis, the trace of the LF movement of *personne* in (98) will be antecedent-governed by the raised INFL at LF, and hence, the ungrammaticality of this example cannot be attributed to the ECP. It can be speculated that the contrast between (97) and (98) is similar to the one between (99) and (100), for which we do not have an account, as noted above, or that the presence of the negative morpheme as a scope marker plays a special role in these examples.

(99) who$_1$ said (that) John bought what$_2$

(100) ?who$_1$ t_1 said (that) who$_2$ bought the book

We leave the contrast between (97) and (98) as a question for future research.

4.3 NP-Movement

4.3.1 Passive and Raising

Thus far, we have analyzed a number of phenomena in terms of the requirement that only a head can be an antecedent governor. All of the cases considered so far have involved movement to an $\bar{A}$-position. We turn now to the implications of our approach for movement to an A-position.

Consider, first, the case of simple passives such as (101).

(101) John$_1$ was arrested t_1

Suppose that the trace of the movement of *John* must, like other traces, be properly governed.[27] The theory we have developed actually provides two ways for the proper government requirement to be satisfied in this case. t_1 is lexically governed by *arrested*, since the latter assigns a θ-role to the former. In addition, t_1 is antecedent-governed by INFL. This is so because INFL is coindexed with the subject, *John*, via agreement, and *John* is coindexed with t_1 via movement. (102) shows the relevant details of the S-structure representation of (101). We assume, following Fiengo (1980) and Chomsky (1981), but departing from Chomsky (1986a), that affix hopping applies in the PF component in English, that is, after S-structure.

(102) John$_1$ [$_{I'}$ INFL$_1$ [$_{VP}$ be arrested t_1]]

In (102), INFL$_1$ c-commands t_1. Further, the former is a head, as required. Finally, no barrier separates INFL$_1$ from t_1, given that VP is not a barrier here, as discussed in chapter 3. Hence, antecedent government obtains.

Next, consider raising structures:

(103) John$_1$ seems [t_1 to be smart]

In this case, lexical government does not obtain, for *seems* neither θ-marks nor Case-marks t_1. Recall that mere government by a head, which does obtain in (103), does not suffice for lexical government. Rather, as argued in L&S, there must be a relationship of θ-role assignment or of Case assignment between governor and governee. The following example, similar to one considered in this regard in L&S (fn. 56), and again in chapter 1 above, provides evidence for this restrictive conception of lexical government:

(104) *Bill$_1$ INFL$_1$ is believed [$_{CP}$ that [$_{IP}$ it$_2$ INFL$_2$ seems [t_1 to be
       smart]]]

Clearly, *seems* governs t_1, but if (104) is to be ruled out by the ECP, such
government without θ-role assignment or Case assignment evidently does
not suffice to license the trace. (Note that antecedent government also fails
in (104). INFL$_2$ in the intermediate clause cannot antecedent-govern t_1
since it is not coindexed with it. INFL$_1$ in the matrix clause is coindexed
with t_1 but is too distant to serve as an antecedent governor for it. The
intermediate IP constitutes a barrier for t_1, and INFL$_1$ is not contained in
the first maximal projection containing that barrier.)

In L&S, we proposed that although lexical government is unavailable in
raising structures such as (103), antecedent government by the moved NP
does hold. That possibility is no longer available, because the NP *John* is
not a head. Antecedent government does obtain, though the relevant antecedent governor is not *John*. Rather, as indicated in the discussion of
(101), it is INFL. The approach we will develop is quite similar to that
of Chomsky (1986a), though differing in certain matters of execution.
In (105), we indicate further relevant properties of the abbreviated
S-structure representation (103).

(105) John$_1$ [$_{I'}$ INFL$_1$ [$_{VP}$ seem [$_{IP}$ t_1 to be smart]]]

Here, as in (102), no barriers separate INFL$_1$ and t_1. VP is not a barrier,
and IP in (105) is the θ-marked complement of *seem*, hence also not a
barrier. Thus, antecedent government obtains in this case as well.

Raising adjectives receive just the same treatment as raising verbs. Consider S-structure representation (106).

(106) John$_1$ [$_{I'}$ INFL$_1$ [$_{VP}$ be [$_{AP}$ likely [$_{IP}$ t_1 to win]]]]

In (106), IP is not a barrier for t_1, because it is the complement of a head,
likely. Similarly, AP is the complement of *be*. Thus, no barriers separate t_1
from INFL, allowing antecedent government.[28]

Let us next consider an infinitival analogue of (106):

(107) I believe [$_{IP}$ John$_1$ [$_{I'}$ to$_1$ [$_{VP}$ be likely [$_{IP}$ t_1 to win]]]]

Here, the INFL of the intermediate clause apparently antecedent-governs
t_1 even though it lacks Tense and AGR. Since the structure is again well
formed, we conclude that INFL is coindexed with the subject even when it
is [$-$Tense, $-$AGR]. An example similar to (107), but seemingly even
more problematic, is given in (108).

(108) I consider [John$_1$ likely [$_{IP}$ t_1 to win]]

In this case, the intermediate clause, which should, by hypothesis, be headed by the INFL that antecedent-governs t_1, is a small clause. Since the sentence is grammatical, we tentatively conclude that even small clauses have INFL, contrary to the analysis proposed by Chomsky (1981) and Stowell (1981). According to this conclusion, which is also argued for by Kayne (1981c) and Kitagawa (1986),[29] small clauses, exactly like other clauses, are projections of INFL.

We have illustrated how the ECP allows passive and raising as in (101) and (103), but rules out illicit "super-raising" as in (104). Thus, the ECP captures much of the locality effect observed in NP-movement. It should be noted, however, that there are examples of "super-raising" that do not readily fall under our ECP account. One such case, which was brought to our attention by Noam Chomsky, who attributes it to Mark Baker, is shown in (109).[30]

(109) *John$_1$ seems [that [it was told t_1 [that [Mary is a genius]]]]

This example involves raising of *John* from the object position of *told* to the matrix subject position, and is clearly ungrammatical. But unlike the trace in (104), t_1 in (107) satisfies the ECP, since it is θ-marked, and hence lexically governed, by the verb *told*. Note that this trace is not antecedent-governed. The only potential antecedent governor for this trace is the matrix INFL, but the intermediate IP is a barrier for it. Given this fact, Chomsky (1986a) suggests the possibility that all traces must be antecedent-governed regardless of whether they are lexically governed or not.[31] We will return to examples such as (109) and will propose an alternative solution in section 4.3.3.

4.3.2 NP-Movement in Nominals
Simple passive in nominals is straightforwardly accommodated under our approach. In (110), t_1 is lexically governed by *destruction* via θ-role assignment.

(110) [$_{NP}$ the city's$_1$ [$_{N'}$ destruction t_1]]

Note that unlike the case of sentential passives, there is no antecedent government here, since there is no INFL. *The city's* cannot be the antecedent governor, because it is not a head. Although simple passive is possible in nominals, it is well known that raising is not. Thus, the following example is ungrammatical:

(111) *[$_{NP}$ John's$_1$ [$_{N'}$ belief [$_{IP}$ t_1 to be intelligent]]]

This result immediately follows from the hypothesis adopted here. As in (110), antecedent government does not obtain. Further, here, the head N *belief* does not assign Case or a θ-role to the position of t_1. Hence, t_1 cannot be properly governed.

The account developed above is quite similar to that of Kayne (1981b), who also rules (111) out as an ECP violation. He proposes that exceptional government is possible for V but not for N, as illustrated in (112).[32]

(112) a. V [$_{IP}$ t
       └────↑

      b. N [$_{IP}$ t
       └────↑
            *

Since government is a necessary condition for Case assignment, the ungrammaticality of (113) also follows from this hypothesis, under the assumption that inserted *of* is an instantiation of oblique Case assigned by N to NP, as proposed by Chomsky (1986b).

(113) *the belief of John to be intelligent

Unlike Kayne, however, we attribute the ungrammaticality of (113), not to the impossibility of exceptional government by N, but to the impossibility of exceptional Case assignment by it. We relate this impossibility of exceptional Case assignment to Chomsky's (1986b) hypothesis that N, unlike V, assigns inherent Case, which crucially involves θ-marking. (See section 4.3.3.) Thus, we can still maintain that N and V are identical in their behavior with respect to exceptional government, and hence, we can still rule out examples such as (114) by the PRO theorem (the theorem that PRO cannot be governed). More specifically, (114) violates Condition B if PRO is governed and coindexed with *John's*, and Condition A if PRO is not coindexed with *John's*.

(114) *John's belief [$_{IP}$ PRO to win]
      (cf. *John believes [$_{IP}$ PRO to win])

Higginbotham (1983) offers another account of (111), one not involving the ECP at all. Under his approach, a genitive NP is (obligatorily) assigned relation R to the head noun. This relation is not limited to any one specific thematic role, but it does count for satisfaction of the θ-Criterion. Examples such as (111) are then directly ruled out by the θ-Criterion. The argument *John* is illicitly assigned two roles: the subject role of *to be intelligent* and the relation R to the head noun *belief*. As Higginbotham notes, this has the effect of ruling out not just raising in nominals but passive in nominals as well. Thus, in (110), also, *the city* will have two roles: object of *destruction* and relation R to that same head. Higginbotham thus concludes that (116), rather than (110), is the appropriate representation for (115).

(115) the city's destruction

(116) [$_{NP}$[$_{NP}$ the city's] [$_{N'}$ destruction]]

Relation R in this case will be theme.

We do not adopt this approach, in part because of the extensive arguments of Anderson (1979, 1983) for movement in nominals. Further, the approach is crucially based on the existence of the process assigning the free relation R, and there is reason to doubt that it exists. Lasnik (1988) points out that there are certain surprising cooccurrence restrictions on the arguments of a noun mirroring those on arguments of a verb. To see this, first observe that the genitive can be an agent, as in (117), or an instrument, as in (118).

(117) the army's destruction of the city

(118) the rocket's destruction of the city

Thus far, this is entirely consistent with Higginbotham's approach, but does not provide any special support for it, since (117) and (118) are mirrored in sentential structures:

(119) the army destroyed the city

(120) the rocket destroyed the city

Now note that either the agent or the instrument can be realized as a by-phrase instead of as a genitive.

(121) the destruction of the city by the army

(122) the destruction of the city by the rocket

Further, both agent and instrument can be realized in the same NP:

(123) the army's destruction of the city with the rocket

(124) the destruction of the city with the rocket by the army

What is not possible, however, is for genitive agent (respectively, instrument) to be realized simultaneously with by-phrase instrument (respectively, agent):

(125) *the army's destruction of the city by the rocket

(126) *the rocket's destruction of the city by the army

This fact is unexplained under the R approach, since nothing should prevent the relation R in (125) from being the agent relation or the relation R in (126) from being the instrument relation. The object of by in these examples will be assigned a θ-role exactly like its counterpart in (121) or (122). Under Anderson's approach, however, (125) and (126) have just the status we should expect. There is no free R relation. Rather, NP can be theme just in case it has moved from a complement position that is assigned that θ-role. If it is base-generated in the subject position, it will have to bear a subject θ-role. Independently, a *by*-phrase necessarily receives the subject role.[33] Thus, (125) and (126) are ruled out as θ-Criterion violations, since two independent arguments are both assigned the subject role. To summarize, there is good reason to believe that NP-movement in nominals does exist, hence that Higginbotham's account of the lack of raising in nominals is overly restrictive. Our account in terms of the ECP runs into no such difficulty.

Before leaving this topic, we want to mention one last approach to the raising problem. Chomsky (1986b:218), based on the observations and proposals of Anderson (1979), suggests that raising in nominals is directly excluded by a semantic condition:

The application of Move α ... [in nominals] is constrained rather narrowly by certain semantic conditions. See Anderson (1979). A consequence is that there can be no NP-movement if there is no semantic relation at all to the head of the NP, as in the nominalizations of exceptional Case-marking constructions. Thus, there are no such forms as "John's belief to be intelligent" from the D-structure $the belief [John to be intelligent]."

The semantic condition alluded to involves "affectedness" of the moved NP by the head. Thus, Anderson points out such ill-formed instances of preposing as the following:

(127) *algebra's knowledge
       (cf. knowledge of algebra)

What Anderson proposes is that "the semantic relation between nominals and their complements determines the kind of complement" (1979:43). In particular, "the bare NP complement must be changed or moved by the action of the head nominal" (p. 44) Thus, the D-structure representation of *the destruction of Rome* will be as in (128), whereas that of *knowledge of algebra* will be as in (129).

(128) [$_{NP}$ the [$_{N'}$ destruction [$_{NP}$ Rome]]]

(129) [$_{NP}$[$_{N'}$ knowledge [$_{PP}$ of [$_{NP}$ algebra]]]]

Then, by general syntactic principles involving preposition stranding and reanalysis, preposing will be allowed in the former case but not in the latter. This plausible account is rather more specific than Chomsky suggests. In particular, the relevance of affectedness is not that it constrains the application of a transformation, but rather, that it determines a lexical property, the subcategorization choice of NP or PP, in a way reminiscent of the proposals of Grimshaw (1979) and Pesetsky (1982).

Given this, note that Anderson's account for (127) in fact does not generalize to the lack of raising in nominals. Since movement itself is free, what would have to be prohibited is a D-structure representation such as (130).

(130) $[_{NP} \ldots [_{N'} \text{N} [_{IP} \ldots]]]$

But nothing in the above account would prohibit such a structure.[34] Thus, raising in nominals must apparently be ruled out independently of Anderson's affectedness constraint. And, as we showed above, under the hypothesis that only X^0 categories can be antecedent governors, such raising is excluded by the ECP.

4.3.3 Extending the Uniformity Condition

Chomsky (1986b) discusses further ungrammatical instances of NP-movement. Some examples similar to his are given in (131)–(133).

(131) $*[_{NP} \text{John's}_1 [_{N'} \text{destruction of} [_{NP} \text{a} [_{N'} \text{portrait} \, t_1]]]]$

(132) $*[_{NP} \text{John's}_1 [_{N'} \text{stories about} [_{NP} [_{N'} \text{pictures} \, t_1]]]]$

(133) $*[_{NP} \text{John's}_1 [_{N'} \text{belief} [_{CP} \text{that} [_{IP} [_{NP} \text{pictures} \, t_1] \text{are on sale}]]]]$

Such examples satisfy the ECP, since the trace t_1 is lexically governed in all cases. Chomsky proposes the following condition (his (272), p. 194) to rule them out:

(134) *Uniformity Condition*
       If α is an inherent Case-marker, then α Case-marks NP if and only if $[\alpha]$ θ-marks the chain headed by NP.

He states that "[(134)] amounts to the requirement that inherent Case must be realized on NP under government by the category that θ-marks NP at D-structure" (p. 194).

For our purposes, the condition can be restated as follows:[35]

(135) a. α assigns inherent Case to β only if α θ-marks β (D-structure (D-structure)

       b. If β bears the inherent Case assigned by α, then α governs β. (S-structure)

The first part of (135) states that θ-role assignment is a necessary condition for inherent Case assignment. This condition accounts for the familiar contrast between (136) and (137), under the assumption that *of* is a realization of the inherent Case assigned by N.

(136)   the destruction [of the city]

(137)   *the belief [$_{IP}$ of John to be intelligent]

The head N, *destruction*, assigns a θ-role to its complement, *the city*, in (136). Thus, the former can assign inherent Case to the latter. But in (137), *belief* assigns a θ-role to the complement IP and not to *John*. In general, exceptional Case marking is impossible with inherent Case. (135a) accounts for this generalization.[36]

(135b) rules out the examples in (131)–(133). Chomsky assumes that the genitive Case in (139) is a realization of the inherent Case assigned by the head N at D-structure.

(138)   [$_{NP}$[$_{N'}$ destruction [the city]]]   (D-structure)
        └_____↑

(139)   [$_{NP}$ the city's$_1$ [$_{N'}$ destruction t_1]]   (S-structure)

(135b) states that an NP bearing inherent Case must be governed by the Case assigner at S-structure. (139) satisfies this condition since *the city's*, which bears the inherent Case assigned by *destruction*, is governed by this head noun at S-structure. (131)–(133), on the other hand, clearly violate the condition. In (131), for example, *John's* bears the inherent Case assigned by *portrait* at D-structure, but is not governed by this N at S-structure.

We noted above that there are ungrammatical examples of "super-raising" that are not accounted for by our formulation of the ECP. A representative example (109), due to Mark Baker, is repeated in (140).

(140)   *John$_1$ seems [$_{CP}$ that [$_{IP}$ it was told t_1 [$_{CP}$ that Mary is a genius]]]

Condition (135b) does not account for this example either, since *John* receives nominative Case, a structural Case, in the matrix subject position at S-structure. No inherent Case is assigned in this example. However, (131)–(133) and (140) share certain features. For example, NP-movement crosses a barrier in all of these examples. The intermediate IP is a barrier for t_1 in (140), and the embedded IP as well as the subject of that IP are barriers for t_1 in (133). Turning now to (131)–(132), recall that we assumed in chapter 3, following Chomsky (1986a), that NPs that are assigned oblique Case constitute barriers for traces within them.[37] Given this assumption, the embedded NPs in (131)–(132) are barriers for the NP-traces. The embedded NP in (131) is assigned oblique Case by *destruc-*

tion, and the one in (132) is assigned oblique case by the preposition *about*. In effect, (131)–(133) and (140) are all Subjacency violations for this reason. The problem is, of course, that they are far worse than mere Subjacency violations and hence demand an independent account.

The property observed in the preceding paragraph can be stated as follows:[38]

(141) Suppose that $C = (\alpha_1, \ldots, \alpha_n)$ is an A-chain. Then, if β is a barrier for α_i, then β dominates every member of C.

(141) states, in effect, that NP-movement across a barrier is prohibited. Since (135b) accounts for most of the examples on which (141) is based (i.e., (131)–(133) but not (140)), we will reformulate (135) in what follows so that it fully captures (141).

(135b) imposes a locality condition on an inherent Case assigner and the NP on which the Case is realized. As stated, (135b) does not account for (140), since no inherent Case is assigned in this example. However, suppose that (135b) is reformulated in terms of θ-role assignment, rather than inherent Case. For example, let us assume (142) as a first approximation.

(142) Suppose that β bears a θ-role assigned by α. Then, if γ is a barrier for α, γ dominates β.[39]

(142) accounts for (131)–(133) straightforwardly. In (131), for example, *John's* bears the θ-role assigned by *portrait*, but is not dominated by the embedded NP, which is a barrier for this N. Hence, (131) violates (142). In addition, (142) rules out the problematic (140). In this example, the matrix subject *John* bears a θ-role assigned by *told*, but is not dominated by the intermediate IP, which is a barrier for *told*. Thus, unlike (135b), (142) accounts for (140) as well as (131)–(133).

Note that (142) correctly allows passive and raising. Consider the following examples:

(143) $John_1$ was arrested t_1

(144) $John_1$ seems $[_{IP} t_1' $ to be likely $[_{IP} t_1$ to win]]

John in (143) bears the θ-role assigned by *arrested*, and given that VP is not a barrier, there is no barrier for *arrested* that does not dominate *John*. Similarly, *John* in (144) bears the θ-role assigned by the most deeply embedded INFL' (or VP), and there is no barrier for this θ-role assigner that does not dominate *John*, since the embedded IPs are both L-marked. Hence, (143) and (144) are both allowed.

According to the hypothesis that (135b) should be reformulated as in (142), the (Extended) Uniformity Condition is as in (145).

(145) a. α assigns inherent Case to β only if α θ-marks β.   (D-structure)

   b. Suppose that β bears a θ-role assigned by α. Then, if γ is a barrier for α, γ dominates β.   (S-structure)

(145b), in particular, accounts for (131)–(133), which involve inherent Case assignment, but also (140), which falls under neither our formulation of the ECP nor Chomsky's (1986b) formulation of the Uniformity Condition.[40] At the same time, (145) also rules out various sentences that have been analyzed in terms of other independent principles, such as the ECP, Condition A, and the Locality Condition on Chains. We will briefly speculate on this redundancy in the following section.

4.4   Conditions on NP-Movement

4.4.1   Redundancies Induced by the Uniformity Condition

The formulation of the Uniformity Condition in (145) independently accounts for the ungrammatical NP-movement examples that we have analyzed in terms of the ECP. First, as noted above, Chomsky (1986b) points out that (145a) rules out examples such as (137), repeated here as (146).

(146) *the belief [$_{IP}$ of John to be intelligent]

The head N, *belief*, cannot assign inherent Case to *John*, since it does not θ-mark it. Though Chomsky did not point it out, this account of (146) immediately extends to examples of "raising in nominals." Consider the following example:

(147) *John's$_1$ belief [$_{IP}$ t_1 to be intelligent]

For (147) to be grammatical, *John's* must be assigned Case by *belief* in the position of t_1 at D-structure. But this is impossible since N assigns inherent oblique Case and *belief* does not θ-mark the position of t_1. Hence, (147) is ruled out for the same reason that (146) is.

This account of (147) relied on the first part of the Uniformity Condition and hence is clearly independent of our revision of the condition. The standard super-raising examples such as (148), on the other hand, like Baker's example (140), fall under Uniformity because of the extension proposed in (145b).

(148) *John$_1$ seems [$_{CP}$ that [$_{IP}$ it is believed [$_{IP}$ t_1 to be intelligent]]]

In (148), the IP *it is believed . . . (γ* in (145b)) is a barrier for the predicate *to be intelligent* (α in (145b)). *John* (β in (145b)) bears the θ-role assigned by α, but is not dominated by γ. This constitutes a violation of the Uniformity Condition. Thus, (148) is excluded independently of the ECP. Given the

Extended Uniformity Condition in (145), then, it is not clear, after all, that the ECP is specifically needed to rule out any ungrammatical instances of NP-movement.

The same seems to be true for Condition A, as it applies to traces of NP-movement. That is, since a stronger condition, (145b), will apply in typical Condition A contexts, the latter condition will be redundant. To see this, consider first the nominative island condition (NIC) subcase of Condition A, illustrated in (149).

(149) *John$_1$ seems [$_{CP}$[$_{IP}$ t_1 is intelligent]]

According to the theory of Chomsky (1981), t_1 in (149) violates Condition A, since it is an anaphor and is free in its governing category, the lower clause. But note that (149) also violates (145b). The embedded IP is a barrier for the θ-role assigner of *John*, and *John* is not dominated by that IP. It should be noted that Chomsky (1986b) dispenses with the NIC subcase of Condition A entirely; thus, trivially, Condition A will not be relevant for (149). Chomsky (1986b) observes that in such a case, Condition A is redundant with respect to the ECP. In (149), t_1 is not lexically governed, and, in our terms, INFL of the matrix clause is too distant to serve as antecedent governor. (149) thus is another example where the ECP is redundant with respect to the Uniformity Condition.

Specified subject condition (SSC) effects for NP-trace as well as NIC effects fall under the Uniformity Condition. Consider (150) and (151), for example.

(150) *John$_1$ seems [$_{CP}$ that [$_{IP}$ Mary likes t_1]]

(151) *John$_1$ seems [$_{CP}$ that [$_{IP}$ Mary is [$_{AP}$ proud t_1]]]

Here, t_1 is free in its governing category, the lower clause, in violation of Condition A. In addition, these examples violate (145b). *John* bears a θ-role assigned by *likes* or *proud*, but the lower IP is a barrier for the θ-role assigner and it does not dominate *John*.[41]

SSC effects for NP-trace within nominals also fall under the Uniformity Condition, as pointed out by Chomsky (1986b), being excluded by (145b).[42] Consider the following example:

(152) *John's$_1$ destruction of [$_{NP}$ Mary's portrait t_1]
(cf. the destruction of [Mary's portrait of John])

In (152), t_1 is free in its governing category, the NP *Mary's portrait t_1*, in violation of Condition A. Once again, the Uniformity Condition is violated as well. *John* bears a θ-role assigned by *portrait*, but there is a barrier for the latter, the oblique Case-marked intermediate NP, which does not dominate the former. Now note that Uniformity is violated in a structure such as (152), even independently of the presence of a "specified subject." The ill-formed example (131), repeated here as (153), is parallel to (152) but lacks an intervening specified subject.

(153) *John's$_1$ destruction of a portrait t_1
       (cf. the destruction of a portrait of John)

Here, although Condition A is irrelevant, the example is correctly excluded by Uniformity in exactly the same way that (152) was, since the presence or absence of a specified subject is irrelevant to that condition.[43]

We have seen that (145) independently accounts for violations of the ECP and Condition A that involve NP-traces.[44] Thus, to the extent that (145) is well motivated, this redundancy raises the possibility (which we leave open for further research) that NP-traces are subject neither to the ECP nor to Condition A. This hypothesis is plausible if NP-traces have no binding features, a possibility investigated by Barss (1986). If NP-traces have no values for the features [± anaphor, ± pronominal], then they will straightforwardly not be constrained by Condition A. Further, they also will not be subject to the ECP, if only [− pronominal] empty categories are subject to this principle, as proposed by Chomsky (1981).

(145b) also creates a redundancy between itself and the Locality Condition on Chains proposed by Chomsky (1981), and argued for by Rizzi (1986a) and Lasnik (1985). Lasnik (1985), observing that examples such as (154) do not violate Condition A, proposes to account for them by the condition in (155), from Chomsky 1981:333.

(154) *John$_1$ seems that he$_1$ likes t_1
       |_____|

(155)   Where α_j, α_{j+1} are successive members of a chain, α_j must locally bind α_{j+1}.

In (154), this condition is violated, since he$_1$, rather than *John*, locally binds t_1. Hence, *John* and t_1 cannot constitute a chain, and the θ-Criterion is violated.

Chomsky (1986b) points out that (154) itself provided only weak motivation for (155), however, since an apparently independent chain condition, barring more than one Case-marked member, is violated as well. Further, given Chomsky's (1986b) proposal that adjectives and nouns are (inherent) Case assigners, (156) also violates this condition, or, if the inherent Case is realized on *John*, the condition against Case conflict.

(156) *John$_1$ seems that he$_1$ is [proud t_1]

(cf. It seems that John is proud of himself)

However, no Case condition is violated by (157).

(157) *John$_1$ seems [$_{CP}$ that [$_{IP}$[$_{NP}$ his$_1$ belief [$_{IP}$ t_1 to be rich]] is crazy]]

Here, t_1 is Caseless, since inherent Case is assigned only under θ-marking, and *belief* does not θ-mark the subject of its complement. Thus, the chain (*John$_1$*, t_1) has but a single Case-marked member, exactly as is required. Further, as in the earlier examples, Condition A is satisfied, with *his$_1$* binding t_1. Precisely because Condition A is satisfied, however, condition (155) is violated, with *his$_1$*, rather than *John$_1$*, locally binding t_1.

Chomsky (1986b) discusses similar examples and proposes to account for most of them on independent grounds, for instance, by the Chain Condition. Further, he speculates that the remaining examples, such as (157), also can be explained by independent principles and hence that (155) can be eliminated altogether. Now note that (157) violates (145b). *John* ($= \beta$) bears the θ-role assigned by the predicate *to be rich* ($= \alpha$). But both the NP *his belief t to be rich* and the IP of which that NP is the subject are barriers ($= \gamma$) for α, and neither dominates *John*.[45] In fact, all locality violations considered in Chomsky 1986b as well as all those considered here are violations of (145b). For example, in both (154) and (156), the embedded IP constitutes a barrier for the θ-role assigner of *John*, *likes* in the former case and *proud* in the latter. Thus, it appears that, as Chomsky (1986b) conjectures, the Locality Condition on Chains is entirely redundant for such cases of NP-movement. This suggests that it might be entirely eliminable.[46]

As we have shown, then, (145b) extends (usually redundantly) to many ungrammatical examples of NP-movement discussed in the literature. In particular, it raises questions about whether NP-traces should be subject to the ECP and Condition A, and also about the very existence of the Locality Condition on Chains. Among the ungrammatical examples of NP-movement that do not fall under (145b) are (158) and (159).

(158) *John$_1$ strikes t_1 that Mary is intelligent

(159) *John$_1$ seems to t_1 that Mary is intelligent

As (160)–(161) demonstrate, the matrix subject positions in (158)–(159) can be non-θ-positions.

(160) it strikes John that Mary is intelligent

(161) it seems to John that Mary is intelligent

Thus, (158)–(159) do not seem to violate the θ-Criterion. As noted above, Chomsky (1986b) proposes a chain condition that bans double Case marking, and this condition would account for (158)–(159). These examples indicate that such a condition is needed independently of the Uniformity Condition.

4.4.2 Chain-Binding Effects and NP-Movement

We have shown that a number of phenomena regarding NP-movement can be straightforwardly accounted for in terms of the Extended Uniformity Condition (145), repeated here as (162).

(162) a. α assigns inherent Case to β only if α θ-marks β.   (D-structure)
   b. Suppose that β bears a θ-role assigned by α. Then, if γ is a barrier for α, γ dominates β.   (S-structure)

Examples such as the following, which are discussed extensively in the literature, are not ruled out by (162), as Jun Abe (personal communication) points out:

(163) [how likely t_1 to win]$_2$ is John$_1$ t_2

Here, *John* bears the θ-role assigned by *to win*. But neither the IP complement of *likely* nor the moved AP in SPEC of CP is a barrier for this predicate. The former is L-marked, and the latter is an $\bar{\text{A}}$-binder. Thus, there is no barrier for *to win* that does not dominate *John*. In this section, we will argue that contrary to appearance, the representation in (163) is ill formed. And we will suggest, on the basis of this conclusion, that NP-movement is constrained by the Proper Binding Condition, as proposed by Fiengo (1977), in addition to the Uniformity Condition.[47]

(163) is generally analyzed as an instance of chain binding in the sense of Barss (1986). In this example, *John$_1$* chain-binds t_1, and according to the analysis, Condition A of the binding theory is satisfied in (163) exactly as it is in (164).

(164) [which picture of himself$_1$]$_2$ does John$_1$ like t_2 best

In (164), *John$_1$* chain-binds *himself$_1$*, since the former c-commands a trace of the NP in SPEC of CP, which contains the latter. Thus, even if Condition A constrains NP-traces as well as lexical anaphors, it is quite reasonable to assume that (163), as well as (164), satisfies this condition. That is, as far as Condition A is concerned, we expect the representation in (163) to be well formed.[48]

However, there is good reason to believe that the representation in (163) is ill formed. In this regard, Anthony Kroch (personal communication) notes that examples such as the following (which he attributes to Mark Baltin) are ungrammatical (see also Kroch and Joshi 1985):

(165) *[how likely t_1 to be a riot]$_2$ is there$_1$ t_2
       (cf. there is likely to be a riot)

(166) *[how likely t_1 to be taken of John]$_2$ is advantage$_1$ t_2
       (cf. advantage is likely to be taken of John)

The matrix subject in (165) is existential *there*, and that in (166) is an idiom chunk. Thus, these sentences are typical examples of raising. Kroch points out that these examples indicate that when raising is clearly involved, chain-binding effects with NP-traces do not obtain.

Saito (1989) argues, on the basis of Kroch's suggestion, that independently of whether or not NP-traces are subject to Condition A, (165)–(166) are ruled out by the Proper Binding Condition (see Fiengo 1977, May 1977, and chapter 3 above). This condition, Saito argues, applies to all traces at both S-structure and LF, and it is, in general, insensitive to chain binding; that is, it requires a trace to have an antecedent that strictly c-commands it. Given this conclusion, not only (165)–(166) but also (163) must be ill formed.

This line of reasoning suggests that (167) is grammatical only when it has the structure in (168).

(167) how likely to win is John

(168) [how likely [PRO$_1$ to win]]$_2$ is John$_1$ t_2

That is, (169) is, in fact ambiguous between (170a) and (170b).

(169) John is likely to win

(170) a. John$_1$ is likely [t_1 to win]
       b. John$_1$ is likely [PRO$_1$ to win]

According to this hypothesis, (165)–(166), unlike (163), do not have corresponding sentences with PRO, since, as is well known, existential *there* and idiom chunks cannot appear in control structures such as those in (171).

(171) a. *there tried [PRO to be a riot]
       b. *advantage wants [PRO to be taken of John]

The proposed hypothesis seems quite plausible, given examples such as (172), discussed by Postal (1974).

(172) ??John's likelihood to win

As was discussed extensively above, raising is impossible in nominals.

Nevertheless, (172) is only marginal. Note now that examples with the head noun *likelihood* that clearly involve raising are completely ungrammatical.

(173) *advantage's likelihood to be taken of John

(174) *headway's likelihood to be made by John
    (cf. headway is likely to be made by John)

The contrast between (172) on the one hand and (173)–(174) on the other indicates that *likely/likelihood* are indeed ambiguous between raising and control predicates. That is, (172) is better than (173)–(174) because this example can involve control rather than raising.[49]

There are other predicates that share these properties of *likely/ likelihood*. Among them are *promise/promise* and *threaten/threat*. The verbs *promise* and *threaten* are ambiguous between raising and control predicates:

(175) a. ?Headway$_1$ promises [t_1 to be made by John]
     b. ?the cat$_1$ threatens [t_1 to be let out of the bag]

(176) a. John$_1$ promises [PRO$_1$ to work on the problem]
     b. John$_1$ threatens [PRO$_1$ to leave]

(175a–b) are somewhat marginal, but contrast sharply with (177a–b).

(177) a. *headway's promise to be made by John
     b. *the cat's threat to be let out of the bag

This is again what we expect, given the impossibility of raising in nominals. As also expected, the nominal counterparts of (176a–b) are perfectly grammatical, as shown in (178).

(178) a. John's promise to work on the problem
     b. John's threat to leave

Our claim here is that *likely* belongs to the same class of verbals as *promise* and *threaten*.

We have argued that the sentence (167) is grammatical only with the representation in (168), and that the structure in (163) is ruled out by the Proper Binding Condition. Since (163) does not violate the Uniformity Condition, it seems that we need two conditions, the Chain Condition (or a condition against double Case marking) and the Proper Binding Condition, in addition to Uniformity, to constrain NP-movement.

4.5 Summary

In this chapter, we considered a variety of phenomena and discussed the consequences of the proposals in chapter 3.

In section 4.1, we argued for the hypothesis, originally proposed by Stowell (1981), that only X^0 categories can be proper governors. Specifically, we showed that this hypothesis interacts with the analysis of topicalization in chapter 3 and makes correct predictions concerning topicalization of subjects. In section 4.2, we considered LF movement of subjects and reanalyzed the relevant phenomena in terms of INFL raising in LF. We considered QR, and also LF WH-movement in English, Chinese, and Japanese. In the course of the discussion, we argued, following Hendrick and Rochemont (1982), that the Superiority Condition is needed independently of the ECP, and we provided additional evidence for this hypothesis. In section 4.3, we discussed NP-movement and proposed a revision of Chomsky's (1986b) Uniformity Condition. We showed that this revision enables us to account for some examples that have been considered problematic. In section 4.4, we argued that as far as NP-movement is concerned, the effects of the revised Uniformity Condition overlap considerably with those of other conditions, such as the ECP and Condition A, and thus, the Uniformity Condition itself raises questions about whether those other conditions apply to NP-traces. Finally, we considered the so-called chain-binding effects on NP-traces and argued that, contrary to initial appearances, the relevant examples provide evidence that the Proper Binding Condition is needed, independently of the Uniformity Condition, to account for the distribution of NP-traces.

Chapter 5
Further Empirical and
Theoretical Considerations

In the preceding chapters, we have developed a theory of proper govern-ment and applied it to a considerable range of phenomena. In this chapter, we will examine additional facts that raise certain difficulties but can po-tentially be accommodated by our framework, or by natural extensions of it. In the course of the discussion, we will consider several alternative analyses and compare them with our own. In section 5.1, we discuss an asymmetry that arises between NPs and PPs, even when the latter are complements. We suggest that the precise formulation of the notion "lexical government" is of central concern in resolving this asymmetry. The quantifier-WH interactions noted by May (1985) are the topic of sec-tion 5.2. Here, we accept May's claim that the ECP does not predict the range of readings he presents, but we argue that an independent LF condi-tion accommodates the facts that raise difficulties for the ECP as well as facts problematic for May's account. The disjunctive nature of the ECP as formulated, for example, in L&S and in preceding chapters has recently been called into question. In section 5.3, we discuss this issue and respond to several arguments of Aoun et al. (1987) that lexical government and antecedent government are not simply two alternative ways of satisfying the proper government requirement, but rather, that a version of lexical government is always demanded, even when antecedent government ob-tains. In section 5.4, we consider a complex of proposals on LF movement developed by Pesetsky (1987) and Nishigauchi (1986). Pesetsky and Nishi-gauchi are concerned with eliminating an asymmetry between S-structure movement and LF movement, only the former being constrained by Sub-jacency. They argue that the asymmetry can be resolved by appeal to two mechanisms, *LF pied-piping* and *D-linking*. The first of these mechanisms permits WH-phrases within certain movement islands to pied-pipe those islands, thus avoiding the necessity of moving out of them. The second mechanism provides for the interpretation of certain instances of WH in situ without appeal to movement. We examine these important proposals and show that at least some of the asymmetries they are intended to resolve actually reemerge, although in slightly different form. Finally, in section 5.5, we consider some specific issues raised by the proposals in Chomsky (1986a) but not yet examined here. Of particular concern are the account for the *that*-trace effect within the CP-IP analysis of clausal structure, and the question of how the notion "barrier" relates to that of "government."

5.1   Lexical Government of PP

The ECP theory we have developed so far, like Huang's (1982) theory, predicts a sharp distinction between complements and noncomplements. We have seen this prediction confirmed by a substantial range of phenomena. However, under certain circumstances, the distinction seems to show up in somewhat different ways. For example, in some cases, a distinction appears to arise between NPs and PPs even when both are complements. In this section, we will discuss such NP-PP asymmetries.[1]

5.1.1   NP-PP Asymmetries

Consider the following contrast from Chomsky 1982, attributed to Adriana Belletti:

(1)   *to whom$_1$ did they leave before speaking t_1

(2)   ??who$_1$ did they leave before speaking to t_1

Both of these examples involve extraction out of an adjunct and hence violate Subjacency. Further, apparently neither of them violates the ECP, since the trace t_1 would seem to be lexically governed in both cases. Yet (1), which involves extraction of a complement PP from an adjunct, is much worse than (2) and has the approximate status of the ECP violation shown in (3).

(3)   *how$_1$ did they leave [before fixing the car t_1]

A similar contrast is found in the case of extraction out of complex NPs:

(4)   ??who$_1$ did you witness John's attempt to give artificial respiration to t_1

(5)   ?*to whom$_1$ did you witness John's attempt to give artificial respiration t_1

In this case, (5) is still somewhat better than the clear ECP violation shown in (6).

(6) *how$_1$ did you witness John's attempt [to give artificial respiration to Bill t_1

But it is clearly worse than (4), which suggests that it is not a mere Subjacency violation.

The NP-PP asymmetry shown in (1)–(2) and (4)–(5) can be accounted for by the ECP, if the PP-traces is (2) and (5) are not lexically governed, since they obviously are not antecedent-governed. Then, we should expect those traces to behave exactly like the adjunct traces in (3) and (6). Recall that lexical government requires Case marking or θ-role assignment by a lexical head. Thus, if the PP-traces in (2) and (5) are not assigned θ-roles, the examples are automatically ruled out by the ECP, since those traces are presumably not Case-marked, not being NPs. Further, it seems quite possible that the PPs are not assigned θ-roles, that is, that it is actually the object of the preposition that is θ-marked, the preposition and the verb jointly assigning a θ-role to the NP, as Stowell (1981) proposes. If this is correct, then antecedent government will always be required when a PP moves. Consequently, what would be just a Subjacency violation for a moved complement NP would be an ECP violation for a moved PP. Notice that the acceptability of (7) and (8) remains unproblematic on this account.

(7) who left before speaking to who

(8) who witnessed John's attempt to give artificial respiration to who

In these examples, if the PP had to undergo LF WH-movement, the ECP would be violated, since, exactly as in the case of syntactic movement, both lexical government and antecedent government would fail. However, as noted by Huang (1982), there is no reason to assume that the PP must move. If instead, only *who* moves, then the resulting trace will be lexically governed, via Case assignment (and perhaps via θ-role assignment as well).

There is another NP-PP asymmetry that may be explicable in similar terms. As is well known, although WH-movement of an NP can license a parasitic gap, WH-movement of a PP cannot. In (9), the movement of an adjunct PP clearly fails to license a parasitic gap.

(9) *by what method$_1$ did you prove the theorem t_1 [after establishing the lemma e_1]

Further, a complement PP behaves like an adjunct in this regard, as the sharp contrast between (10) and (11) indicates.

(10)   who$_1$ did you speak to t_1 [before sending a paper to e_1]

(11)   *to whom$_1$ did you speak t_1 [before sending a paper e_1]

If the trace of a PP cannot be lexically governed, then both (9) and (11) are ruled out by the ECP, assuming, as argued in Chomsky 1982 and section 4.1.2.2, that parasitic gaps must be properly governed. The parasitic gap, e, in both examples will fail to be antecedent-governed, given that *before* in COMP, as a lexical head, blocks SPEC-head agreement (see section 5.5). These examples will thus receive the same treatment as (12), repeated from chapter 4, example (33).

(12)   *who$_1$ did you telephone t_1 [after e_1 arrived]

Thus far, we have shown how the nonexistence of PP parasitic gaps might be explained by the ECP. In fact. more generally, only arguments may be parasitic gaps. In (13), WH-movement of an AP does not make a parasitic AP possible.

(13)   *how angry$_1$ can John appear t_1 [without becoming e_1]

Similarly in (14) and (15), a parasitic AdvP is ungrammatical.

(14)   *how quickly$_1$ did John solve the problem t_1 [after proving the theorem e_1]

(15)   *why$_1$ did John resign t_1 [after criticizing his boss e_1]

Thus, the following interpretation, though coherent, is unavailable for (14):

(16)   what is the speed such that John solved the problem at that speed after proving the theorem at that very same speed

Likewise, (17) is impossible as an interpretation of (15).

(17)   what is the reason such that John resigned for that reason after criticizing his boss for that very same reason

Finally, even predicate nominals are bad as parasitic gaps:

(18)   *what (kind of teacher)$_1$ did Mary become t_1 [without considering John e_1]

All of these cases are accounted for in the same way as the PP cases. Lexical government of the parasitic gap will not obtain, since the AP, AdvP, and predicate NP do not receive Case or a θ-role. And antecedent government fails for the reason discussed above: the COMP is occupied by a lexical head. Thus, (13), (14), (15), and (18) all violate the ECP.

It is interesting to note that this approach correctly predicts that alongside the NPs that cannot license parasitic gaps (predicate nominals), there are apparently non-NPs that can. In particular, (19) indicates that CP parasitic gaps are possible.

(19) that John is here$_1$, Mary claimed t_1 [without really believing e_1]

In this case, e is lexically governed, because it is assigned a θ-role by *believing*. No ECP violation results, apparently a correct consequence.[2]

5.1.2 Complement-Noncomplement Asymmetries with PPs

Though the analysis just suggested has a number of desirable consequences, it raises certain problems as well. First, observe that the theory predicts a precise bifurcation. NP (and CP) argument traces can be lexically governed; all other traces must be antecedent-governed. Though this correctly accounts for the lessened acceptability of, for example, (5) vis-à-vis (4), it does not account for the further contrast between (5) and (6). PP complements are substantially worse than NP complements when extracted out of certain islands, but somewhat better than adjuncts. This latter property remains mysterious.

WH-island configurations also seem to exhibit this now mysterious property. As expected, (21) is worse than (20). But (21) also seems substantially better than (22).

(20) ?what shelf$_1$ do you wonder whether to put the book on t_1

(21) ??on what shelf$_1$ do you wonder whether to put the book t_1

(22) *why$_1$ do you wonder whether to put the book on the shelf t_1

Once again, this three-way contrast is unexpected. In fact, it is hard to see how to accommodate it at all. If, as suggested above, PPs behave like adjuncts with respect to the ECP, then an example like (21) should be fully as bad as (22). If, on the other hand, a complement PP is treated in the same way as a complement NP, then (21) should be as good as (20),[3] and, more significantly, (1) should be as good as (2).

Whether or not complement PPs are lexically governed remains a problem. On the one hand, the NP-PP asymmetries indicate that PPs are never lexically governed. On the other hand, examples such as (21) suggest that complement PPs can be lexically governed. Given our definition of lexical government, where Case assignment or θ-role assignment is a necessary condition, this problem reduces to the question of whether a complement PP is directly θ-marked by a verb or not.[4]

One further problem arises for the attempt to deduce the NP-PP asymmetry we noted from the ECP. Consider again extraction out of an adjunct, but this time from a more deeply embedded position:

(23) ??who did they go home without believing Mary spoke to

(24) *to whom did they go home without believing Mary spoke

(24) is completely impossible, whereas (23) is somewhat better, essentially repeating the asymmetry of (1)–(2). This time, however, there is a derivation that conforms to the demands of the ECP. Consider S-structure representation (25).

(25) to whom$_1$ [did they go home [without believing [$_{CP}$ t_1' [$_{IP}$ Mary spoke t_1]]]]

Here, *to whom* moved into the SPEC of the most deeply embedded CP. From there, it moved directly to the SPEC of the matrix CP, leaving t_1'. This second step, as it should, violates Subjacency. But now note that t_1' is in just the right position to make the lowest COMP an antecedent governor for t_1. Further, although t_1' itself is not properly governed, it can be deleted in the LF component. The incorrect result is that although "short" movement of a PP out of an adjunct is excluded, "long" movement is not. This problem is strikingly reminiscent of one discussed in section 2.3.4. There too, the issue was how to prevent long movement out of an island via an intermediate SPEC of CP. A relevant example is given in (26).

(26) *how$_1$ do you wonder whether John said [$_{CP}$ t_1' [$_{IP}$ Mary solved the problem t_1]]

As in (25), the most deeply embedded COMP can assign $[+\gamma]$ to the initial trace at S-structure, and the intermediate trace can subsequently delete in LF. The difference is that in (26), the moved phrase was an adjunct. We suggested the following condition in chapter 2 to account for (26):

(27) a. Every trace must be a member of a chain.
    b. Every chain must have as its tail an empty category that is licensed.

We argued that at S-structure, nothing would license an adjunct trace, so such a trace could not exist at that level. Hence, an adjunct trace could not be γ-marked at S-structure, the desired result. In the present instance, as well, we would like to be able to say that t_1 in (25) cannot be γ-marked at S-structure. Then, at LF, t_1' would have to be present, and it would be $[-\gamma]$ ultimately resulting in an ECP violation. But (27b), which forced the right result for an adjunct, is of no help here. t_1 is in fact licensed, via the Projection Principle, by the subcategorization properties of *speak*. Thus, if the contrast between (23) and (24) is to follow from the ECP, we must stipulate a difference between NPs and PPs. (27) evidently will not suffice.

5.2 Quantifier-WH Interactions

May (1985) presents an intriguing paradigm that, he argues, cannot be handled by the ECP. His argument, whose basic outline we will present here, seems to us correct in its essentials. May first observes that (28) displays an ambiguity.

(28) what did everyone buy for Max

In May's words, (28) "... may be understood, loosely as either a single question, asking for the identity of the object such that everyone bought it for Max, or as a 'distributed' question, asking of each individual what it is that that person bought for Max" (p. 38). (29), on the other hand, displays no similar ambiguity, lacking the distributed question reading.[5]

(29) who bought everything for Max

In the theory presented by May (1985), the QNPs in (28)–(29) can have scope over the WH-phrases if QR can adjoin them to S (= IP) at LF. Thus, the facts mentioned above imply that (28) can have the LF representation in (30), but (29) cannot have the one in (31).

(30) $[_{S' (= CP)}$ what$_1$ $[_{S (= IP)}$ everyone$_2$ $[_{S (= IP)}$ t_2 bought t_1 for Max]]]

(31) $[_{S' (= CP)}$ who$_1$ $[_{S (= IP)}$ everything$_2$ $[_{S (= IP)}$ t_1 bought t_2 for Max]]]

On May's account, *what* and *everyone* in (30), and *who* and *everything* in (31), govern each other; hence, their relative scope is free. May points out that the impossibility of the LF representation (31) does not follow from the ECP as formulated in L&S. For an ECP analysis to work, the trace t_1 should violate that principle in (31). But under the theory of L&S (as well as the one adopted here), since the trace of *who*, t_1, is properly governed at S-structure, its $[+\gamma]$ marking carries over to LF, regardless of what configuration is later created. Thus, the ECP is ineffective in excluding this reading.

5.2.1 May's Path Containment Analysis

May ultimately appeals to the Path Containment Condition (PCC) of Pesetsky (1982) to account for the nonambiguity of (29). Consider again (31), with "paths" indicated:

(32) $[_{S' (= CP)}$ who$_1$ $[_{S (= IP)}$ everything$_2$ $[_{S (= IP)}$ t_1 bought t_2 for Max]]]

In (32), the paths of *who* and *everything* illicitly "cross," rendering this LF representation ill formed.[6] Thus far, not only is a wide scope reading excluded for *everything* in (29), but a narrow scope reading is as well. To allow the narrow scope reading, May proposes that QR can adjoin a quantifier to VP as well as to S ($=$ IP). Consider (33).

(33) $[_{S' (= CP)}$ who$_1$ $[_{S (= IP)}$ t_1 $[_{VP}$ everything$_2$ $[_{VP}$ bought t_2 for Max]]]]

(33) licitly represents the narrow scope reading, since the PCC is satisfied. Further, the wide scope reading is still unavailable since the two operators do not govern each other and hence cannot commute. As mentioned above, mutual government is, for May, the licensing condition for commutation. Note that (30), on the other hand, is in accord with the PCC, as shown in (34).

(34) $[_{S' (= CP)}$ what$_1$ $[_{S (= IP)}$ everyone$_2$ $[_{S (= IP)}$ t_2 brought t_1 for Max]]]

This one well-formed representation provides both readings, as indicated above.

Thus, May's theory provides an account for the contrast between (28) and (29), which the ECP does not explain. However, there are data that seem to fall under neither the ECP nor May's theory. First, consider the following example discussed by May (1985):

(35) who$_1$ do you think everyone saw t_1 at the rally

This example is ambiguous between the single question reading and the distributed question reading. May (1985) assigns the following LF representation to (35):

(36) $[_{S' (= CP)}$ who$_1$ $[_{S (= IP)}$ everyone$_2$ $[_{S (= IP)}$ you think $[_{S' (= CP)}$ $[_{S (= IP)}$ t_2 saw t_1 at the rally]]]]]]

In (36), *who* and *everyone* may commute since they govern each other. Thus, the scope ambiguity of (35) is predicted.

Williams (1986) notes, however, that this account of (35) assumes that QR of *everyone* is not clause-bound, though examples such as (37) indicate that it is.

(37) someone thinks (that) everyone saw you at the rally

This example does not have the reading where *everyone* takes wide scope over *someone*, which *indicates* that QR of *everyone* is clause-bound, or at least, that it cannot adjoin the embedded subject *everyone* to the matrix IP.[7] And if *everyone* in embedded subject position cannot be adjoined to the matrix IP by QR, (36) cannot be a possible LF representation for (35). The following example seems to pose a similar problem:

(38) I wonder who$_1$ t_1 saw everyone

This example lacks the distributed question reading and is as unambiguous as (29). This implies that *everyone* cannot have wide scope over *who* in this example. The following LF representation for (38), which allows a wide scope reading for *everyone*, is excluded by the PCC, exactly as (32) was:

(39) $[_{IP}$ I wonder $[_{CP}$ who$_1$ $[_{IP}$ everyone$_2$ $[_{IP}$ t_1 saw $t_2]]]]$

However, if QR is not clause-bound, nothing seems to prevent (38) from having the LF representation in (40).

(40) $[_{IP}$ I $[_{VP}$ everyone$_2$ $[_{VP}$ wonder $[_{CP}$ who$_1$ $[_{IP}$ t_1 saw $t_2]]]]]$

Hence, unless QR is clause-bound, the unambiguity of (38) is prob'ematic. Thus, either (38) is problematic (on May's assumption about QR) or (35) is (on the assumption that QR is clause-bound).

5.2.2 Group versus Quantificational Interpretations

We have shown that questions arise under either an ECP treatment or a PCC treatment of the WH-quantifier scope phenomenon. In this section, we will examine the relevant data more closely, and reconsider the nature of the generalization to be accounted for.

Let us consider again the ambiguous (28), repeated here as (41).

(41) what$_1$ did everyone buy t_1 for Max

Recall that according to May, when *everyone* has narrow scope, (41) represents a single question asking for the identity of the object such that everyone bought it for Max. To this question, (42) is an appropriate answer.

(42) everyone bought Max a Bosendorfer piano

On the other hand, when *everyone* has wide scope, we have, according to May, a "family of questions," to which the appropriate response would be a family of answers as in (43).

(43) Mary bought Max a tie, Sally a sweater, and Harry a piano

Williams (1986) challenges May's analysis, proposing instead that what May treats as wide scope *everyone* is not a quantifier at all, but rather is an NP with "a nonquantificational 'group' interpretation." May (1988) replies that if the notion "group interpretation" is taken to mean, simply, that the NP in question denotes a set or a collective, then this precisely fails to give the wide scope reading (the one for which (43) is an appropriate answer) and instead gives only the narrow scope reading. May thus concludes that Williams must have had something else in mind and then proceeds to explore the possibilities, arguing that none of them provides a real account for the phenomena under discussion.

May's argument that the simple notion of "group interpretation" fails to give the wide scope reading seems to us a strong one. We would like to suggest that group interpretation could, nonetheless, be playing some role in quantifier-WH interaction. As May points out, if anything is a group interpretation, it is the *narrow* reading of *everyone*. However, May stops short of considering the implications of this possibility. Consider, again, the reading of (41) anticipating a collective answer as in (42). Is *everyone* here truly a narrow scope quantifier (as May's theory has it), or does it denote a group? It turns out that there is evidence for the latter position. As is well known, the third person singular pronoun can take *everyone* as its antecedent just in case it is bound as a variable by it.[8] In particular, when the structural requirements on variable binding do not obtain, only a *plural* pronoun can be associated with *everyone*:

(44) after I spoke to everyone, $\left\{ \begin{matrix} \text{they} \\ \text{*he} \end{matrix} \right\}$ left

Now consider (45), a slightly modified version of (41).

(45) what did everyone$_1$ buy for Max with his$_1$ bonus money

(46) what did everyone$_1$ buy for Max with their$_1$ bonus money

(45), unlike (46), does not seem capable of anticipating the collective answer in (42). This is exactly as would be expected if the interpretation of (41) that goes with (42) is not a quantificational one, but rather, necessarily involves a true "group" reading. If, on the other hand, this reading involves narrow scope *everyone*, it is quite unclear why the presence of the singular pronoun should suppress it.

If the putative "narrow scope reading" of *everyone* in (41) necessarily results from the "group interpretation" of this NP, as we have suggested, then it follows that when *everyone* in (41) is interpreted as a universal quantifier, it always takes scope over the WH. There is one more case to consider, however, before we can reach this conclusion. Note that (41) can also be answered, for example, as in (47), interpreted to mean that everyone bought a different book, or even different copies of the same book, for Max.

(47) everyone bought Max a book

But the interpretation of (41) that goes with this interpretation of (47) actually also involves wide scope interpretation of *everyone*. This can be seen from the fact that the relevant interpretation of (47) is represented as follows:

(48) [for all x: x a person] [there is a y: y a book] [x bought Max y]

Hence, it seems that, in fact, *everyone* in (41), when interpreted as a universal quantifier, invariably takes wide scope over the WH. We next consider why this should be.

5.2.3 Scope and Rigidity
Given the discussion above, the relative scope of WH and quantifiers seems to be determined by their D-structure position. The one that asymmetrically c-commands the other at D-structure takes wide scope at LF. Let us consider again (28)–(29), (35), and (38).

(28) what$_1$ did everyone buy t_1 for Max

(29) who$_1$ t_1 bought everything for Max

(35) who$_1$ do you think everyone saw t_1 at the rally

(38) I wonder who$_1$ t_1 saw everyone

In (28) and (35), *everyone* asymmetrically c-commands the WH at D-structure and correspondingly takes wide scope at LF. In (29) and (38), on the other hand, the WH asymmetrically c-commands *everyone*, and correspondingly, *everyone* cannot have the distributive interpretation.

A question now arises, given that QR is basically clause-bound, as noted earlier in (37).

(37) someone thinks (that) everyone saw you at the rally

Why is this clause-boundedness constraint relaxed so as to allow *everyone* in (35) to have scope over the WH at LF? Let us consider the LF configurations of the conflicting cases. In the following representations, we assume, essentially with May, that the adjunction site for QR is not limited to IP. In particular, we allow CP as an adjunction site (a possibility rejected by May). We will not, however, adopt May's assumption that when two quantifiers govern each other at LF, either can have wider scope.[9] Thus, we assume that LF configurations unambiguously represent scope relations as in the theory of May (1977). We offer (49) as the LF representation of (37), and (50) as the LF representation of (35).[10]

(49) [$_{IP}$ someone$_1$ [$_{IP}$ t_1 thinks [$_{CP}$ (that) [$_{IP}$ everyone$_2$ [$_{IP}$ t_2 saw you at the rally]]]]]

(50) [$_{CP}$ everyone$_2$ [$_{CP}$ who$_1$ [$_{IP}$ do you think [$_{CP}$[$_{IP}$ t_2 saw t_1 at the rally]]]]]]

Note that in (50), the c-command relation of the operators *everyone* and *who* preserves that of their respective traces. On the other hand, were *everyone* to move to the matrix in (37) to take wider scope than *someone*, the c-command relation of the respective traces would be reversed in the operators. (51) illustrates this.

(51) $[_{IP}$ everyone$_2$ $[_{IP}$ someone$_1$ $[_{IP}$ t_1 thinks $[_{CP}$ (that) $[_{IP}$ t_2 saw you at the rally$]]]]]$

On the basis of the above observations, we tentatively state the relevant generalization as the following LF well-formedness condition:[11]

(52) Suppose that Q_1 and Q_2 are operators (quantified NP or WH). Then, Q_1 cannot take wide scope over Q_2 if t_2 c-commands t_1.

Then, we specify QR as follows:

(53) QR adjoins a quantified NP to a minimal node to satisfy (52).

In (37), the embedded IP is the minimal node that *everyone* can adjoin to, without violating (52). Hence, by (53), the LF representation of (37) must be as in (49). In (35), on the other hand, *everyone* must adjoin to the matrix CP to satisfy (52). Thus, the LF representation of this example must be as in (50). (52)–(53) also capture the nonambiguity of (29) and (38). Let us consider (29), repeated here as (54).

(54) who$_1$ t_1 bought everything for Max

The minimal node that *everything* can adjoin to in LF is the VP.[12] The resulting LF representation is (55).

(55) $[_{CP}$ who$_1$ $[_{IP}$ t_1 $[_{VP}$ everything$_2$ $[_{VP}$ bought t_2 for Max$]]]]$

(55) satisfies (52) because t_1 c-commands t_2, and *everything* does not have scope over *who*. Hence, (55) is the LF representation for (54), and *who* must take wide scope over *everything*.

(52) is, in effect, the "rigidity condition" on quantifier scope proposed by Huang (1982), and later by Hoji (1985) for Japanese. Huang and Hoji discuss the scope relations among quantified NPs, but as we have shown, the generalization seems to extend to scope relations of quantified NPs and WHs in English as well. The rigidity condition as such is, of course, not without potential problems. First consider (56).

(56) someone loves everyone

It is generally assumed that (56) is ambiguous: it can have either the LF representation in (57a) or the one in (57b).

(57) a. $[_{IP}$ someone$_1$ $[_{IP}$ everyone$_2$ $[_{IP}$ t_1 $[_{VP}$ loves t_2]]]]$
     b. $[_{IP}$ everyone$_1$ $[_{IP}$ someone$_2$ $[_{IP}$ t_2 $[_{VP}$ loves t_1]]]]$

(57a), which represents the preferred reading, satisfies (52), but (57b) does not. Hence, it seems that (52) has exceptions.[13] However, we believe that this does not affect our discussion. Note that certain other existential quantifiers are like *who* in their quite strict obedience to (52). There is no clear contrast between (58) and (59).

(58) who loves everyone

(59) some woman loves everyone

In both cases, *everyone* strongly favors narrow scope, probably to the exclusion of any other possibility. Even in (56), there is a preference in this direction. How to account for the difference between (56) and (59) is unclear. It is possible that (52) reflects a preference, rather than an absolute, and that there is lexical variability associated with the preference. Alternatively, (52) might be absolute in general but its effects might be weakened, for whatever reason, in the case of certain quantifiers, such as *someone*. But in any case, given the properties of examples such as (59), we can maintain our account of (54).[14]

Second, once we extend the rigidity condition so that it covers WH-phrases as well as quantified NPs as in (52), a question may arise with respect to examples such as (60).

(60) ??what$_1$ do you wonder who$_2$ t_2 bought t_1

If *what* takes scope over *who* in (60), then this example clearly violates (52). Yet the example is no worse than a weak Subjacency violation. We conclude that (52) is not an independent condition on LF, but is part of a condition on the application of QR. That is, (52) is part of (53), which specifies the operation of QR. Then, it is irrelevant for examples such as (60), since QR is irrelevant. This change does not affect our analysis of examples such as (54), since QR of *everything* applying in LF is still constrained by (52).

5.3 The Disjunctive Nature of Proper Government

In the theory of Chomsky (1981), the ECP—that is, the proper government requirement for traces—can be satisfied in two distinct ways: by lexical government or by antecedent government. This disjunctive nature of the ECP is inherited in later works such as Huang 1982, L&S, and this monograph itself.[15] It is of course desirable conceptually to dispense with this (or any) disjunction, and efforts have been made toward this goal. In this section, we will briefly discuss two works that are concerned with this issue: Chomsky 1986a and Aoun et al. 1987 (henceforth AHLW).

5.3.1 Antecedent Government

Chomsky (1986a) suggests that antecedent government is not merely one of two alternative ways of licensing a trace, but rather, is required of every trace. The empirical motivation for this suggestion comes from the following example, discussed in section 4.3.3, and originally due to Mark Baker:

(61) *John$_1$ seems [$_{CP}$ that [$_{IP}$ it was told t_1 [$_{CP}$ that [$_{IP}$ Mary is a genius]]]]

(61) has the same grammatical status as (62), which is another super-raising example.

(62) *John$_1$ seems [$_{CP}$ that [$_{IP}$ it is believed [$_{IP}$ t_1 to be a genius]]]

In L&S, (62) was ruled out by the ECP, t_1 being the offending trace, because antecedent government clearly fails, and lexical government does as well under the assumption, first articulated in that work, that lexical government is contingent on θ-role or Case assignment. However, (61) is not susceptible to the same analysis, since t_1 is in fact assigned a θ-role by *told* and hence is lexically governed by it. Under our theory, this should suffice for t_1 to satisfy the ECP, even though the trace is not antecedent-governed. Chomsky thus concludes that antecedent government is a necessary condition for satisfying the ECP, rather than one of two alternative modes of satisfying it.

However, this conclusion can now be challenged, since, in chapter 4, we proposed an extension of Chomsky's (1986b) Uniformity Condition that rules out (61) independently of the ECP.[16] Under this extension, no barrier can interrupt an A-chain. Thus, since the embedded finite IP containing t_1 in (61) is a barrier (under the theory developed in chapter 3), this example violates the Extended Uniformity Condition. Given this extension of the Uniformity Condition, we need not appeal to failure of antecedent government to rule out (61). Thus, (61) does not establish antecedent government as a necessary requirement on traces. This is a desirable result, since, as Epstein (1987) shows, (63) raises problems for antecedent government as a necessary condition.

(63) who read what

As discussed in chapter 2, the LF trace of the WH in situ will not be antecedent-governed by the moved WH-phrase or the matrix COMP. We therefore appealed to lexical government to license the LF trace of *what*, since *what* is the complement of a lexical head. But if antecedent government is necessary, this account of (63) is not available. Chomsky (MIT class lectures, 1986) suggests that this problem can be avoided in the following way: *what* can first adjoin to VP and from there move to SPEC of CP. The VP-adjoined intermediate trace is clearly close enough to the initial trace to serve as an antecedent governor for it. However, aside from the problem of how this intermediate trace is itself properly governed, the initial trace is in fact not antecedent-governed, given the condition on antecedent governors that we proposed in chapter 4. There, we argued that only an X^0 can be an antecedent governor. Since the intermediate trace of *what* is an NP, it will not qualify. Thus, given the theory developed here, (63) indicates that lexical government suffices for licensing.[17]

5.3.2   Lexical Government

5.3.2.1   NP-Movement within NPs

There has been another closely related proposal aimed at eliminating the disjunction in the ECP. AHLW, among others, argue that lexical government is required of all traces. More specifically, they propose that empty elements must be governed by a lexical head, and further, that this requirement applies at PF.[18] They first present examples like (64) as evidence for their proposal:[19]

(64) a picture of John's

AHLW note that in (64), there is no "object" reading for *John's*—that is, that *John* cannot be understood as the complement of *picture*. Thus, they argue, the representation in (66) is allowed but the one in (65) must be excluded.

(65) a picture of [$_{NP}$ John's$_1$ e t_1]

(66) a picture of [$_{NP}$ John's e]

In (65) and (66), e is an empty category whose interpretation is determined by the head noun *picture*. AHLW hypothesize that this empty category is not a suitable governor for the trace of *John* in (65). Thus, (65) is correctly excluded as a violation of the head government requirement. In (66), on the other hand, there is no trace that needs to be head-governed, so this representation is permitted. In their analysis of (64), AHLW assume that t_1 in (65) is antecedent-governed by *John*, as we did in L&S. Hence, they conclude that the head government requirement applies to all traces, regardless of whether or not they are antecedent-governed.

There are, however, reasons to doubt that (64) constitutes direct evidence for the head government requirement. First, Anderson (1983) discusses examples such as (64) and proposes an independent analysis. According to her analysis, (64) has a base-generated empty N, as shown in (67).

(67) a picture of [$_{NP}$ John's [$_N$ e]]

She proposes that the interpretive property of (64) follows from the hypotheses in (68), which she argues are motivated on independent grounds.

(68) a. Base-generated empty Ns are not θ-role assigners.

  b. The only θ-role that *'s* can assign is the possessor θ-role.

By (68a), *John* in (67) cannot be assigned a θ-role by the empty N, and hence, *'s* is the only potential θ-role assigner for it. Then, by (68b), it follows that *John* is assigned the possessor θ-role. Here, we will not discuss Anderson's plausible analysis in any detail. But it should be clear that if it is correct, the fact that *John* in (64) cannot assume the object θ-role is accounted for independently of any head government requirement.

Second, suppose, contrary to Anderson (1983), that the interpretive property of (64) has to do with the ill-formedness of (65) as a representation and in particular is to be attributed to the trace in (65) violating some sort of proper government requirement, as AHLW assume. It is true that given the formulation of the ECP in L&S, for example, the trace in (65) is antecedent-governed by *John's*. Thus, it may be claimed, as AHLW do, that antecedent government is not sufficient for a trace to satisfy the proper government requirement. However, given our proposals in chapter 4, this conclusion no longer follows. We argued there that only X^0 categories can be antecedent governors. Given this hypothesis, *John's* in (65), being a maximal projection, cannot antecedent-govern the trace in question. Thus, if the trace is not lexically governed, it will be filtered out by our ECP. In fact, we obtain the desired result if we translate the core of AHLW's proposal into our terms, and suppose that empty Ns are not lexical governors. Thus, the ill-formedness of (65) can be explained by our ECP without an additional head government requirement.

Third, and most important, although the phenomenon addressed by AHLW can easily be accommodated in our theory, it is not entirely clear that AHLW's generalization is the correct one. For example, as they note, there do exist grammatical sentences that seem to contain the offending portion of (65). They give (69) as one such case.

(69) Lincoln$_1$'s portrait t_1 was bad but Wilson$_2$'s *e* t_2 was worse

They do not offer an account of (69), but speculate that it involves a discourse process that "seems to affect coordinate structures in particular ..." However, as Jackendoff (1971:543, fn. 6) observes, this process of "N'-deletion" is actually relatively free and in particular is not limited to coordinate structures. The following examples cited by Jackendoff are all acceptable:

(70) a. Tureck's performance of Bach on the piano doesn't please me as much as Glenn Gould's
   b. Tom's dog with one eye attacked Fred's
   c. I borrowed Fred's diagram of a snake's eye because Steve's had been stolen

In all of these configurations, acceptability is preserved even if the elided N′ contains a trace (that is, even if the second genitive NP is understood as complement to the missing N). This is illustrated in (71).

(71) a. Lincoln's portrait didn't please me as much as Wilson's

 b. I destroyed Lincoln's portrait because Wilson's had been stolen

Given the generality of the N′-deletion phenomenon, there does not seem to be any bar to analyzing (64) as an instance of this phenomenon.[20] Then, the problem turns out to be why (66), and not (65), is possible as an example of N′-deletion.

If this is the correct way to approach the contrast between (65) and (66), then AHLW's head government account for (65) faces a more general problem. Jackendoff (1971) argues that N′-deletion has essentially the same properties as VP-deletion. In standard VP-deletion constructions, however, quite generally the residual NP is allowed to be an underlying complement, as in (72).

(72) Harry was arrested after Bill was

Parallel to (65), the relevant portion of the structure of (72) might be assumed to be as in (73).

(73) Bill$_1$ was e t_1

But if e is not an appropriate head governor for t in (65), presumably the same should be true in (73). Since (72) is perfect, we conclude that the head government requirement is not responsible for the ungrammaticality of (65).

This leaves open the question of what (65) does violate. The first question to be addressed here is why the N′-deletion process responsible for (71) is not available in a structure like (65). To explore this, we must first consider under what circumstances N′-deletion is possible. As mentioned above, Jackendoff points out that N′-deletion is relatively free. In fact, he argues that it has essentially the same distribution as VP-deletion. Thus, for example, it is not limited to coordinate structures. VP-deletion has further well-known properties as well. For example, the antecedent need not be represented in the phrase marker containing the deleted VP. As shown by Hankamer and Sag (1976), however, there must be a linguistically represented antecedent. If it is not in the same phrase marker, then it must be elsewhere in the discourse. Pragmatic control is not available. Consider the following context-utterance events:[21]

(74) a. [Sag produces an uncooked egg and goes into a windup motion as if in preparation for throwing the egg into the audience.]

Hankamer: #Don't be alarmed, ladies and gentlemen. He never actually does.
  b. [Same context]
Hankamer: ... He never actually does it.

Compare (74a) with a situation that provides a discourse antecedent:

(75) Audience member: I'm afraid Sag will throw an egg.
     Hankamer: He never actually does.

N'-deletion shares these properties of VP-deletion as well. It requires a linguistic antecedent, as illustrated by (76).

(76) [Lasnik and Saito are in a yard with several barking dogs belonging to various people.]
    Lasnik: #Harry's is particularly noisy.

And a discourse antecedent renders the utterance in (76) acceptable:

(77) Lasnik: These dogs keep me awake with all their barking.
    Saito: Harry's is particularly noisy.

Having established that N'-deletion, like VP-deletion, requires a linguistic antecedent, we now return to (64) and (71a), repeated here with their structures as (78a) and (78b).

(78) a. a picture of [$_{NP}$ John's$_1$ [$_{N'}$ e]]
    b. [$_{NP}$ Lincoln's$_1$ [$_{N'}$ portrait t_1]] did not please me as much as
       [$_{NP}$ Wilson's$_2$ [$_{N'}$ e]]

It is not surprising that N'-deletion is allowed in (78b). The deleted N' has an antecedent, [$_{N'}$ portrait t]. in the same sentence. The problem is why *John* cannot have the object θ-role in (78a). Let us assume, as seems plausible, that the structure of (78a) is as in (79).

(79)

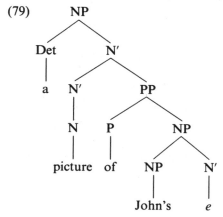

If *John's* is understood to be the possessor, then the N′-deletion in (79) is correctly allowed. The deleted N′ has an antecedent, [N′ picture]. However, if *John's* assumes the object θ-role, then the deleted N′ in (79) must have an antecedent containing a trace, exactly like the deleted N′ in (78b). But there is no instance of [N′ picture *t*] in (79). Hence, if (78a) is an instance of N′-deletion, as we assume to be the case, then the absence of the object reading of *John* in (78a) is straightforwardly explained.

There are certain other problems to be discussed concerning (78a). Note first that (78a) is quite different from (80) in meaning.

(80) a picture of John's picture

The only possible interpretation of (80) is 'a picture of a particular picture', and the only interpretation of (78a) is 'one of John's pictures'. The nonambiguity of (78a) indicates that N′-deletion does not apply in the configuration shown in (81).

(81)

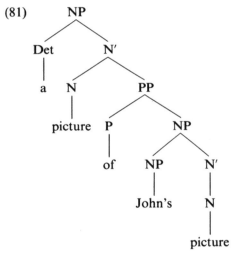

(81) is the structure corresponding to the reading 'a picture of a particular picture'. Hence, if N′-deletion could delete *picture* in this structure, we would expect (78a) to have this reading as well. But such N′-deletion is clearly precluded, since there is no occurrence of [N′ picture] that serves as the antecedent of the N′ to be deleted. Thus, the nonambiguity of (78a) is straightforwardly explained.

The nonambiguity of (80), on the other hand, indicates that N′-deletion is obligatory in the structure shown in (82).

(82)

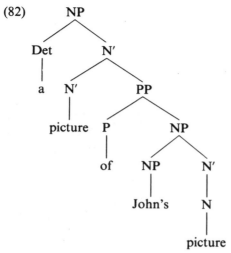

If we apply N'-deletion to (82), we obtain (78a) with its only possible interpretation, 'one of John's pictures'. But if N'-deletion need not apply in (82), then (80) should also have this interpretation, contrary to fact. The question then arises why N'-deletion is obligatory in (82). We speculate that if N'-deletion does not apply in (82), the configuration violates Condition C of the binding theory.

Suppose that Condition C applies to N's as well as to NPs. Then, the configuration in (82) can be ruled out by this condition.[22] Now, suppose further that empty N's resulting from N'-deletion are not R-expressions and hence are not subject to Condition C. Then, the "obligatoriness" of deletion in (82) follows from Condition C. Although the account sketched here is quite speculative, there is evidence that deletion can in fact save examples from Condition C. For example, consider (83).

(83) if Mary can solve John's$_1$ problem, he$_1$ can (*solve John's$_1$ problem)

In (83), if the VP, *solve John's problem*, is not deleted, then the example violates Condition C. However, the example improves considerably with the deletion of the VP. This lends support to our speculation about the apparent obligatoriness of N'-deletion in (82).

5.3.2.2 Gapping and Movement Processes
In addition to the facts about nominals discussed in the preceding subsection, AHLW present an argument for the necessity of head government based on interactions between gapping and movement processes. We will first consider their evidence from WH-movement.[23] ((84a–c) are based on AHLW's (12a–c).)

(84) a. (??)Fay introduced Kay to Ray and Jon GAP Don to Ron
     b.   *which man$_i$ did Fay introduce e_i to Ray and which woman$_j$
           Jon GAP e_j to Ron
     c.   *Fay wondered what$_i$ Kay gave e_i to Ray and what$_j$ Jon GAP e_j
           to Ron

In (84b) and (84c), e_j is antecedent-governed by (the COMP associated with) *which woman$_j$* and *what$_j$*, respectively, yet the examples are ungrammatical. AHLW argue that these traces must be head-governed (and that the GAP does not count as a suitable governor). Before we accept this tempting conclusion, it is important to consider whether other independent constraints might be at work here.

It is well known that gapping is very heavily constrained. For example, coordination is required; subordination will not license gapping. Compare (85) with (86).

(85)   John saw Bill and Mary Susan

(86)   *John saw Bill because Mary Susan

Further, the clauses involved in gapping must themselves be coordinate, not merely parallel constituents of larger coordinate structures:

(87)   *Harry said that John saw Bill and Tom said that Mary Susan

In fact, the coordination must be precisely at the IP level; even CP coordination will not suffice:

(88)   I think that [$_{IP}$[$_{IP}$ John saw Bill] and [$_{IP}$ Mary Susan]]

(89)   *I think [$_{CP}$[$_{CP}$ that John saw Bill] and [$_{CP}$ that Mary Susan]]

But now notice that this constraint, whatever its ultimate explanation might be, will almost certainly exclude AHLW's (84b–c). In both of those examples, coordination is at the CP level, rather than at the IP level:

(90) (= structure of (84b))
      [$_{CP}$[$_{CP}$ which man did Fay introduce e_i to Ray] and [$_{CP}$ which woman$_j$
      Jon GAP e_j to Ron]]

(91) (= structure of (84c))
      Fay wondered [$_{CP}$[$_{CP}$ what$_i$ Kay gave e_i to Ray] and [$_{CP}$ what$_j$ Jon
      GAP e_j to Ron]]

AHLW briefly consider the possibility of a general limitation of gapping to conjoined Ss (= IPs), but they reject this, based on the acceptability of (92) (their (13b)), as compared with the predictably unacceptable (93) (their (13a)).

(92)   I wonder whether Fay visited Kay and whether Ron did GAP Jon

(93)   *I wonder whether Fay visited Kay and whether Ron GAP Jon

However, it is doubtful that the same process is operative in the two examples. In particular, the phenomenon in (92) does not conform to any of the gapping diagnostics described above. Note, first, that it does not require coordination:

(94)   John visited Bill after Susan *(did) Mary

Further, unlike gapping (and like VP-deletion), the operative process here can have an antecedent earlier in the discourse, not merely in the same sentence:

(95)   Speaker 1: John visited Bill yesterday
       Speaker 2: Mary did Susan today

Compare what happens in a clear case of gapping like (96).[24]

(96)   Speaker 1: John visited Bill yesterday
       Speaker 2: *Mary Susan today

It must be noted that AHLW claim that the deletion process in (92) is like gapping with respect to WH-trace licensing. In particular, they claim that (84b–c) are equally bad with an overt auxiliary, as in (97a–b).[25]

(97)   a.   *which man$_i$ did Fay introduce e_i to Ray and which woman$_j$ did
        Jon GAP e_j to Ron
    b.   *Fay wondered what$_i$ Kay gave e_i to Ray and what$_j$ Jon did
        GAP e_j to Ron

Since, as we have shown, the deletion process that leaves behind an auxiliary verb patterns with VP-deletion rather than with gapping, the IP coordination requirement on the latter process cannot be relevant here. Thus, there is apparently evidence for the head government constraint. (97a–b) will be excluded since GAP is not a suitable head governor for e_j. However, for the construction in question, this constraint seems too strong. Examples structurally identical to those in (97) but with other auxiliary verbs seem reasonably acceptable, and clearly better than the examples in (84):

(98)   ?Fay wondered what Ray will give to Ray and what Jon will to Ron

We therefore conclude that the phenomenon in (97), whatever its precise nature, should not be accounted for in the same way as that in (84).

   There is one final instance of true gapping that should be mentioned. AHLW present (99) (their (13d)) as a further counterexample to the IP coordination requirement.

(99) I wonder which man saw Fay and which woman Kay

This does seem genuinely inconsistent with the requirement, though the vacuous movement hypothesis of Chomsky (1986a) would allow *which man* and *which woman* to be in situ in subject position at S-structure. Under that assumption, which we will not pursue here, IP coordination could be maintained.[26]

The final gapping paradigm to be considered involves heavy NP shift. AHLW observe that heavy NP shift and gapping are incompatible. They present the following examples (in their (12d, f)):

(100) *Fay admired e_i greatly [her uncle from Paramus]$_i$ but Jon GAP e_j only moderately [his uncle from New York]$_j$

(101) *Fay gave e_i to Ray [her favorite racket]$_i$ and Jon GAP e_j to Ron [his favorite plant]$_j$

AHLW argue, again, that these examples display a failure of head government, the GAP not constituting a suitable head governor for the trace of heavy NP shift. It is not entirely clear that this phenomenon bears on the present concerns, since, for example, (100) is quite degraded even without heavy NP shift:

(102) ?*Fay admired her uncle from Paramus greatly but Jon GAP his uncle from New York only moderately

This seems to reflect two additional independent properties of gapping. The first is that only coordination with *and* or *or* strongly supports this process. Even simple instances of gapping are at best marginal with *but*:

(103) a. John likes Mary and Bill Susan
       b. ?*John likes Mary but Bill Susan

The second independent property is that, as noted by Jackendoff (1971), in the most acceptable instances of gapping, only one constituent remains to the right of the GAP. But in (100)–(102), there are two constituents following the GAP.

However, for present purposes let us put aside these considerations and simply accept the facts as presented by AHLW. Note that as with the phenomena involving nominals discussed in section 5.3.2.1, this result would seem to follow directly from our analysis. Suppose that GAP is not a possible lexical governor (just as, for AHLW, it is not a possible head governor). Then the trace in (100) and (101) will violate the ECP, since, as argued in chapter 4, a shifted heavy NP cannot antecedent-govern its trace. Thus, the trace in (100) and (101) would be neither lexically governed nor antecedent-governed.

5.4 Subjacency as a Condition on S-Structure Move α

We have so far assumed, following Huang (1982) and others, that Subjacency is a constraint on S-structure movement and that LF movement, in particular LF WH-movement, is not subject to this condition. This hypothesis is supported by contrasts such as the following:

(104) ??what$_1$ does John wonder whether Mary bought t_1

(105) who$_1$ t_1 wonders whether Mary bought what

In (104), *what* is moved out of a WH-island at S-structure in violation of Subjacency. In (105), on the other hand, *what* moves to the SPEC of the matrix CP only in LF. If Subjacency constrains LF movement as well as S-structure movement, then we predict falsely that (105) should be as bad as (104). Hence, the grammaticality of (105) indicates that Subjacency is a condition only on S-structure movement and not on LF movement.

However, hypotheses have been proposed to resolve this S-structure versus LF asymmetry by making Subjacency a condition on both S-structure and LF movement, while still accounting for contrasts such as (104)–(105). In this section, we will briefly consider two such hypotheses: the LF pied-piping hypothesis, developed in detail by Nishigauchi (1986), and the D-linking hypothesis of Pesetsky (1987).

5.4.1 The LF Pied-Piping Hypothesis

The LF pied-piping hypothesis assumes that LF movement is subject to Subjacency, and it appeals to pied-piping to save grammatical sentences that seemingly violate this condition in LF. Consider the following examples:

(106) ?*what$_1$ did you see [$_{NP}$ the man that bought t_1]

(107) who$_1$ t_1 saw [$_{NP}$ the man that bought what]

In (107), if *what* moves to the matrix SPEC of CP in LF, the movement violates Subjacency. Under the pied-piping hypothesis, not just *what*, but the whole complex NP, moves to the matrix SPEC of CP. Then, there is no violation of Subjacency. Formalizing the pied-piping hypothesis, Nishigauchi (1986) proposes roughly that the pied-piping of the complex NP in (107), for example, is made possible by the percolation of the [+WH] feature of *what* to the complex NP. With this feature percolation, the whole complex NP is a WH-phrase and hence moves into the matrix COMP (SPEC of CP) in LF.

However, as noted by Nishigauchi, the percolation of the [+WH] feature cannot be totally free. Consider the following example:

(108) *who$_1$ t_1 saw [$_{NP}$ the man that bought the book why]

Under the ECP analysis, the LF movement of *why* inevitably produces a trace that violates this principle. However, if the whole complex NP in (108) can pied-pipe and move into SPEC of CP in LF, as in the case of (107), then (108) does not violate any principle, in particular, the ECP or Subjacency. It should, in fact, have the status of the perfect (109).

(109) who$_1$ t_1 saw who

Thus, it is necessary to stipulate that pied-piping is possible in (107) but not in (108). Nishigauchi proposes that "a WH-phrase must be identical in syntactic category with the dominating node in order for the [+WH] feature to be percolated to the latter" (p. 120). Given this assumption, the distinction between (107) and (108) follows. In (107), the complex NP and the WH in situ are identical in syntactic category. Hence, the [+WH] feature percolates up to the complex NP, and pied-piping is possible. In (108), on the other hand, pied-piping is impossible since the WH in situ and the complex NP do not agree in syntactic category, and hence, the [+WH] feature of the former does not percolate up to the latter.

The pied-piping hypothesis has the attractive feature of making Subjacency a condition on both S-structure and LF movements. In addition, it appears that the hypothesis has only a minimal effect on the rest of the theory. The ECP would, it seems, continue to rule out examples such as (110) and (111).

(110) *who$_1$ do you think that t_1 left

(111) *how$_1$ do you know whether [$_{IP}$ John fixed the car t_1]
      (cf. ??what$_1$ do you know whether John fixed t_1)

And the pied-piping mechanism that is utilized for LF WH-movement appears to be independently needed for S-structure WH-movement, as in examples like (112).

(112) on which table$_1$ did you put the book t_1

However, a closer examination reveals that the pied-piping hypothesis is incomplete in certain key respects and, at this point, leads to bifurcations elsewhere in the theory.

First of all, it is still not entirely clear exactly when LF pied-piping is possible. That is, in Nishigauchi's terms, it is not clear when the [+WH] feature can percolate up. As mentioned above, Nishigauchi hypothesizes that [+WH] can percolate up only to nodes that are identical to the WH in syntactic category. But more refinement is clearly needed to account for contrasts such as those in (113)–(114).

(113) a. who$_1$ t_1 left after buying what
      b. ?*what did John leave after buying t_1

(114) a. who$_1$ t_1 fell asleep during what
      b. ?*what$_1$ did John fall asleep during t_1

If Subjacency applies in LF, then the grammaticality of (114a), as opposed to (114b), shows that what moves in LF in this example is not *what* but rather the PP *during what*. However, *what* is an NP and is therefore not identical to *during what* in syntactic category. The same question arises with respect to S-structure pied-piping, as in (112).

Second, whatever the mechanism is that allows LF pied-piping, it is different in crucial respects from the one that licenses S-structure pied-piping. S-structure pied-piping, especially for WH-questions, is severely restricted, as shown in (115).

(115) a. [on which table]$_1$ did you put the book t_1
      b. *[after buying what]$_1$ did John leave t_1
      c. *[the man that bought what]$_1$ did John see t_1

If Subjacency constrains LF WH-movement, then LF counterparts of (115b–c) must be allowed to account for the grammatical (116)–(117).

(116) who$_1$ t_1 left after buying what (= (113a))

(117) who$_1$ t_1 saw the man that bought what (= (107))

Thus, the mechanism that licenses pied-piping must be different for S-structure WH-movement and LF WH-movement. In particular, it must be far more permissive in the latter case. Consequently, we have a trade-off. Given the pied-piping hypothesis, there is no need to stipulate that S-structure and LF movements differ with respect to Subjacency. But instead, it seems necessary to stipulate a nearly corresponding difference between S-structure and LF WH-movements with respect to the possibility of pied-piping.

Since the conceptual question does not weigh heavily in either direction, we turn now to some of the empirical evidence that has been offered for the pied-piping hypothesis. For example, Nishigauchi, among others, discusses question-answer pairs such as the following:

(118) a. [[dono kyoozyu-ga   suisensiteiru] hito]-ga
          which professor-nom recommend   person-nom
          saiyoosare-soo   desu ka
          be appointed-likely be   Q
          'the person that *which professor* recommends is most likely to get the position'

b. i. *Suzuki-kyoozyu desu
Suzuki-professor be
'(it's) Professor Suzuki'

ii. [[Suzuki-kyoozyu-ga   suisensiteiru] hito]   desu
Suzuki-professor-nom recommend   person be
'(it's) the person that Professor Suzuki recommends'

Nishigauchi assumes that a short answer like (118bi) or (118bii) to a WH-question must correspond to the WH-phrase in COMP (SPEC of CP) in the LF representation of the WH-question. Given this assumption, the fact that (118bii) is a more acceptable answer to (118a) than (118bi) implies that in the LF representation of (118a), not just *dono kyoozyu* 'which professor', but the whole complex NP containing it, must be in COMP (SPEC of CP). And such an LF representation is possible only with LF pied-piping. The LF representation with only *dono kyoozyu* in COMP (SPEC of CP) is excluded, as desired, if Subjacency applies to LF WH-movement.

Although the facts here seem clear enough, the theoretical assumption is less firmly established. In this regard, consider the following examples:

(119) a. who$_1$ did you give a book to t_1
b. to whom$_1$ did you give a book t_1

(120) a. John
b. to John

Given Nishigauchi's correspondence assumption, we expect that (120a) is a proper answer only for (119a), and (120b) only for (119b). However, (120a) and (120b) are both appropriate answers for either (119a) or (119b). It seems, then, that a "short answer" to a WH-question need not precisely correspond to the WH-phrase in SPEC of CP.

Nishigauchi (1986) himself discusses another potential problem for the argument for LF pied-piping based on examples like (118). He points out that as an answer for the question in (121a), (121bi) and (121bii) are both possible.[27]

(121) a. kimi-wa [[dare-ga   kaita] hon]-o   yomimasita ka
you-top who-nom wrote book-acc read   Q
'you read the book that who wrote'

b. i. Austen desu
Austen be
'(it's) Austen'

ii. [Austen-ga   kaita] hon   desu
    Austen-nom wrote book be
    '(it's) the book that Austen wrote'

For (118), it was claimed that the answer (118bi) is impossible since the LF movement of *dono kyoozyu* to COMP (SPEC of CP) violates Subjacency. Similarly, in (121), the LF movement of *dare* 'who' to the matrix COMP (SPEC of CP) violates Subjacency. Thus, according to the pied-piping hypothesis, the answer in (121bi) should be impossible. Nishigauchi argues that "(79a) [= (121bi)] is actually a truncated form which derives from (79b) [= (121bii)] via some sort of deletion operation, the conditions on which would be essentially pragmatic in nature" (p. 67). This speculation may turn out to be correct. But in the absence of a clearer statement of the conditions on the hypothesized deletion, (121) considerably weakens the force of the argument based on (118).

Our discussion of the arguments for LF pied-piping is by no means exhaustive. The LF pied-piping hypothesis clearly has certain attractive features, and presumably it can be developed further to overcome some of the problems that it faces. Yet, for reasons stated above, it seems to us at this point that the hypothesis does not have clear advantages, conceptual or empirical, over the approach that stipulates that Subjacency applies only to S-structure Move-α

5.4.2 Pesetsky's D-Linking Analysis

Pesetsky's (1987) D-linking hypothesis maintains that not all WH-phrases move. That is, even at LF, some WH-phrases in situ remain in situ. In particular, a WH-phrase may remain in situ if it is *discourse (D-) linked*. For example, for a question involving a D-linked WH-phrase, the range of felicitous answers is limited by a set of objects of type N that both speaker and hearer have in mind. Pesetsky proposes that *which* phrases are always D-linked, noting that "If the hearer is ignorant of the context assumed by the speaker, a *which*-question sounds odd" (p. 109). A *which* phrase in situ in an island is then predicted to be grammatical even if Subjacency does constrain LF movement. We agree with the prediction, of course, since we have claimed, with Huang, that Subjacency does *not* constrain LF movement. For *which* phrases, the two proposals have the same effect. A relevant example is (122), with *which books* in a WH-island.

(122) who knows where we bought which books

As expected under either account, *which books* can be understood as having matrix scope.[28]

In addition to Subjacency, Superiority provides another diagnostic for movement, according to Pesetsky.[29] (123) exhibits the usual superiority effect, but (124) does not.

(123) *Mary asked [what$_2$ [who read t_2]]

(124)   Mary asked [which book$_2$ [which man read t_2]]

Pesetsky argues that this is precisely predicted if (123) involves LF movement and (124) does not, given that Superiority is a constraint on (the result of) LF movement.

On the face of it, this account of (123) seems to conflict with another of Pesetsky's examples:

(125) who wonders where we bought what

Pesetsky implies, and we agree, that *what* can have matrix scope here, just as *which books* can in (122). But this indicates that *what* can be D-linked, just as *which books* can be. For if *what* were to attain matrix scope via LF movement, an LF Subjacency violation should result. Thus, *what* may be interpreted in situ. But the same should be true of *who* in (123). It should be able to avoid violating Superiority in just the way that *which man* does in (124). Pesetsky states, however, that this is only an apparent conflict. He argues that *who* and *what* may in fact be D-linked, and that under appropriate discourse conditions, superiority effects disappear. He presents (126) (due to Bolinger (1978)) as an illustration.

(126) I know what just about everybody was asked to do, but what did who (actually) do

According to Pesetsky, "the context implies D-linking of *what* and *who*" (p. 108).[30] But it is not entirely clear in what sense the first conjunct in (126) does establish D-linking. Presumably, Pesetsky intends that *everybody* establishes the relevant context for the D-linking of *who*. True, *everybody* narrows the relevant set down to all *human beings* in the universe of discourse. But *who* itself already embodies this restriction. Thus, the question portion of (126), as in (127), should be just as good in isolation. Of course, if this were true, there would be no superiority effects at all.

(127) (*)what did who do

To the extent that this problem is unresolved, the account of the relative acceptability of (126) seems incomplete. A related descriptive problem arises with respect to (125). Pesetsky does not indicate that any special context is needed to allow the wide scope reading of *what* in that example, and we feel that none in fact is needed. This raises questions about the pragmatic and/or semantic substance of the notion "D-linking."

The final phenomena we will consider involve what Pesetsky terms "aggressively non-D-linked" WH-phrases. These are WH-phrases that are incompatible with overt markers of D-linking, such as *which*. Pesetsky gives the following minimal pair, involving the aggressively non-D-linked *the hell*:

(128) a.   what the hell book did you read that in

     b.   *which the hell book did you read that in

If a ... *the hell* phrase cannot be D-linked, then it must move to COMP (SPEC of CP), since those are the only two possibilities that will lead to an interpretation. Pesetsky suggests that Japanese *ittai* functions like English *the hell*. In (129), an *ittai* WH-phrase is possible in situ since nothing prevents LF movement.

(129)   Mary-wa John-ni ittai   nani-o   ageta no
       Mary-top John-dat the hell what-acc gave Q
       'what the hell did Mary give to John'

When the *ittai* phrase is within an island, however, the result is ungrammatical, even though without *ittai*, the corresponding example is fine:

(130)   *Mary-wa [$_{NP}$[$_{CP}$ John-ni ittai   nani-o   ageta] hito]-ni
       Mary-top   John-to the hell what-acc gave   person-dat
       atta no
       met
       'Mary met the person [that gave what the hell to John]'

(131)   Mary-wa [$_{NP}$[$_{CP}$ John-ni nani-o ageta] hito]-ni atta no

This follows if an *ittai* phrase, being aggressively non-D-linked, must undergo LF movement.[31]

Notice that the notion "aggressively" does a substantial amount of work in this analysis. We assume that an example such as (132) is perfectly grammatical even if *what* does not happen to be D-linked.

(132)   who read what

Yet (133) is impossible.

(133)   *who read what the hell

Thus, an aggressively non-D-linked WH-phrase is one that (1) cannot be D-linked (example (128)) and (2) must undergo WH-movement as soon as possible (example (133)). The logical connection between these two properties is not entirely clear. That a non-D-linked WH-phrase must undergo WH-movement is, of course, fundamental. But that it cannot do it in LF, in a language that has both syntactic and LF WH-movement, does not directly follow from this property. Interestingly, the distribution of such phrases is very much like that of WH-adjuncts. As discussed in earlier chapters, a WH-adjunct is impossible in situ within an island even in a language that freely allows WH in situ. (134) has just the status of (130).

(134) *Mary-wa [$_{NP}$[$_{CP}$ John-ni naze hon-o   ageta] hito]-ni   atta no
       Mary-top   John-to why book-acc gave   person-to met
       'Mary met the person [that gave a book to John why]'

Further, a WH-adjunct is bad as the unmoved WH in a multiple interrogation. (135) is rather like (133).

(135) *Who left why

Finally, syntactic extraction of either sort of WH-phrase out of an island is bad:

(136) *why$_1$ do you wonder [$_{CP}$ who left t_1]

(137) *what the hell$_1$ do you wonder [$_{CP}$ who wrote t_1]
       (cf. ??what$_1$ do you wonder [$_{CP}$ who wrote t_1])

It is rather tempting, then, to construct an analysis based, not on "aggression," but on some adjunct-like characteristic of these phrases. Here, we will merely outline some of the properties that such an analysis might have. Suppose that a WH-*the hell* phrase must be in an adjunct position at some point in the derivation, due to its focused nature, and that this adjunct position becomes the focus position. Then, there are two possible LF representations for (133), depending on whether *what the hell* adjoins to VP or to IP on its way to SPEC of CP. (138) illustrates the first possibility and (139) the second.

(138) [$_{CP}$ [[what the hell]$_1$ [who]$_2$]$_2$ [$_{C'}$ C$_2$ [$_{IP}$ t_2 [$_{VP}$ t_1' [$_{VP}$ read t_1]]]]]

(139) [$_{CP}$ [[what the hell]$_1$ [who]$_2$]$_2$ [$_{C'}$ C$_2$ [$_{IP}$ t_1' [$_{IP}$ t_2 [$_{VP}$ read t_1]]]]]

In both (138) and (139), t_1' represents the focus position. Now consider the proper government requirements of the traces. t_1 is uniformly properly governed, by virtue of lexical government by the verb. Further, t_2 is uniformly properly antecedent-governed by COMP at S-structure and hence is marked [$+\gamma$] at that level. But in neither example is t_1' properly governed, since neither lexical government nor antecedent government obtains. Both representations are thus excluded and (133) is correctly ruled out.

   The analysis of (137) is similar. There will have to be an intermediate "focus trace" adjoined to the lower VP or IP, and this trace will fail to be properly governed, the desired result. Note, though, that there is one additional derivation that must be excluded: one in which *what the hell* moves directly to the higher VP, and from there to the higher SPEC of CP. The resulting representation would be as follows:

(140) $[_{CP}$ [what the hell]$_1$ $[_{C'}$ C$_1$ $[_{IP}$ do you $[_{VP}$ t_1' $[_{VP}$ wonder $[_{CP}$ who$_2$ $[_{C'}$ C$_2$ $[_{IP}$ t_2 wrote t_1]]]]]]]]]

The first movement of *what the hell* will violate Subjacency, but apparently nothing else is violated, since t_1' is antecedent-governed by the matrix COMP. Yet (137) is much worse than a mere WH-island violation, as in (141).

(141) ??what$_1$ do you wonder $[_{CP}$ who wrote t_1]

Thus, we must prohibit the long first movement of *what the hell* in (140), forcing the intermediate focus trace to be in the lower clause. Then, as noted above, it will fail to be properly governed, the required result. Suppose that this movement is, like QR, very local. In particular, suppose, as in the discussion of QR in section 5.2, that the movement must normally be to the minimal dominating category. Then, the first movement in the derivation of (137) will necessarily be to the embedded VP, creating the necessary focus position there. The subsequent movement out of the lower clause will leave a focus trace that will fail to be properly governed, as already discussed.

Grammatical instances of long-distance movement of *the hell* phrases will still be permitted. Consider (142).

(142) what the hell$_1$ do you think [John wrote t_1]

Here, the initial movement will again be to the lower VP. But this time, the subsequent movement can be to the lower SPEC of CP, and from there to the higher SPEC of CP. The resulting configuration is as in (143).

(143) $[_{CP}$ [what the hell]$_1$ $[_{C'}$ C$_1$ $[_{IP}$ do you think $[_{CP}$ t_1'' $[_{C'}$ C$_1$ $[_{IP}$ John $[_{VP}$ t_1' $[_{VP}$ wrote t_1]]]]]]]]]

The lower COMP properly antecedent-governs the focus trace t_1', and the initial trace t_1 is, of course, lexically governed by *wrote*. Thus, there is no violation.

Abstractly, the long movement of *what the hell* in (142) is reminiscent of the wide scope possibility for *everyone* in (35), repeated here as (144).

(144) who do you think everyone saw at the rally

Here, *everyone* evidently can move out of its clause. But now consider (145), which is abstractly like (137).

(145) ??who do you wonder whether everyone saw at the rally

Note first that, as usual, this has the status of a Subjacency violation. But now notice that the wide scope reading for *everyone* is impossible. This is so even though the exemption to clause-boundedness that we proposed for (144) should carry over to (145). We suggest that this contrast between (144) and (145) can be analyzed in the same terms as that between (142) and (137). Suppose that the initial movement of this quantifier must be to the minimal dominating category. For both (144) and (14S) this will be the lower IP. Suppose further that QR is a sort of focusing—in other words, that a focus trace must be created. The lower IPs in (144) and (145) will then be as shown in (146) and (147), respectively, for the wide scope reading.

(146) ... $[_{CP} t_1'' [_{C'} C_1 [_{IP} t_1' [_{IP} t_1 \text{ saw } t_2 \text{ at the rally}]]]]$

(147) ... $[_{CP} \text{whether } [_{C'} C [_{IP} t_1' [_{IP} t_1 \text{ saw } t_2 \text{ at the rally}]]]]$

In (146), t_1', the focus trace, will be properly antecedent-governed by COMP. But in (147), t_1' is not properly governed at all. Thus, the wide scope reading is correctly excluded.[32] Note that the narrow scope reading for (145) will be allowed, with *everyone* itself as the focus:

(148) $[_{CP} \text{whether } [_{C'} C [_{IP} \text{everyone}_1 [_{IP} t_1 \ldots$

The analysis of *what the hell* suggested above extends to *ittai* in Japanese as well. Consider (130), repeated here as (149).

(149) *Mary-wa $[_{NP}[_{CP}$ John-ni ittai   nani-o   ageta] hito]-ni
     Mary-top   John-to the hell what-acc gave   person-to
     atta no
     met
     'Mary met the person that gave what the hell to John'

If *ittai nani-o* must adjoin to the VP of the relative clause first and leave a trace in that adjoined position, as we suggested for *what the hell* in (133), then the LF representation of (149) will be as in (150).

(150) ... $[_{NP}[_{CP} \text{Op}_2 [_{C'}[_{IP} e_2 [_{VP} t_1' [_{VP} \text{John-ni } t_1 \text{ ageta}]]] C_2]] \text{hito}_2] \ldots$

The trace t_1' is not properly governed and hence violates the ECP.[33]

An alternative analysis for Japanese *ittai* would be to treat it directly as an adjunct. As shown in (151), *ittai* can be separated from the WH that it is associated with.

(151) John-wa ittai   Mary-ni nani-o   watasita no
     John-top the hell Mary-to what-acc handed
     'What the hell did John hand to Mary'

Hence, it is not clear that *ittai* and *nani* form a constituent in (149). If not, then *ittai* can be regarded as an adverbial polarity item associated with Q-morphemes in COMP. And if *ittai* itself must move to the SPEC of a [+WH] COMP in LF, then given that it is not a complement, we would expect it to pattern exactly like *naze* 'why'. Thus, (149) can be accounted for in exactly the same way as (134).[34]

In conclusion, we note again that Pesetsky's D-linking analysis is supported by data such as (123) and (124), repeated here as (152) and (153).

(152) *Mary asked [$_{CP}$ what$_2$ [$_{IP}$ who read t_2]]

(153) Mary asked [$_{CP}$ which book$_2$ [$_{IP}$ which man read t_2]]

The contrast between (152) and (153) suggests that some notion like D-linking may play a role in the grammar. However, we have argued that many of the central phenomena used to motivate the D-linking analysis receive an adequate, or even more adequate, account in terms of the ECP as developed in this monograph.

5.5 CP, VP, and Barrierhood

5.5.1 *That*-Trace Effect Revisited

We noted in chapter 2, when we abandoned the traditional S' analysis of clause structure in favor of the CP hypothesis, that *that*-trace effects were no longer straightforwardly accounted for in the terms of L&S, since now there are two "positions in COMP" rather than just one. We will now explore how the blocking effect of *that* on antecedent government can be recaptured.

First, given our conclusion in chapter 4 that only X^0 categories can be antecedent governors, even in an example like (154), the WH-phrase cannot be the antecedent governor for the trace.

(154) who$_1$ t_1 left

The structure of (154) is more precisely as in (155).

(155) [$_{CP}$ who$_1$ [$_{C'}$ C [$_{IP}$ t_1 left]]]

We assumed in this case that COMP is assigned the index of the WH-phrase through SPEC-head agreement. Then, COMP antecedent-governs the subject trace in (155). The following example can be analyzed in the same way:

(156) who$_1$ do you think [$_{CP}$ t_1' [$_{C'}$ C [$_{IP}$ t_1 left]]]

By SPEC-head agreement, the embedded COMP receives the index *1* and antecedent-governs the subject trace.

Now, consider the *that*-trace violation in (157).

(157) *who$_1$ do you think [$_{CP}$ t_1' [$_{C'}$ that [$_{IP}$ t_1 left]]]

If the presence of *that* in the COMP blocks SPEC-head agreement, then (157) is accounted for as an ECP violation. The intermediate trace t_1', being an X^{max}, does not antecedent-govern the subject trace. And the COMP, without SPEC-head agreement, does not have the index *1*, which is necessary for the COMP to antecedent-govern the subject trace. The question, then, is why SPEC-head agreement in CP fails when *that* is present.

Here, we suggest that SPEC-head agreement fails in (157) because the intermediate trace and *that* do not share appropriate features. We have assumed so far that verbs taking sentential complements select for a [+WH] COMP or a [−WH] COMP. Verbs such as *think* select for a [−WH] COMP, whereas those such as *wonder* select for a [+WH] COMP. Further, we proposed, on the basis of examples such as (158)–(159), that *that* and intermediate traces both have the feature [−WH].

(158) a.   John thinks [that [Mary left]]
       b.   who$_1$ does John think [t_1' [t_1 left]]
(159) a.   *John wonders [that [Mary left]]
       b.   *who$_1$ does John wonder [t_1' [t_1 left]]

The examples in (158) indicate that *that* can appear in a [−WH] COMP, and that intermediate traces can appear in the SPEC position of a [−WH] COMP. Those in (159), on the other hard, show that neither can be in the head or the SPEC position of a [+WH] COMP. (159b), in particular, shows that intermediate traces, unlike WH-phrases, cannot serve to satisfy the requirement that a [+WH] COMP must have a [+WH] SPEC.

The important distinction here is that between those elements with the feature [+WH] and those without. So, let us assume now that verbs like *think* select, not for a [−WH] COMP, but for a COMP without the feature [+WH].[35] Then, the head COMP of a CP complement of such verbs can have either the feature [−WH] or no feature at all. Given these two possibilities, we can now assume that *that* is [−WH], whereas traces are not marked for the [±WH] feature. Since *that* in effect is a marker for a proposition as opposed to a question, the assumption that *that* is substantively [−WH] seems reasonable. On the other hand, traces can have a [+WH] or [−WH] antecedent, and thus it also seems reasonable to assume that traces lack the [±WH] feature altogether.

With this slight modification of the [±WH] feature system, let us now return to the *that*-trace effects. The relevant examples, (154), (156), and (157), are repeated here, with appropriate structures, as (160)–(162).

(160) [$_{CP}$ who$_1$ [$_C$ +WH] [$_{IP}$ t_1 left]]

(161) who$_1$ do you think [$_{CP}$ t_1' [$_C$ e] [$_{IP}$ t_1 left]]

(162) *who$_1$ do you think [$_{CP}$ t_1' [$_C$ that] [$_{IP}$ t_1 left]]
                                              [−WH]

In order to account for the *that*-trace phenomenon, we must block COMP Indexing by SPEC-head agreement in (162), but not in (160)–(161). The desired result is obtained immediately if we assume the following condition:

(163) The index of SPEC is copied onto the head only if the SPEC and the head agree with respect to the feature [±WH].

In (160), both *who* and the COMP have the feature [+WH]. Hence, COMP receives the index *1* from the WH-phrase, and it antecedent-governs the subject trace. In (161), the intermediate trace t_1' and the empty COMP both lack the [±WH] feature. Thus, this COMP also is coindexed with, and hence antecedent-governs, the subject trace. In (162), however, the embedded COMP fails to obtain the index *1* because of (163). (The intermediate trace t_1' lacks the [±WH] feature, and the embedded COMP, dominating *that*, is [−WH].) Hence, the COMP does not antecedent-govern the subject trace, and the latter violates the ECP.

This modification of the [±WH] feature system not only allows us to account for *that*-trace effects, but at the same time enables us to extend the empirical coverage of the ECP to other well-known facts. Consider the following relative clause paradigm:

(164) a. [$_{NP}$ the man [$_{CP}$ Op$_1$ (that) [$_{IP}$ Mary saw t_1]]]
       b. [$_{NP}$ the man [$_{CP}$ Op$_1$ *(that) [$_{IP}$ t_1 saw Mary]]]
       c. [$_{NP}$ the man [$_{CP}$ Op$_1$ (that) [$_{IP}$ Mary said [$_{CP}$ t_1' [$_{IP}$ t_1 left]]]]]

Chomsky and Lasnik (1977) account for the gap in paradigm (164) with the following filter:

(165) *[$_{NP}$ NP tense VP]

Since the data in (164a–b) show the kind of subject-object asymmetry characteristic of the ECP, the null hypothesis is that the contrast does, in fact, follow from this principle.[36]

The desired result is obtained if we hypothesize that empty operators have the feature [−WH]. Then, if *that* is present in (164b), it agrees with the empty operator and receives its index. Consequently, the COMP ante-

cedent governs the subject trace. On the other hand, if *that* is absent, the
COMP node lacks the [±WH] feature altogether. Hence, the empty operator, which is [−WH], is unable to copy its index to the COMP, and
consequently COMP fails to antecedent-govern the subject trace. Thus, it
follows from the ECP that the complementizer *that* is required in (164b).
In (164a), on the other hand, the trace is in the object position. Hence, it
is lexically governed and need not be antecedent-governed. It is thus
irrelevant whether SPEC-head agreement obtains in the relative clause
CP. Finally, in (164c), the trace is in the subject position and needs to be
antecedent-governed. But the required antecedent government obtains
from the most deeply embedded COMP. This COMP is empty and hence
lacks the [±WH] feature. Thus, it receives the index of the intermediate
trace, which also lacks the [±WH] feature, and antecedent-governs the
subject trace in question. Since the intermediate trace can delete in LF,
whether the relative clause COMP receives the index of the operator
is again irrelevant. Note that this analysis of (164) is made possible by
the revised [±WH] feature system, and thus it provides support for the
proposed revision.

Another set of facts that our revised feature system may capture involves the distribution of empty complementizers. Consider the following
examples:

(166) a. John believes [(that) Mary won the race]
       b. [*(that) Mary will win the race] is obvious
       c. [*(that) Mary won the race], John already knows

These examples illustrate the general property that the complementizer
that is optional in a complement CP, but is obligatory when CP is the
subject or a topic. Stowell (1981) notes that the contrast between (166a)
and (166b), in particular, shows the kind of subject-object asymmetry
characteristic of ECP phenomena, and he proposes an account based on
this principle.[37] He first assumes that when *that* is not present in COMP,
the COMP is occupied by an empty category that is subject to the ECP. He
then proposes that COMP is the head of S′ (CP) and that lexical government percolates down to the head as follows:

(167) If Y lexically governs XP, then it lexically governs X, the head of
       XP.

Since the embedded CP in (166a) is lexically governed by the matrix verb,
its COMP is also lexically governed, due to (167). Hence, when *that* is
absent from this COMP, the empty category in its place satisfies the ECP.
On the other hand, the embedded CPs in (166b–c) are not lexically gov-

erned. Hence, when *that* is absent, the empty category in its place is neither lexically governed nor antecedent-governed. Thus, the ECP requires that *that* be present in (166b–c).

Stowell's ECP account for (166), which is based on the S′ analysis, crucially assumes that a verb can "govern into" COMP, as illustrated in (168).

(168) V $[_{S'}[_{COMP} e]$ $[_S$

This kind of lexical government is made possible by (167) and the assumption that COMP is the head of CP.[38] However, we argued in L&S and chapter 1 above, where we also assumed the S′ analysis, that verbs cannot "govern into COMP." (169) was one of the crucial examples.

(169) *how$_1$ does Bill wonder whether Mary said $[_{S'}$ t_1' $[_S$ John solved the problem t_1]]

This example has the status of an ECP violation. But the initial trace cannot violate this principle, for if it does, (170) should also be ruled out.

(170) how$_1$ did Mary say $[_{S'}$ t_1' $[_S$ John solved the problem t_1]]

Hence, it must be the intermediate trace t_1' that violates the ECP in (169). And this in turn implies that lexical government of the form shown in (171) is impossible.

(171) V $[_{S'}[_{COMP} t]$ $[_S$

Thus, Stowell's ECP account of the distribution of empty COMPs appears to be inconsistent with the theory developed here.[39]

However, the CP structure proposed by Chomsky (1986a) resolves this inconsistency directly. According to this hypothesis, intermediate traces are not in COMP, but are in the SPEC of CP position. Thus, the structures (168) and (171) are revised to (172) and (173), respectively.

(172) V $[_{CP}[_{C'}[_C e]$ $[_{IP}$ ...

(173) V $[_{CP}$ t $[_{C'}[_C e]$ $[_{IP}$ ...

The difference in the positions of the relevant empty categories in (172)–(173) enables us to make the necessary distinction: a verb cannot govern an intermediate trace. This is so because the lexical government in (172) follows directly from Stowell's (167) as before; but now, (167) has nothing to do with the case shown in (173). According to (167), lexical government "percolates down" to the head, but it does not "percolate down" to the

SPEC. To the extent that lexical government here follows from θ-marking, this distinction between head and SPEC seems well motivated. The semantic selection features of a category plausibly reside in its head, but not in its SPEC. Thus, the analysis of CP proposed by Chomsky (1986a) solves an old problem.

But it creates a new problem as well. Consider the following example:

(174) what John read is unclear

This example is not at all problematic if its structure is as in (175).

(175) $[_{S'}$ what$_1$ $[_S$ John read $t_1]]$ is unclear

However, according to the CP analysis under consideration, the structure of (174) should be as in (176).

(176) $[_{CP}$ what$_1$ $[_{C'}[_C$ $e]$ $[_{IP}$ John read $t_1]]]$ is unclear

Here, a CP with an empty head appears in the subject position. Hence, according to Stowell's analysis, (176) should be an ECP violation, exactly as (177) is.

(177) *$[_{CP}[_{C'}[_C$ $e]$ $[_{IP}$ John left]]]$ is obvious

Thus, the question arises why (176) is good.

The [±WH] feature system suggested above provides a way to distinguish between the empty COMPs in (176) and (177). The empty COMP in (176) clearly has the feature [+WH]. According to the standard analysis, the empty COMP in (177) has the feature [−WH]. But recall our suggestion that a non-[+WH] COMP is [−WH] if and only if it contains *that*. According to this suggestion, the empty COMP in (177) has no feature at all. Hence, (176) and (177) can be correctly distinguished if only those empty COMPs without the [±WH] feature are subject to the ECP. We suggest here more concretely that the [±WH] feature provides "content" to the empty COMP and consequently exempts the COMP from the ECP, perhaps for the same reason that the feature [+pronominal] exempts PRO from this principle.

Although the [+WH] feature system suggested here resolves the difficulty posed by (176)–(177), it does not provide a straightforward solution to another problem of Stowell's ECP account of the distribution of empty COMPs. It is well known that the distribution of infinitival CPs is quite free and that they occur in noncomplement positions as well as complement positions, as shown in (178).

(178) a. I tried $[_{CP}$ e $[_{IP}$ PRO to win the race]]
      b. $[_{CP}$ e $[_{IP}$ PRO to win the race]] is important
      c. John took steroids $[_{CP}$ e $[_{IP}$ PRO to win the race]]

Since the infinitival CPs in (178) have an empty COMP, their distribution should be constrained by the ECP exactly as in the case of finite CPs, according to Stowell's ECP analysis. Our revised [±WH] feature system at least provides a way to make the data in (178) consistent with Stowell's analysis. We suggested above that only those empty COMPs without a [±WH] feature are subject to the ECP. Hence, if we assume that an empty COMP in an infinitival CP, unlike an empty COMP in a finite CP, can freely have the feature [−WH], then the examples in (178) are not ruled out by the ECP. This "account" is of course hardly an explanation. Thus, the facts in (178) remain problematic, and our revised feature system merely enables us to state the problem in a more coherent way.

In this section, we suggested a slight revision of the [±WH] feature system to make the ECP account of the *that*-trace phenomenon consistent with Chomsky's (1986a) CP structure. Although the full implications of the revised [±WH] feature system remain to be seen, it does seem to facilitate an ECP account for Chomsky and Lasnik's (1977) NP-tense-VP filter facts, as well as a Stowell-type ECP account for the distribution of empty COMPs consistent with Chomsky's CP structure.

5.5.2 The Barrierhood or VP

In section 1.3.2, we noted that VP never effectively functions as a barrier for Subjacency or antecedent government. This property of VP formed the empirical basis for Chomsky's (1986a) proposal that adjunction to a maximal projection provides a path of escape from that maximal projection. But, as we discussed, that path of escape must often be prevented, necessitating, in Chomsky's theory, a set of stipulations prohibiting adjunction under many circumstances. Further, one of those stipulations, the one prohibiting adjunction of a WH-phrase to IP, turned out to be insufficient to handle the full range of WH-island effects it was designed for. Thus, as an alternative, we essentially stipulated that VP is not a barrier. We will now briefly consider what this stipulation might follow from.

Recall from chapter 3 that (non-)barrierhood is defined in terms of L-marking. An L-marked maximal projection is not a barrier. L-marking (following Chomsky (1986a)) is defined as follows:

(179) α *L-marks* β if α is a lexical category that θ-governs β.

Chomsky actually suggests in passing that INFL can θ-govern VP, its complement. Then, L-marking—hence, nonbarrierhood—of VP trivially follows if INFL is suitably lexical.[40] However, there is reason to doubt this simple account. In particular, it is not clear that the relation between

INFL and VP has any of the semantic import of that between a lexical head and its complement. Let us then consider more closely the range of configurations in which a VP complement to INFL can occur. First, INFL might itself be a V (as in the case of a sentence with a modal). Here, it might be reasonable to posit a relation of θ-government—hence, of L-marking—between the modal INFL and its complement VP. Where there is no modal, however, there is presumably no θ-government of the VP. Escape from VP must still be permitted, however, in a configuration involving an affix INFL and a main verb. In this case, as argued by Lasnik (1981), in English INFL lowers to the verb. We suggested in note 18 of chapter 4 that a structure resulting from INFL movement is no longer an IP, but rather, is a projection of V. But then, even if VP is not L-marked and hence is a barrier, movement out of VP will still be allowed, as long as it is to the immediately dominating maximal projection. Thus, both of these configurations do yield the desired permeability of VP, under plausible assumptions. However, the third possible configuration involving VP is problematic. Where VP is headed by a verb that raises to INFL (an "auxiliary" verb), IP will clearly have a head and we will thus surely not dispense with IP by the result of this raising. Further, it cannot be that the raised verb L-marks the VP it has left behind, since, given the Projection Principle, transformational operations cannot create new configurations of θ-government. Thus, the raised *has* in (180) should θ-mark the lower VP, and not the VP complement to INFL.

(180) Mary wonders [who$_1$ [Bill has$_2$ [$_{VP_j}$ t_2 [$_{VP}$ seen t_1]]]]

Hence, the permeability of VP$_j$ in the embedded clause in (180) is still unexplained.[41]

Given this difficulty, let us consider an alternative. Note that L-marking distinguishes between NPs that are or are not θ-governed (complements vs. subjects) and similarly between CPs that are or are not θ-governed (complements vs. adjuncts). If it is the case, as hinted above, that VP is never θ-governed, then for this category, there is no such distinction to be made.[42] That is, L-marking is simply irrelevant for VP. Suppose, then, that lack of L-marking results in barrierhood only for those categories for which L-marking is relevant. By hypothesis, VP would thus never be a barrier.[43] Given the lack of an alternative, we will tentatively adopt this hypothesis.

5.5.3 Barriers and the Definition or Government

Chomsky (1986a) had as one of his goals the unification of the locality requirement not only for Subjacency and antecedent government but also for government. Our project, ultimately, has necessarily been less ambitious than this. We have repeatedly found that the locality demanded for movement and antecedent government is not as strict as that necessary for government. For example, VP is a barrier for government, but not for movement or antecedent government. This entails that, to the extent that "antecedent government" is defined in terms of barriers, "government" should not be.

As far as we can tell, this conclusion raises no major difficulties. Aoun and Sportiche's (1982/83) characterization of government in (181a), with one slight extension in (181b) proposed by Stowell (1981) and Belletti and Rizzi (1981), serves adequately for our purposes.

(181) a. α *governs* β if every maximal projection dominating α dominates β and conversely.

b. If α governs β, then α governs the head of β.

One case that is explained nicely in Chomsky's (1986a) theory, but which may be problematic for (181), is "exceptional" government, as in exceptional Case marking configurations:

(182) I believe [$_{IP}$ John to be clever]

Here, *believe* apparently governs *John* despite the presence of an intervening maximal projection boundary. According to Chomsky's (1986a) theory, where maximal projections block government only when they are barriers, exceptional government is directly accommodated. The IP in (182) is L-marked by *believe* and hence is not a barrier. The definition in (181), on the other hand, disallows such government, apparently an incorrect consequence. However, following Davis (1984), we suggest that appearances are deceiving and that in (182), *believe* does not actually govern *John*. Rather, *believe* governs its IP complement, in the normal fashion; then, by (181b), *believe* governs the head INFL of that IP, thus transferring its accusative Case assigning feature to that INFL. INFL then assigns Case to its specifier as in finite constructions. The only difference is with respect to the specific Case assigned.

Notes

Chapter 1

1. The principles-and-parameters approach is explained in detail in Chomsky 1981, 1982.

2. (1b) is acceptable as an echo question, but not as a "normal" question. We are concerned here only with the latter.

3. The following constraint proposed by Chomsky (1973:281) seems to have a similar effect: "A [+WH] COMP is interpreted only when it contains a WH-phrase [i.e., at S-structure]."

4. More precisely, X and Y not only must be lexical but also must both be immediate constituents of COMP for the filter to apply.

5. Those languages satisfy (14) trivially. Since there is no syntactic WH-movement, a [−WH] COMP cannot have a [+WH] head at S-structure.

6. *Koto* 'the fact that' is added to the end of some example sentences in Japanese to avoid the unnaturalness resulting from the lack of a topic in a matrix sentence.

7. See Hong 1985, where a similar account is proposed for Korean. Note that *ka* is here assumed to be equivalent to the feature [+WH], and not a complementizer occupying the head position of COMP. Consequently, the presence of *ka* in a [+WH] COMP does not by itself satisfy the filter (13).

8. Matrix questions are usually uttered with rising intonation at the end, and such rising intonation is obligatory in matrix questions without *ka* such as (25b).

9. See, for example, Baker 1970, Chomsky 1973, May 1977, AHS, Kayne 1981a. Baker and Chomsky did not explicitly make use of an LF level, but their observations and analyses can easily be translated into a framework with such a level.

10. As noted earlier, the matrix COMP of a WH-question in French need not be specified [+WH] at S-structure. We assume that such a COMP will be [+WH] at LF. Then, in French, a WH can move in LF into a COMP that is not headed by a WH-phrase at S-structure.

11. See Huang 1982 for a detailed discussion of similar facts in Chinese.

12. Another [+WH] that can be base-generated in COMP is *if*.

13. Noting that a WH in COMP cannot move to a different COMP in LF, AHS state that an instance of LF WH-movement can originate only from an A-position. The account in terms of (39) in the text gives this result for the relevant cases.

14. As pointed out in note 5, (51) is trivially satisfied at S-structure in languages without syntactic WH-movement. But given that satisfaction is trivial, there is no particular reason to assume that (51) actually acts as a *filter* at S-structure in those languages. We will assume that it does not, so that we may group (50) and (51) together, as seems natural.

15. See Cattell 1976 and Kayne 1981b for similar proposals. For the definition of *proper government*, see section 1.3.

16. Since the movement in (60) crosses NP and S, the question arises why the example does not violate Subjacency. See Chomsky 1977a for relevant discussion. This problem does not arise with the formulation of Subjacency in Chomsky 1986a, which we discuss in detail in chapter 3.

17. LF WH-movement is indicated by an arrow in (61)–(64). For some speakers, some of these examples are slightly degraded. But they are clearly far better than examples with corresponding syntactic WH-movement. For example, (64) contrasts sharply with (i), which involves syntactic WH-movement out of a subject.

(i) ?*who$_1$ did Mary say that friends of t_1 hit Bill

Similarly, (ii) is perhaps marginal, but it contrasts sharply with (iii).

(ii) ?who$_1$ did pictures of who impress t_1

(iii) ?*who$_1$ did pictures of t_1 impress who

18. The particle *no* at the end of the examples is often used in matrix questions. It differs from *ka* in that it cannot be used as a Q-morpheme in embedded questions, as shown in (i).

(i) John-ga [$_{S'}$ Mary-ga nani-o katto $\left\{ \begin{array}{c} \text{ka} \\ \text{*no} \end{array} \right\}$] siritagatteiru koto

John-nom Mary-nom what-acc bought   want-to-know fact
'the fact that John wants to know what Mary bought'

19. Contrasts such as those in (67)–(68) are observed independently by Bolinger (1978). Bolinger also notes that *where* and *when* pattern with *what*, rather than with *why*, citing examples such as (i) and (ii).

(i) who gets her groceries where

(ii) who got his answer when

For these and related phenomena, Huang proposes that locative and temporal interrogative forms contain a phonetically null preposition. This preposition serves as a "lexical governor" in a sense to be made precise immediately below.

20. AHS assume that (72) applies at S-structure. Following Huang (1982), we assume that it applies at LF as well.

21. (75) is somewhat marginal. In general, there is an LF effect that superficially resembles the WH-island effect in Japanese. However, the WH-island constraint

does not straightforwardly extend to LF movement, given the acceptability of such English examples as (61), or of (48) on the matrix scope interpretation of *what*.

22. In (75)–(76), the WH in situ cannot move to the embedded COMP and take scope there. In general, a COMP containing *whether* does not allow another WH. For example, the following sentence is unambiguous:

(i) who$_1$ t_1 wonders whether John bought what

The WH in situ, *what*, must be in the matrix COMP and cannot be in the embedded COMP at LF. We assume that this is because *whether* does not undergo absorption (in approximately the sense of Higginbotham and May (1981)) with any other WH.

23 We will return directly to the question of whether traces in COMP are themselves subject to the ECP.

24. We assume, although not crucially, that the objective Case marker is stranded by the LF movement of the object and functions as a proper governor for the trace. See Saito 1989 for an alternative possibility.

25. An alternative way to rule out (94) as an LF representation of (91) would be to assume as in AHS that each instance of LF WH-movement can originate only from an A-position. (See note 13 above.) Then, LF COMP-to-COMP movement is disallowed, and hence, (94) is an impossible LF representation for (91). However, we will not adopt this approach here, since, as we will show in section 1.4, there is evidence that LF COMP-to-COMP movement is in fact possible.

26. Another possibility, which we will not pursue here, is that VP is not a maximal projection—in particular, that S′ is a projection of V. See Kayne 1981b and Bouchard 1982 for relevant discussion.

27. More precisely, we proposed in section 1.1 that the trace is in the head position of the COMP, and the COMP is the head of the S′. We assume here that "X is a head of Y" is a transitive relation. Then, the trace in (104) is in the head position of the S′, since it is in the head position of COMP, which heads the S′.

28. The notions "bind" and "c-command" are defined as follows (Reinhart 1981):

(i) α *binds* β if
 a. α c-commands β, and
 b. α and β are coindexed.

(ii) α *c-commands* β if neither α nor β dominates the other and the branching node most immediately dominating α dominates β.

29. We assume here that the trace of *why* is bound after absorption (in the sense of Higginbotham and May (1981)) applies to LF representations, thus satisfying the condition against free variables in semantic representations.

30. Given our assumption that S is a maximal projection, it is of course not clear why it is not a barrier to government.

31. Further, as noted in Chomsky 1981, the structure in (117) is excluded quite generally, even in languages in which S is not a bounding node.

32. See L&S for discussion of the intermediate status of (i) (= L&S (154)).

(i) ?*someone who John expected *t* would be successful though believing *e* is
    incompetent

33. Hence, this analysis of (131) implies that LF COMP-to-COMP movement is possible. Huang (1982:552) presents exactly the same argument for LF COMP-to-COMP movement on the basis of the behavior of the "A-not-A" operator, which we will discuss below (136).

34. In chapter 2, we will argue that Move α need not produce a trace unless the trace is required by independent principles, such as the ECP and the Projection Principle. Given this assumption, relativization in (149)–(150) need not leave an intermediate trace in COMP, provided that Subjacency is a condition on movement rather than on representation.

35. The embedded S′ in (156) has the complementizer *to* in the COMP, and we might expect this complementizer to block antecedent government of the trace of *naze* 'why' at LF. However, as indicated by (i), there are no *that*-trace effects with adjunct traces in general.

(i) why$_1$ do you think [that [John left t_1]]

This is curious since overt complementizers do block the antecedent government of subject traces:

(ii) *who$_1$ do you think [that [t left]]

We will discuss this subject-adjunct asymmetry in detail in chapter 2.

36. (159) is somewhat marginal, but it is far better than (157). See note 21. In addition, (159)–(160) are both quite awkward, presumably because of the processing difficulty inherent in center-embedded constructions.

Chapter 2

1. In these examples, we have used a WH-phrase as the scrambled item to ensure that scrambling, rather than some sort of left dislocation, is what is involved. WH-phrases do not left-dislocate in Japanese. See Saito 1985 for discussion of this and other relevant properties of scrambling.

2. See Koopman and Sportiche 1985 for the clausal structure in (15). The structure in (15) is supported independently for Japanese sentences in Kitagawa 1986, Fukui 1986, and Kuroda 1988, among others. See also Whitman 1986 for relevant discussion.

3. For example, if there were symmetric binding between subject and object, (i) would incorrectly violate Condition C.

(i) John$_1$-no hahaoya-ga kare$_1$-o aisiteiru (koto)
    John-'s   mother-nom he-acc love   fact
    'John's mother loves him'

See Saito 1985, Hoji 1985, Whitman 1986, and the references cited there for various binding asymmetries between subject and object in Japanese.

4. Part of the motivation for the VP-internal subject hypothesis was to provide an answer to this question. (See Koopman and Sportiche 1985, Kuroda 1988, Fukui

1986, and Kitagawa 1986.) The hypothesis states, roughly, that the D-structure representation of English sentences is as in (17), and that the subject NP moves to the SPEC of IP position to receive Case. According to this hypothesis, then, the hierarchical structures of English and Japanese sentences are identical, except for the S-structure position of the subject NP.

5. This is denied by Aoun et al. (1987), who claim that *why* does show *that*-trace effects. Perhaps there is some sort of dialect difference at work here, because speakers we have consulted find no such effects. Incidentally, Aoun et al. acknowledge that "Some speakers claim to get a lower-clause interpretation for *why* in [an example like (19b)] even if a complementizer is present" (p. 563). But they reject these judgments because "we have found that when asked to repeat the sentence, those speakers omit *that*, as if it was not perceived." This argument is rather difficult to evaluate, since no information is provided about controls with complement extraction or, indeed, with no extraction at all. We suspect that when it is deletable, *that* will be rather freely deleted. If this is correct, no conclusions can be drawn about *that*-trace effects with adjuncts.

6. Some dialects of Japanese do allow complementizer deletion. See Saito 1984, 1986 for discussion of these dialects.

7. Kyle Johnson (personal communication) suggests that in a language with syntactic complementizer deletion, like English, COMP is deletable in LF only in a configuration in which it would be deletable in the syntax. That is, whatever prevents deletion in one component would likewise prevent it in the other. If this is correct, then LF *that*-deletion would be impossible in (31a–b).

8. If *that* is deleted, and another intermediate trace created, then the latter violates the ECP.

9. A problem arises concerning the status of *whether*. If it is under COMP in (i), then the COMP, which is [+WH], violates the filter in (48).

(i) John wonders [$_{CP}$[$_{C'}$[$_C$ whether] [$_{IP}$ Mary left]]]

We will thus assume here, following a suggestion by Caroline Heycock (personal communication), that *whether* is base-generated in the SPEC of CP position.

There is one further phenomenon that tends to support this assumption. Examples like (ii) are somewhat degraded as compared with (iii).

(ii) ??what do you wonder whether John bought *t*

(iii) what do you think that John bought *t*

The derivation of (iii) is now straightforward. *What* moves out of the embedded clause via the SPEC of CP. Subjacency is thus not violated. If a similar derivation is available for (ii), there should be no difference in status between the two examples, contrary to fact. Thus, the contrast between (ii) and (iii) once again points to the conclusion that *whether* is generated in SPEC of CP, rather than in COMP.

10. Stowell (1981) and Chomsky and Lasnik (1977) assume (62) in the syntax. We are extending it to LF as well, the null hypothesis.

11. We assume, as in L&S, that movement need not leave a trace unless the trace is required by independent principles. This is, of course, the null hypothesis, since it does away with the stipulation that movement must produce a trace.

12. The superficially similar, but well-formed, (i) will be shown in chapter 4 to have a different structure.

(i) how likely to win is John

13. For another lowering analysis, see May 1977, 1985, where the scope ambiguity of examples such as (i) is accounted for in those terms.

(i) someone is likely to win the race

14. See Chomsky 1976 for discussion.

15. See Lasnik 1976 for discussion.

16. Samuel David Epstein (personal communication) suggests that the deletion of the trace in (84) is blocked possibly not only by the EPP part of Conservation, but also by recoverability as well. We may assume, for example, that if the subject trace is deleted, then the θ-role, or the Case it bears, would not be recoverable.

17. For detailed discussion of chain formation, see Rizzi 1986a, Barss 1986, and Epstein 1987.

18. This trace thus differs from an adjunct trace, which is not required by the EPP.

19. The S-structure representation (93) is generated if the movement of *how* does not leave an initial trace, or if the initial trace is deleted.

20. See Epstein 1987 for an alternative reduction of principle (86).

Chapter 3

1. (2) might seem to be a condition on representation, but Chomsky apparently does not intend that it be necessarily construed that way.

2. Based on a suggestion made by Kyle Johnson, Chomsky speculates that (17) might follow from the θ-Criterion.

3. Chomsky's analysis of the *that*-trace effect relies on the notion "minimality." In (i), $t_1{}'$ fails to antecedent-govern t_1 because *that* constitutes a closer governor.

(i) ... $[_{C'' (=S')} t_1{}' [_{C'}$ that $[_{IP} t_1$ won the race]]]

Where *that* is absent, we have (ii).

(ii) ... $[_{C''} t_1{}' [_{C'} e [t_1$ won the race]]]

In this case, e, being featureless, does not count as a relevant governor and minimality is not invoked.

4. Chomsky (1986a) has *how* originating within VP. This difference will ultimately not be crucial in most cases. But see note 24 below.

5. Samuel David Epstein (personal communication) points out that the following example may be problematic for Chomsky's formulation of the ECP:

(i) *how$_1$ do you $[_{VP} t_1{}' [_{VP}$ resent $[_{NP}$ the destruction of the city $t_1]]]$

There is no barrier between $t_1{}'$ and t in this example; hence, the former should be able to antecedent-govern the latter. Thus, this example is not ruled out by the ECP.

One possible solution for this problem, suggested by Stowell (1989), would be to adopt the DP analysis, proposed by Fukui and Speas (1986), among others, and to assume that the NP complement of D is a barrier. According to this hypothesis, the structure of (i) is as in (ii), and the NP constitutes a barrier for antecedent government.

(ii) *how$_1$ do you [$_{VP}$ t_1' [$_{VP}$ resent [$_{DP}$ the [$_{NP}$ destruction of the city t_1]]]]

Essentially the same analysis is given for Japanese examples similar to (i) by Saito and Murasugi (1989). As far as we know, this analysis is consistent with Chomsky's (1986a) theory, and with the modification of it that we propose here. However, the exact implications of the DP analysis for the ECP still need to be investigated. For relevant discussion, see Stowell 1989 and the references cited there.

6. We reserve the term *left dislocation* for constructions involving a bound position: either a pronoun, as in (28), or an anaphoric epithet, as in (i).

(i) John$_1$, I like the nut$_1$

This construction is occasionally confused with the *as for* construction, as in (ii), but their properties are quite different.

(ii) as for John, I like him

Unlike the former construction, the latter does not demand predication:

(iii) *sports, I like baseball

(iv) as for sports, I like baseball

Another difference is that the possibility of left dislocation is subject to substantial dialectal variation, whereas the *as for* construction apparently is not.

7. Examples such as (42) are not totally unacceptable, for some speakers. We speculate that for those speakers, the embedded clause can be construed as a matrix clause in some sense, possibly along the lines suggested by Bresnan (1969), who analyzes certain superficial matrix clauses as adsententials. When no such analysis is available, for example, in the case of sentential subjects, the results are clearly ungrammatical for all speakers. See (43)–(44) in the text.

8. Syntactically, topicalization seems quite similar to scrambling in Japanese. According to the analysis proposed in Saito 1985, scrambling is a leftward adjunction operation. Thus, when the object NP precedes the subject NP in Japanese, as in (i), the former is adjoined to IP, as shown in (ii).

(i) John-o   Mary-ga   nagutta
    John-aac Mary-nom hit
    'Mary hit John'

(ii) [$_{IP}$ John-o$_1$ [$_{IP}$ Mary-ga t_1 nagutta]]

9. Chomsky presents only one argument that INFL does not L-mark VP: VP must be a barrier for V-raising to prevent "long" raising as in (i).

(i) *[how tall]$_2$ be$_1$ [$_{IP}$ John [$_{I'}$ will [$_{VP}$ t_1 t_2]]]

Chomsky argues that t_1 must be in violation of the ECP, but that this result obtains only if VP is a barrier. We have no concrete alternative to offer, but one might conjecture that this head constraint is actually a Condition A effect rather than an ECP effect.

10. Baltin's account is based on essentially the formulation of Subjacency presented in Chomsky 1973 and Rizzi 1980.

11. Note that the matrix IP, though it is a barrier, is not a relevant barrier, since movement is to a position within CP, the maximal projection immediately dominating IP.

12. At this point, we do not offer any account for the rather surprising contrast between (86) and (87). In fact, island violations with NPs are generally less severe than those with non-NPs. See section 5.1 for further discussion.

13. We speculate, following Chomsky (1986a), that Case is adjoined to the maximal projection, creating a barrier. This, however, raises certain other problems (e.g., for the θ-criterion).

14. Other facts that may be accounted for by assuming that oblique Case assignment creates a barrier are shown in (ic) and (iib).

(i) a.   who$_1$ did you see a picture of t_1
   b.   ?who$_1$ did you see friends of t_1
   c.   ?*who$_1$ did you see a picture of friends of t_1

(ii) a.   what$_1$ did you put your paper under t_1
   b.   ?*who$_1$ did you put your paper under a book about t_1

If N assigns oblique Case to its complement, then *friends of t_1* in (ic) constitutes a barrier. In addition, if P assigns oblique Case as well, then the ungrammaticality of (iib) is accounted for since *a book about t_1* is a barrier.

15. Fiengo's definition of *bound* was somewhat different from current ones. But his central point carries over. The relevant notion of binding that we assume here is the one statable in terms of "strong" c-command:

(i) α *c-commands* β iff neither α nor β dominates the other and every branching node dominating α dominates β.

See Reinhart 1976 for discussion.

16. Samuel David Epstein (personal communication) points out that given our account, the following example provides support for free indexing of A-positions at S-structure, as proposed by Chomsky (1980, 1982):

(i) ?*the coach$_1$ is too important [$_{CP}$ Op$_1$ for [$_{IP}$[$_{NP}$ close friends of t_1] to [$_{VP}$ win]]]

(i) has the same status as (89). However, in this example, if *the coach$_1$* is coindexed with t_1, it seems that the operator can first adjoin to VP, and then move to SPEC of CP, without violating the Generalized Proper Binding Condition. Epstein observes that (i) is ruled out by the condition if free indexing applies at S-structure. Under this assumption, *the coach* does not receive its index until this level and therefore cannot serve as the binder of t_1 when the movement takes place.

17. For our purposes here, we assume the following, somewhat simplified formulation of Kuno's (1973) Clause Nonfinal Incomplete Constituent Constraint:

(i) ... [$_\alpha$ X β Y]

Extraction out of β is prohibited if α immediately dominates β and Y is nonnull.

It is not clear to us at this point what the exact statement of this generalization should be, or how this generalization can be explained in a principled way.

18. In section 4.1.2.2, we provide further evidence for this structure.

19. May's discussion was actually couched in terms of the framework of Chomsky 1980, but its essentials carry over to that of Chomsky 1981.

20. See Epstein 1986 for important discussion of the notion "local binding." For present purposes, the following characterization, adapted from Chomsky 1981:59, suffices:

(i) α locally binds β iff α binds β and there is no γ that binds β and is bound by α.

21. While acknowledging the similarities between configurations allowing antecedent government and those satisfying Subjacency, we argued against the unification of those two configurations in L&S. The strongest evidence for this conclusion was the existence of parametric variation for Subjacency (Rizzi 1980, Sportiche 1981/82, Torrego 1984) and the lack of such variation for antecedent government. For example, extraction of a complement out of a WH-island results in a Subjacency violation in English, but it is allowed in Spanish, as shown in (i) (= L&S's (126)).

(i) qué libro$_1$ no   sabes   [por qué$_2$ te   habrán regalado t_1 t_2]
    what book NEG (you) know why   (they) to you have   given
    'what book don't you know why they have given to you'

On the other hand, extraction of an adjunct out of a WH-island is, as far as we know, disallowed in any language. The following Spanish example (= L&S's (127)) violates the ECP:

(ii) *por qué$_2$ no   sabes   [qué libro$_1$ te   harbrán regalado t_1 t_2]
     why   NEG (you) know what book (they) to you have   given
     'why don't you know what book (they) have given to you'

If the locality relations involved in antecedent government and Subjacency are the same, then we expect, contrary to fact, that the same variation is observed in the Subjacency phenomenon and the ECP phenomenon.

Here, we will simply assume the formulation of Subjacency proposed above, and continue to examine its consequences. But it should be noted that the parametric variation in Subjacency (e.g., why (i) is good) remains unexplained. See Chomsky 1986a for relevant discussion.

22. In chapter 4, we will show that (114) is ruled out independently of the Subjacency requirement for antecedent government. Such is not the case for (115), however.

23. It might be claimed that (113), (116), and (117) violate the crossing constraint and hence need not be ruled out by the ECP. However, they are worse than the following examples, which similarly involve crossing but do not violate the ECP:

(i) ?*John$_1$, this book$_2$, Mary thinks [$_{CP}$ t_1' [$_{IP}$ t_1 likes t_2]]

(ii) ?*I know who$_1$, this book$_2$, Mary thinks [$_{CP}$ t_1' [$_{IP}$ t_1 likes t_2]]

The subject trace t_1 in these examples, unlike that in (113), (116), and (117), is antecedent-governed by the intermediate trace t_1'. Thus, we assume that (113), (116), and (117) violate the ECP in addition to crossing.

24. If the initial trace of *how* must be in VP, as assumed by Chomsky (1986a), this analysis must be modified. See chapter 4, note 18.

25. Chomsky assumes that *after* in (131)–(132) is a P taking a CP complement. The analysis of these examples outlined in the text is not affected in any essential way even if we adopt this assumption.

26. This result directly generalizes to (i).

(i) which book$_1$ did you buy t_1 [$_{CP}$[$_{IP}$ PRO to read PG$_1$]]]

In this case, the IP in the adjunct is not L-marked, since it is not the complement of any lexical head. But this is irrelevant if the empty operator moves to the SPEC of CP position as in (ii).

(ii) ... [$_{CP}$ Op$_1$ [$_{IP}$ PRO to read t_1]]

The adjunct CP is a barrier for Op$_1$, but the operator is still subjacent to t_1, since the maximal projection immediately dominating this CP dominates t_1 as well.

27. In the latter case, it is actually movement to and from VP that potentially led to the undesired derivation. The latter movement need not leave a trace in VP.

28. (143b) seems to have as one of its consequences the effect of L-marking via a chain. Thus, in (141b), the constituent [pictures of t_1] is not in an L-marked position, but it heads a chain whose tail, t_2, is L-marked by *wanted*. There is no such L-marking in (141a). Note that these chain effects are crucially limited to $\bar{\text{A}}$-chains, as implied by (143b). This is necessary since a derived subject behaves as though it were non-L-marked (i.e., like a barrier) with respect to extraction, even if it heads an A-chain whose tail is in an L-marked position. This is illustrated in (i).

(i) ?*who$_1$ did you think that [pictures of t_1]$_2$ were painted t_2

However, as shown by (144b), (143b) covers cases that cannot be analyzed as L-marking via a chain.

29. Chomsky (1986a) takes (144a–b) as evidence that the embedded WH-phrases in these examples are L-marked. He suggests that when α is L-marked, its SPEC is also L-marked. In (144a–b), the embedded CP is L-marked, and the embedded WH-phrase is in the SPEC position of this CP. Hence, the embedded WH-phrases in (144a–b) are L-marked (although not θ-governed) and consequently are not barriers.

Although this hypothesis seems plausible, we will not adopt it here, since it does not extend to cases such as (141b) and (144c). The embedded topics in these examples are adjoined to IP and hence are neither L-marked nor in the SPEC position of an L-marked constituent.

30. A typical example of crossing is given in (i).

(i) *what$_1$ do you wonder who$_2$ John gave t_1 to t_2

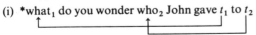

Although it is not clear how to characterize "crossing" precisely, (145) will be a case of crossing under either Baker's (1977) or Pesetsky's (1982) formulation. Examples such as (ii) also fall under Baker's (1977) formulation of crossing.

(ii) ?*who$_1$ did you give t_2 to t_1 [$_{NP}$ a book about syntactic theory]$_2$

31. The contrast between (147a) and (147b) can be accounted for if in the former, the NP *friends of* t_1 constitutes a barrier, as a result of oblique Case assignment by the preposition *to*. See note 14 for discussion.

32. The contrast between (ib) and (iib), which is somewhat weaker than that between (146) and (147), suggests that not only P but also V cannot be [+top].

(i) a. ??Mary thinks that [$_{VP}$ read this book]$_1$, she should t_1
     b. *Which book$_2$ does Mary think that [$_{VP}$ read t_2]$_1$ she should t_1

(ii) a. ??Mary thinks that [$_{VP}$ find a picture of John]$_1$, she should t_1
     b. ?*which man$_2$ does Mary think that [$_{VP}$ find a picture of t_2]$_1$, she should t_1

33. We have considered "extraposed" relative clauses in the text, and for these, some sort of predication mechanism seems appropriate. "Extraposed" complements, however, do not seem amenable to such a treatment. Consider (i) and (ii).

(i)   the proof that John was guilty was presented

(ii) the proof was presented that John was guilty

If *that John was guilty* is the complement of *proof* in (ii), then the θ-Criterion and Projection Principle evidently demand that that CP originate in complement position and leave a trace. But we have seen that no such derivation is possible. Here, we conjecture that, contrary to appearances, the relationship in (ii) is not one of complementation but one of modification, with *that John is guilty* base-generated in situ.

Some support for this conjecture comes from the following paradigm:

(iii)   the proof that John was guilty was interrupted

(iv)   ?*the proof was interrupted that John was guilty

We assume that the "process" reading necessary here must involve complementation. Unlike the situation with (i)–(ii), the noun cannot be designating an object, but rather, is a true nominalization of a verb. But then, the ungrammaticality of (iv) is predicted. In this case, the θ-Criterion would demand a movement derivation. However, as we have shown in the text, such a derivation is unavailable.

Chapter 4

1. More precisely, we embed "inheritence" in our definition of *subjacent*. According to the definition in (2), the "actual barriers" that break subjacent relations are those maximal projections immediately dominating a barrier. Thus, we could consider those the "genuine" barriers and say, instead of (5d), that all barriers are barriers by inheritance and that there are no "inherent" barriers.

2. Recall that the SPEC position of the embedded CP is available for the successive-cyclic movement of *John* in (7). On such a derivation, (7) is not ruled out by the Subjacency Condition.

3. See (35) of chapter 2, and the subsequent discussion of its status as a principle.

4. (17) is in certain respects reminiscent of Jaeggli's (1982) hypothesis that traces must be both lexically governed and antecedent-governed. (Also see Stowell 1986, Aoun et al. 1987, Jaeggli 1985, and Chomsky 1986a.) Under this hypothesis, t_1 in

(9) is antecedent-governed, but may fail to be lexically governed and hence violate the ECP. However, we are not adopting Jaeggli's conjunctive ECP here, but rather are accepting Stowell's and Rizzi's assumption that both lexical governors and antecedent governors must be X^0 categories. We will return to Rizzi's argument for this hypothesis in section 4.1.2.

Note also that (17) is incompatible with Chomsky's (1986a) analysis of examples such as (i), where the intermediate trace adjoined to VP is assumed to antecedent govern the initial trace.

(i) how$_1$ [$_{IP}$ did you [$_{VP}$ (t_1') [$_{VP}$ solve the problem t_1]]]

(17) implies that such antecedent government is impossible. The empirical difference between Chomsky's approach and ours is much narrower than these considerations might suggest, however. This is so because for Chomsky, almost all adjoined intermediate traces are used to circumvent the barrierhood of VP. But for us, VP is not a barrier at all, hence, such circumvention is irrelevant.

5. Notice that in addition to the possibilities discussed in the text, a topicalized anaphor can be bound by virtue of the position of its trace, as in (i).

(i) Mary thinks that himself, John likes t

See Barss 1986 for extensive discussion of these and related cases.

6. For our purposes here, we can assume the statement of Condition A in (i), the definition of *governing category* in (ii), and the definition of *accessible SUBJECT* in (iii), which closely follow the proposals in Chomsky 1981.

(i)   An anaphor must be bound in its governing category.

(ii) α is the *governing category* for β if α is the minimal maximal projection dominating (a) β, (b) a governor of β or of a member of an $\bar{A}$-chain containing β, and (c) a SUBJECT accessible to β.

(iii) α is a *SUBJECT accessible to β* if
      a. α is a subject or AGR, and
      b. α c-commands or directly agrees with β (or alternatively, α m-commands β, in the sense of Chomsky (1986a)).

7. Chomsky (1986b) proposes a rather different treatment of Condition A effects than that assumed here. However, our basic point seems to carry over. That is, we see no way that the relation between *John* and *himself* in (21b) can be distinguished from the corresponding relation in (23b). Hence, as in the theory we assume, the offending relation in (23b) must be that between *himself* and its trace.

8. Juan Uriagereka (personal communication) points out one possibly problematic consequence of our account. Given that long topicalization of a subject is always possible (via SPEC of CP), nothing should prevent long topicalization of a nominative anaphor as in (i). However, the example is degraded, as indicated.

(i) ??John thinks that himself, Mary said t won the race

Compare (ii):

(ii) John thinks that himself, Mary thinks Susan likes t

We have no account for the less acceptable status of (i) vis-à-vis (ii). However, we suggest that the ECP is not involved since (i) seems substantially better than (23).

9. (24b) is somewhat odd, probably because of the topicalization of a nonspecific phrase. But if the topicalized phrase were specific, then WH-extraction would be inhibited, as it is in (i).

(i) ??which athletes did you buy the pictures of

10. Note that (25a) indicates that string-vacuous movement of a subject to SPEC of CP must be permitted.

11. See section 3.4.2 for an analysis of this phenomenon. See also Torrego 1985 and Pesetsky 1982 for discussion of examples such as (24a) and (25a).

12. See Ross 1967, Postal 1974, Fiengo 1974, Rochemont 1980, and Johnson 1986, among many other references.

13. Johnson (1986) argues for IP in the latter case. That proposal is potentially problematic, in that the extra IP created may block government, hence lexical government, of t_1 by *believe*. We leave this issue open here.

14. There is one further restriction on HNPS that we have not dealt with. As is well known, this rule cannot operate *successive*-cyclically. Thus, the heavy object of the embedded clause in (i) cannot escape to the higher clause to produce (ii).

(i)   John said [that Mary will solve all of the phonology problems] yesterday

(ii)   *John said that Mary will solve yesterday all of the phonology problems
       cf. *Susan* solved yesterday all of the phonology problems

Particularly in light of our analysis of long-distance topicalization, this is mysterious. Why can't the heavy NP move first to the lower SPEC of CP, and from there to a position in the higher clause? Here, we offer a conjecture. Suppose that "heaviness" is truly a feature relevant to the operation of this process. Then, it is conceivable that when a constituent crucially possessing this feature moves to SPEC of CP, the CP itself acquires the feature via SPEC-head agreement and upward percolation of the features of the head. The resulting configuration has one [+heavy] constituent contained within another. The next step of the derivation, rightward movement to the ultimate landing site, now would see two potentially movable [+heavy] phrases, the CP and the NP (assuming, as seems reasonable, that HNPS, despite its customary name, is not limited just to NPs). But then, the A-over-A constraint will precisely prevent the process from moving the NP.

15. Conceptually, this is virtually identical to what we have proposed. The only apparent differences are with respect to trivial technical details. For example, for us, the notion "head position" is not relevant. Rather, what is crucial is whether a potential antecedent governor is a head. Further, it is not a WH-phrase or trace in COMP (or SPEC of CP in the CP analysis) that antecedent-governs, but rather the COMP itself.

16. (42) is somewhat degraded, as are all parasitic gap constructions involving adjuncts with subjects other than PRO. For example, compare (42) with (i), which is perfect.

(i) who$_1$ did you telephone t_1 after mentioning e_1

It is unclear what accounts for this contrast.

17. Stowell (1986) argues that empty operators and their intermediate traces cannot play any role in antecedent government in general. Our proposal differs from his in that we attribute the failure of antecedent government by Op in (45) to the X^0 hypothesis, and we allow COMP that is coindexed with Op to be an antecedent governor. There are also empirical differences between Stowell's analysis and ours, for example, with respect to examples such as (46). We predict that such examples do not violate the ECP. This prediction is in accord with our judgments, as indicated in the text, but not with those of Stowell, who finds examples similar to (46) comparable to ones like (41).

18. A technical problem arises with respect to examples such as (i).

(i) why$_1$ [$_{IP}$ does everyone think [$_{CP}$ that John left t_1]]

A possible LF representation for this sentence is shown in (ii)

(ii) [$_{CP}$ why$_1$ [$_{IP}$ everyone$_2$ [$_{IP}$ INFL$_2$ [$_{IP}$ t_2 think [$_{CP}$ $t_1{}'$ [$_{IP}$ ... t_1 ...]]]]]]

Here, t_2 is antecedent-governed by INFL$_2$, as in (62). However, the intermediate trace of *why*, $t_1{}'$, is not antecedent-governed by the matrix COMP because of the intervening IP nodes.

One plausible solution to this problem relies on our general assumption that Move α need not leave a trace unless the trace is required by independent principles. After QR and INFL raising apply to (i), the structure can be as in (iii), if INFL raising does not leave a trace.

(iii) [$_{CP}$ why$_1$ [$_{IP}$ INFL$_2$ [$_{IP}$ everyone$_2$ [$_{IP}$ t_2 [$_{I'}$ [$_{VP}$ think [$_{CP}$ $t_1{}'$ ...]]]]]]]

Here, I′ lacks a head, and hence, we can assume that the node disappears. We can assume further that the higher IP nodes become projections of VP. Then, (iii) can be rewritten as (iv).

(iv) [$_{CP}$ why$_1$ [$_{VP(IP)}$ INFL$_2$ [$_{VP}$ everyone$_2$ [$_{VP}$ t_2 [$_{VP}$ think [$_{CP}$ $t_1{}'$ ...]]]]]]

The second VP in (iv) is L-marked by INFL and hence is not a barrier for t_2 or $t_1{}'$. The third and fourth VPs are not barriers either, if we assume with Chomsky (1986a) that L-marking percolates down to a head. Thus, there is no barrier intervening between INFL$_2$ and t_2, and the former antecedent-governs the latter. In addition, the highest VP (or the IP) is the only barrier that separates $t_1{}'$ from the matrix COMP. Since the matrix COMP is contained in the minimal maximal projection dominating this barrier, namely, the CP, antecedent government obtains for $t_1{}'$ also.

Note that this general line of reasoning can be extended to example (120) of chapter 3, repeated here as

(v) ??how do you think (that) this problem, John solved

Recall that we permitted antecedent government of the initial trace of *how* by the assumption that this trace is not (or need not be) present at S-structure and is thus created by LF adjunction, as in (vi).

(vi) ... [$_{CP}$ $t_1{}'$ [$_{C'}$ C$_1$ [$_{IP_3}$ t_1 [$_{IP_2}$ this problem$_2$ [$_{IP_1}$ John solved t_2]]]]]

Here, t_1 is antecedent-governed by COMP, as desired. However, if, as assumed by Chomsky (1986a), the initial trace of how must be in a position to modify the original VP, this analysis fails. Consider (vii).

(vii) ... $[_{CP} t_1' [_{C'} C_1 [_{IP_2}$ this problem$_2$ $[_{IP_1}$ John $[_{VP_2} t_1 [_{VP_1}$ solved $t_2]]]]]]$

Here, t_1 is not antecedent-governed. IP_1 constitutes a barrier for t_1, and IP_2, the maximal projection immediately dominating that barrier, does not contain a binder for t_1.

We can still accept Chomsky's assumption, however, on an analysis parallel to the one in (iv):

(viii) ... $[_{CP} t_1' [_{C'} C_1 [_{VP(IP)}$ INFL$_3$ $[_{VP}$ this problem$_2$ $[_{VP}$ John$_3$ $[_{VP} t_1 [_{VP}$ solved $t_2]]]]]]]$

Here, the highest VP (IP) is the only barrier, and a binder for t_1 is contained in CP, the maximal projection immediately dominating that barrier. Although we believe that the account of (i) and (v) proposed here is quite plausible, for ease of exposition, we will put it aside in the remainder of the discussion.

19. For example, (i) violates the Superiority Condition, and it is accounted for independently by the ECP.

(i) *which problem did you solve how

20. Pesetsky (1982) proposes the Path Containment Condition (PCC) to account for the ECP effects and all of the superiority effects. However, even this condition fails to distinguish the possible and impossible readings of (66). See note 25 for more detailed discussion.

21. An additional fact that follows from the formulation of the Superiority Condition in (76) is the nonambiguity of examples such as (i).

(i) who$_1$ t_1 wonders whether John bought what

As noted in chapter 1, *what* in this example can take matrix scope, but it cannot take embedded scope. There, we proposed that *whether* cannot undergo absorption with any other WH-phrase. However, if *whether* is an operator, this fact follows straightforwardly from (76). According to (76a), *whether* must be Op-disjoint from any WH-phrase that it c-commands.

An outstanding problem for (76) is the lack of the standard superiority effects in Spanish, discussed in detail by Jaeggli (1982).

(ii) a. Juan sabe   quién dijo qué
        Juan knows who   said what
     b. Juan sabe   qué dijo quién
        Juan knows what said who
        'Juan knows who said what'

Jaeggli presents independent evidence that the postverbal subject position in Spanish is properly governed, like the object position and unlike the preverbal subject position. (See also chapter 2 above for relevant discussion.) He then argues that the grammaticality of (iib) provides support for the ECP account of the superiority phenomenon. Given the Superiority Condition as in Chomsky 1973, or as in (76) in the text, we falsely predict (iib) to be ungrammatical. On the other hand, if we do away with the Superiority Condition and appeal to the ECP to account for the relevant facts, then we predict (iib) to be grammatical.

Although we have no answer to Jaeggli's argument, given the evidence we presented *for* a Superiority Condition independent of the ECP, we will provisionally maintain (76) as such.

22. WH-phrases in Japanese do exhibit some sort of weak WH-island effect, and hence, (81) is marginal under the reading indicated there. Further, (81) lacks the reading in which *dono hon* takes matrix scope and *dare* takes embedded scope. We do not have an account for this fact either, but the following generalization seems to hold in Japanese:

(i) Suppose that a sentence contains two WH-phrases α and β, and α precedes β.
    Then, β cannot have scope over α at LF.

23. As noted in chapter 2, the structure in (94) is also proposed by Koopman and Sportiche (1985), Kitagawa (1986), Kuroda (1988), and Fukui (1986), among others.

24. Alternatively, we may adopt the following from Chomsky 1986a:

(i) If α L-marks β, then α L-marks the specifier of β. (See pp. 22–28).

Given our assumption that INFL L-marks VP, (i) implies that it L-marks the subject NP in the configuration in (94).

Yet another possibility is that V raises to INFL in (94), and the subject NP is L-marked by virtue of this V-raising. Then, subject in Japanese would be L-marked in basically the same way as the embedded subject in English ECM constructions.

25. Pesetsky's (1982) Path Containment Condition (PCC) may be considered a natural candidate for such a principle. The PCC was proposed as a principle to subsume the ECP, the Superiority Condition, and the "crossing constraint," which rules out examples such as the following:

(i) *what$_1$ do you wonder who$_2$ John gave t_1 to t_2

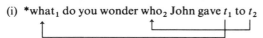

However, it is not clear how the ECP and the Superiority Condition can both be subsumed under this condition, given contrasts such as the following:

(ii) ?who said that who left

(iii) *who said that John left why

And it is not clear how the superiority effects described in (76) can be captured by this condition because of the following contrast discussed in the text:

(iv) ?who wonders what who bought

(v) *what did who buy

See Pesetsky 1982 and May 1985 for the exact formulation of the PCC, and much relevant discussion.

26. Kayne (1981a) discusses this phenomenon in terms of the nominative island condition. This aspect of the NIC was later incorporated into the ECP.

27. Of course, t_1 must exist for the Projection Principle to be satisfied (and, arguably, for *John* to receive a θ-role).

28. Unlike Chomsky (1986a), we do not call upon head-to-head agreement between *likely*, on the one hand, and merged INFL and *be* on the other, to provide an antecedent governor for t_1 here. See Chomsky 1986a: sec. 11 for further details of his analysis.

29. Kayne's (1981c) and Kitagawa's (1986) arguments are based on certain assumptions not adopted here, and hence, we cannot treat them as additional arguments for the same conclusion in this context.

30. Note that (109), like (104), does not seem to be a simple binding theory violation, since it contrasts sharply with examples such as (i) and (ii).

(i)   ?*they think that it was told to each other that Mary is a genius

(ii) ??they said that it seemed to each other that Mary is a genius

As is well known, an expletive and the corresponding AGR constitute only "weak accessible SUBJECTs."

31. Jaeggli (1982), Aoun et al. (1987), Stowell (1986), and Koopman and Sportiche (1985), argue for a similar conclusion, but for different reasons. The hypothesis, which is more precisely stated in (i), is attractive on conceptual grounds.

(i)   All traces must be both antecedent-governed and lexically governed.

But at present, as noted by Epstein (1987), it is not clear how it can accommodate examples such as (ii) in a principled way.

(ii) who$_1$ t_1 bought what$_2$

After the LF movement of *what*, its trace is not antecedent-governed in the usual sense. See the references above, and also chapter 5 in the text, for more detailed discussion.

32. In Kayne's (1981b) formulation of the ECP, there is virtually no antecedent government, and hence, the question of whether *John's* in (111) can be an antecedent governor does not arise. See Kayne 1981b for details.

33. See Marantz 1984 and Lasnik 1988 for further discussion.

34. In fact, for this reason, Anderson (1979) appeals to the NP-*to*-VP filter of Chomsky and Lasnik (1977) to rule out raising in nominals.

35. Chomsky (1986b) assumes that inherent Case is assigned at D-structure and realized at S-structure, whereas structural Case is assigned and realized at S-structure.

36. Although this conclusion seems valid, the example motivating it, (137), is not entirely compelling. (137) might be ruled out not because *belief* fails to assign inherent Case exceptionally, but rather because it fails to assign inherent Case at all. Note that "*of*-insertion" fails even with a complement of *belief*:

(i)   *John's belief of the rumor
      (cf. John believed the rumor)

(ii) *John's belief of Mary
      (cf. John believed Mary)

For a clearer test, we need a verb that is like *believe* in taking an NP or a clause as its complement, and in assigning exceptional Case, but whose nominal is unlike *belief* in inherently Case-marking an NP complement. One such verb is *prove*, with its associated nominal *proof*:

(iii) a.   John proved that Harry was the murderer
    b.   John proved Harry to be the murderer

(iv) a.   John's proof that Harry was the murderer
    b.   *John's proof (of) Harry to be the murderer

(v) a.   John proved Harry's guilt
    b.   John's proof of Harry's guilt

This paradigm provides more direct evidence for (135a).

37. This assumption enabled us to account for examples such as the following:

(i)   ??who$_1$ did you hear a report [$_{CP}$ that Bill hit t_1]

(ii) ??who$_1$ did you hear stories about [$_{NP}$ pictures of t_1]

The CP in (i) and the NP in (ii) are assigned oblique Case and hence constitute barriers for WH-movement. See section 3.3.

38. (141) can be considered as a generalization of the observation made by Aoun (1981) and Bouchard (1982) that CP breaks an A-chain.

39. The effects of (142) are roughly equivalent to those of a condition requiring traces of NP-movement to be antecedent-governed. Thus, (142) is similar in some respects to Chomsky's (and others') hypothesis that all traces must be antecedent-governed. However, since it is not clear how this hypothesis can be generalized to traces of WH-movement in a principled way, as we pointed out in note 31, we assume (142) as a part of the Uniformity Condition, and as a condition independent of the ECP.

40. There is another possible approach to (140), which we would like to mention in passing. First, as pointed out in note 30, (140) is much worse than (i).

(140)   *John$_1$ seems [that [it was told t_1 [that [Mary is a genius]]]]

(i)   ?*they$_1$ think [that [it was told to each other$_1$ [that [Mary is a genius]]]]

Since expletives are only "weak accessible SUBJECTs," as in (i), we concluded in note 30 that (140) cannot be a simple binding theory violation.

However, Chomsky (1986b) hypothesizes that (i) is not a strong binding theory violation because expletives are not "possible binders" of anaphors. Given this approach, it seems possible to distinguish (140) from (i) on the basis of binding theory. Expletives may be "possible binders" for NP-traces, but not for lexical anaphors. Support for this speculation comes from the fact that expletives can be actual binders of NP-traces, as in (ii), but generally not of lexical anaphors.

(ii) it$_1$ seems t_1 to be likely that John will win

If this is the correct approach, then binding theory will by itself account for (140) and the standard super-raising examples such as (iii).

(iii) *John$_1$ seems that it is likely t_1 to win

But since this approach leads to certain complications with respect to the exact formulation of the binding conditions, we will not pursue it further here.

41. In the theory of Chomsky (1986b), (150) violates the condition that a chain can have only one Case-marked member (Chomsky's "last resort" principle), and (151) violates this condition or the condition against Case conflict. (151) violates the Uniformity Condition independently of our reformulation.

42. (152), like (151), violates Uniformity independently of our reformulation.

43. Where Uniformity is irrelevant (i.e., in the case of lexical anaphors), SSC effects are quite evident, as the contrast between (i) and (ii) demonstrates.

(i)   John's destruction of a portrait of himself

(ii) *John's destruction of Mary's portrait of himself

44. This statement is not entirely correct, strictly speaking. Since (145b) is stated in terms of θ-role assignment, it does not extend to examples such as (i) in which an expletive is NP-moved.

(i) *there$_1$ seems that it is likely t_1 to be a riot

We assume that this is not a major problem, since there are various ways to account for this example independently of the ECP and the binding theory. One possibility is to reformulate (145b) as follows:

(ii) Suppose that $(a_1, a_2, \ldots, a_n)$ is an A-chain. Then, if β is a barrier for a_i, then β dominates a_j.

(ii) is a restatement of the generalization in (141) as a principle, and amounts to saying that all NP-traces must be antecedent-governed. Hence, if we assume (ii), we approach even more closely Chomsky's proposal to account for Baker's (140) in terms of the ECP. See note 39. Alternatively, if the Extended Uniformity Condition constrains LF, then the expletive chain in S-structure (i) would become a deviant argument chain at LF, under the expletive replacement analysis of Chomsky (1986b).

45. (157) also violates the ECP, given our formulation of this principle. t_1 is not lexically governed, since, though *belief* governs it, it neither Case-marks nor θ-marks it; nor is it antecedent-governed, since it is not subjacent to INFL of the matrix clause, and *his*$_1$ is a specifier, not a head. Thus, (157) is also an example of redundancy between (145b) and the ECP.

46. Rizzi (1986a) examines certain ungrammatical interactions between anaphoric cliticization and NP-movement in Romance languages. He argues that the anaphoric clitic creates a locality violation. The examples he presents do not appear to fall under (145b); but see Uriagereka 1988 for a suggestion that they fall under antecedent government.

47. Note that if the ECP applies to NP-traces, t_1 in (163) also violates this principle. This trace is not lexically governed, and there is no possible antecedent governor for this trace that c-commands it.

48. See Barss 1986 and the references cited there for detailed analysis of (163)–(164).

49. The question of course remains why (172) is not perfect.

Chapter 5

1. Huang (1982) discusses this very issue and argues that complement PPs are lexically governed. One of his arguments is based on examples such as the following:

(i) who$_1$ did you speak to t_1

A WH is extracted out of a complement P^n in this example. Hence, if complement PPs are not lexically governed (L-marked), (i) should be a CED (Subjacency) violation. (See section 1.2.1 and chapter 3 for relevant discussion.) An alternative analysis for (i) is proposed by Hornstein and Weinberg (1981). They argue that in examples such as (i), V and P are reanalyzed as a V. Then, (i) does not truly involve extraction out of a PP.

2. See Safir 1982 for argument that an empty category associated with a moved CP is actually an NP. If this is correct, then e in (19) is evidently Case-marked as well as θ-marked by the verb.

3. Apparently, this is precisely what happens in Spanish. Extraction of a PP complement, as in (i), is just as good as extraction of an NP complement. (In fact, both are perfect, a phenomenon that remains mysterious under our account, as it does under that of Chomsky (1986a).) On the other hand, extraction of an adjunct, as in (ii) is completely out as usual.

(i)　　a qué trabajador$_1$ [no sabes　　[por qué$_2$ [despidió Juan t_1 t_2]]]
　　　　to what worker　　not know-you why　　fired　　Juan
　　　　'which worker$_1$ don't you know [why$_2$ John fired t_1 t_2]'

(ii) *por qué$_2$ [no sabes　　[a qué trabajador$_1$ despidió Juan t_1 t_2]]
　　　why　　　not know-you to what worker　　fire　　Juan
　　　'why$_2$ don't you know [which worker$_1$ John fired t_1 t_2]'

4. The following contrast provides a further complication:

(i) a. ?tell me who$_1$ t_1 should dress how
　　b. *tell me who$_1$ t solved the problem how

Presumably (ia) is better than (ib) because *dress* and *how* in (ia) have a close relation reminiscent of subcategorization. But it is not clear what the precise nature of this close relation is.

5. (29) is actually a somewhat unfortunate example. What is at issue is a sort of object-subject asymmetry, but even in subject position, it is very difficult to interpret *everything* as part of a distributed question:

(i) who did everything please

(ii) seems to be a more relevant example.

(ii) who met everyone

6. For the definition of *path*, see Pesetsky 1982 and May 1985.

7. Below, we will return to the issue of the clause-boundedness of QR.

8. For example, May (1985:69) notes that anaphora between an *every* phrase and a singular pronoun "... is a hallmark of bound variable anaphora."

9. This assumption played a crucial role given certain of May's other assumptions, which we do not adopt here.

10. Notice that t_2 in (50) does not violate the ECP, given our formulation of the principle in chapter 4.

11. (52) means that the "rigidity" of quantifier scope observed in Chinese and Japanese applies in essence to English as well. (See Kuroda 1971, Kroch 1974, Huang 1982, and Hoji 1985 for much relevant discussion.) (52) is in fact quite similar to the LF condition that Hoji (1985) proposes to account for the relevant facts in Japanese. We will return to this point immediately below.

12. For present purposes, it does not matter whether the minimal node is VP or IP. If VP is a possible adjunction site for QR, as assumed to be the case in May (1985) and here, then *everything* adjoins to VP. Otherwise, it adjoins to IP.

13. Huang (1982) proposes that when *everyone* takes wide scope in (56), it is moved in the syntax to a position that c-commands *someone*. Given this proposal, (56) is not an exception to the rigidity condition, as it is formulated by Huang (1982).

14. The rigidity phenomenon observed in Japanese by Kuroda (1971) and Hoji (1985) also seems to be a matter of preference, at least in some cases. It is widely assumed that (i), as opposed to (56), is unambiguous and allows only the interpretation where *dareka* 'someone' takes wide scope.

(i) dareka-ga   daremo-o   aisiteiru
    someone-nom everyone-acc love
    'someone loves everyone'

Although there is certainly a strong preference in this direction, the wide scope reading of *daremo* 'everyone' is at least easier in (i) than in (ii), where it is completely impossible.

(ii) dareka-ga   [cp daremo-ga   Hanako-o   aisiteiru to]   omotteiru
     someone-nom   everyone-nom Hanako-acc love   COMP think
     'someone thinks that everyone loves Hanako'

This fact indicates that the contrast between (56) and (37) in English obtains in Japanese as well, and further, that there may be no difference between the two languages with respect to the rigidity phenomenon. Thus, the claimed difference, based on examples like (56) and (i), may be purely idiolectal rather than cross-linguistic. There seems to be considerable variation among individuals with respect to the possible ambiguity of (56) and (i) both in English and in Japanese.

15. As noted in chapter 1, it is technically possible to subsume lexical government under antecedent government by coindexing the lexical governor and the governee, as suggested by Stowell (1981). However, as also noted in chapter 1, it is not yet clear that this is a truly substantive way of eliminating the disjunction.

16. That extension of the Uniformity Condition rules out (62) as well. Hence, there is no reason at this point to appeal to the ECP to rule out this example.

17. See Epstein 1987 for further discussion.

18. As far as we know, the proposal that lexical government is a necessary PF condition for traces was first advanced by Jaeggli (1982). AHLW argue that all

traces must not only be governed by a lexical head but also be antecedent-governed; consequently, they propose conjunctive rather than disjunctive requirements. For them, the antecedent government requirement is subsumed under the generalized binding theory of Aoun (1981, 1985), which we will not discuss here. See Lasnik and Uriagereka 1988 for potential problems with such an approach to antecedent government.

19. The actual example that AHLW discuss is (i).

(i) each picture of John's

We discuss the simpler (64) instead since, as far as we can tell, the presence of *each* is not crucial for AHLW's argument.

20. Although Anderson's (1983) analysis of (64) is quite attractive, we assume here that the example does not involve an empty N, as she assumes, but is an instance of N'-deletion. Saito and Murasugi (1989) argue that other examples considered by Anderson (1983) can also be reanalyzed as instances of N'-deletion if we adopt the DP hypothesis of Fukui and Speas (1986) and Abney (1985), among others. This raises the question of whether empty Ns exist at all. But we will not go into this question here.

21. # indicates incompatibility of the utterance with the indicated context.

22. Wasow (1972) argues that not only NPs but also other phrases exhibit Condition C type effects. The analysis of (82) suggested in the text becomes even more plausible under the DP hypothesis proposed by Fukui and Speas (1986) and Abney (1985), among others. What is subject to Condition C in examples like (82) will then be not an N', but an NP. See Lobeck (1990) and Saito and Murasugi (1989) for a reanalysis of N'-deletion as NP-deletion based on the DP hypothesis.

23. Unlike AHLW, we find (84a) degraded. On this point, see the discussion following example (103).

24. The precise analysis of the process in (92) is not clear, but as observed in the text, it has much in common with VP-deletion. It is reasonable to conjecture that VP-deletion is in fact involved, but in combination with a heavy NP shift–like rightward movement of the complement.

25. The judgments are AHLW's. We find these examples substantially degraded, but not completely impossible.

26. Another example relevant to this issue is (i) (= AHLW's (13c)).

(i) I wonder where Fay bought the books and where the records

This example seems reasonably good even though there is no obvious alternative to CP coordination. Interestingly, this example is equally problematic for AHLW's account, since there is no head governor for the trace of *where* in the second conjunct of the embedded question.

27. See Kuno and Masunaga 1986 for more examples of the same kind.

28. According to Pesetsky, D-linked WH-phrases in situ are assigned scope, but by a mechanism other than movement. Note that a D-linked WH-phrase may undergo syntactic WH-movement:

(i) which books did you buy

Further, the moved D-linked WH-phrase may satisfy the requirements of a verb of the *wonder* class:

(ii) a.   I wonder which book you bought
     b.   *I wonder you bought which book

Since, according to Pesetsky, *which* phrases are necessarily D-linked, there are evidently two different modes of interpretation for such phrases, one based on movement and the other not. Thus, D-linking does not precisely divide structures along movement–in situ lines.

29. This diagnostic is evidently neutral with respect to the precise treatment of Superiority. In particular, it does not depend on whether the relevant condition is the ECP, nested dependency, or our version of the Superiority Condition, discussed in chapter 4.

30. Note that presence or absence of D-linking of *what* should actually not be relevant, since it is only for WH in situ that the question of LF movement arises.

31. This assumes that *ittai* phrases cannot undergo pied-piping, as Pesetsky notes.

32. In (146), we assume, as discussed in chapter 4, that the initial trace t_1 may be properly governed by INFL raised in LF. Thus, (146) can be as in (i).

(i) ... $[_{CP} t_1'' [_{C'} C_1 [_{VP(IP)} t_1' [_{VP(IP)} INFL_1 [_{VP} t_1$ saw t_2 at the rally]]]]] ...

Here, the question arises why (147) cannot have the structure in (ii) with INFL properly governing both t_1 and t_1'.

(ii) ... $[_{CP}$ whether $[_{C'} C [_{VP(IP)} INFL_1 [_{VP(IP)} t_1' [_{VP(IP)} t_1$ saw t_2 at the rally]]]]] ...

We propose that antecedent government requires local binding, and hence, the presence of t_1' blocks the proper government of t_1 by INFL, even if $INFL_1$ and t_1 are "close enough" for the proper government relation to obtain. See note 18 of chapter 4 for related discussion.

33. It is not clear whether relative clauses in Japanese have operators in SPEC of CP. If the SPEC of CP is empty, then the movement of *ittai nani-o* can go through this position, leaving a trace there. In this case, the COMP properly governs t_1', but then, the intermediate trace in the SPEC of CP will not be properly governed.

34. Or more precisely, *ittai* adjoins in LF to the WH-phrase it is associated with. If *ittai* and the WH-phrase are coindexed, and the trace of *ittai* is an adjunct trace, then the contrast between (129)/(151) and (149) follows.

35. We essentially follow Tiedeman (1989) on this point.

36. Our account of this contrast can, in some respects, be thought of as a modernization of the NIC treatment proposed by Pesetsky (1981/82).

37. See also Kayne 1981b for a proposal of the same kind.

38. Stowell (1981) in fact argues that COMP is the head of CP, based on this analysis. His conclusion is of course adopted here, and in many other works.

39. But see Saito 1984, 1986 for an attempt to make these theories consistent.

40. In section 3.3.1, we assumed that VP fails to be a barrier for precisely this reason.

41. This line of reasoning does not preclude a raised V from being an L-marker under all circumstances. In particular, if a V θ-marks an argument but is not in an appropriate configuration for L-marking (at D-structure), and V-raising creates such a configuration, then L-marking by the raised V would obtain. This provides an alternative to the chapter 2 treatment of the lack of subject condition effects in Japanese. There, we suggested that given the phrase structure configuration of Japanese, as opposed to English, INFL in the former language L-marks the subject. But such L-marking would be impossible if L-marking requires θ-marking. However, if V raises to INFL in Japanese, as seems plausible, then even this strict condition will be satisfied, given that V θ-marks its subject.

42. See Jackendoff 1971 for a conceptually similar suggestion about why VP-deletion demands an overt auxiliary as a residue, where there is no such requirement for the otherwise parallel N'-deletion, since there is no such possibility. See also Lasnik 1989a for the proposal that θ-visibility (in the sense of Aoun (1979)) demands that an argument have Case at both LF and S-structure, but, crucially, not at D-structure, because Case is simply unavailable at that level.

43. See Tiedeman 1989 for a conceptually similar argument, but based on slightly different assumptions.

References

Abney, S. (1985). "Functor Theory and Licensing: Toward the Elimination of the Base Component." Ms., MIT.

Anderson, M. (1979). "Noun Phrase Structure." Doctoral dissertation, University of Connecticut.

Anderson, M. (1983). "Prenominal Genitive NPs." *The Linguistic Review* 3, 1–24.

Anderson, S. R., and P. Kiparsky, eds. (1973). *A Festschrift for Morris Halle*. Holt, Rinehart and Winston, New York.

Aoun, J. (1979). "On Government, Case-marking, and Clitic Placement." Ms., MIT.

Aoun, J. (1981). "The Formal Nature of Anaphoric Relations." Doctoral dissertation, MIT.

Aoun, J. (1985). *Generalized Binding*. Foris, Dordrecht.

Aoun, J., N. Hornstein, D. Lightfoot, and A. Weinberg (1987). "Two Types of Locality." *Linguistic Inquiry* 18, 537–577.

Aoun, J., N. Hornstein, and D. Sportiche (1981). "Some Aspects of Wide Scope Quantification." *Journal of Linguistic Research* 1.3, 69–95.

Aoun, J., and D. Sportiche (1982/83). "On the Formal Theory of Government." *The Linguistic Review* 2, 211–236.

Baker, C. L. (1970). "Notes on the Description of English Questions: The Role of an Abstract Question Morpheme." *Foundations of Language* 6, 197–219.

Baker, C. L. (1977). "Comments on the Paper by Culicover and Wexler." In Culicover, Wasow, and Akmajian 1977.

Baltin, M. R. (1982). "A Landing Site Theory of Movement Rules." *Linguistic Inquiry* 13, 1–38.

Baltin, M. R. (1984). "Extraposition Rules and Discontinuous Constituents." *Linguistic Inquiry* 15, 157–163.

Baltin, M. R., and A. Kroch, eds. (1989). *Alternative Conceptions of Phrase Structure*. University of Chicago Press, Chicago.

Barss, A. (1986). "Chains and Anaphoric Dependence: On Reconstruction and Its Implications." Doctoral dissertation, MIT.

Belletti, A., L. Brandi, and L. Rizzi, eds. (1981). *Theory of Markedness in Generative Grammar*. Scuola Normale Superiore, Pisa.

Belletti, A., and L. Rizzi (1981). "The Syntax of *ne*: Some Theoretical Implications." *The Linguistic Review* 1, 117–154.

Bolinger, D. (1978). "Asking More Than One Thing at a Time." In Hiz 1978.

Borer, H., ed. (1986). *Syntax and Semantics, Volume 19: The Grammar of Pronominal Clitics*. Academic Press, New York.

Bouchard, D. (1982). "On the Content of Empty Categories." Doctoral dissertation, MIT.

Bresnan, J. (1969). "Remarks on Adsententials." Ms., MIT.

Cattell, R. (1976). "Constraints on Movement Rules." *Language* 52, 18–50.

Choe, J. W. (1987). "LF Movement and Pied-Piping." *Linguistic Inquiry* 18, 348–353.

Chomsky, N. (1957). *Syntactic Structures*. Mouton, The Hague.

Chomsky, N. (1965). *Aspects of the Theory of Syntax*. MIT Press, Cambridge, Mass.

Chomsky, N. (1973). "Conditions on Transformations." In Anderson and Kiparsky 1973. [Reprinted in Chomsky 1977b.]

Chomsky, N. (1976). "Conditions on Rules of Grammar." *Linguistic Analysis* 2, 303–351. [Reprinted in Chomsky 1977b.]

Chomsky, N. (1977a). "On *Wh*-Movement." in Culicover, Wasow, and Akmajian 1977.

Chomsky, N. (1977b). *Essays on Form and Interpretation*. North Holland, Amsterdam.

Chomsky, N. (1979). Unpublished transcript of lectures presented at the Scuola Normale Superiore, Pisa.

Chomsky, N. (1980). "On Binding." *Linguistic Inquiry* 11, 1–46.

Chomsky, N. (1981). *Lectures on Government and Binding*. Foris, Dordrecht.

Chomsky, N. (1982). *Some Concepts and Consequences of the Theory of Government and Binding*. MIT Press, Cambridge, Mass.

Chomsky, N. (1986a). *Barriers*. MIT Press, Cambridge, Mass.

Chomsky, N. (1986b). *Knowledge of Language*. Praeger, New York.

Chomsky, N., and H. Lasnik (1977). "Filters and Control." *Linguistic Inquiry* 8, 425–504. [Reprinted in Lasnik 1990.]

Cinque, G. (1990). *Types of A'-Dependencies*. MIT Press, Cambridge, Mass.

Culicover, P., T. Wasow, and A. Akmajian, eds. (1977). *Formal Syntax*. Academic Press, New York.

Davis, L. (1984). "Arguments and Expletives." Doctoral dissertation, University of Connecticut.

Elliott, W. N. (1982). "Local Binding and Extraction from NP." Ms., MIT.

Epstein, S. D. (1986). "The Local Binding Condition and LF Chains." *Linguistic Inquiry* 17, 187–205.

Epstein, S. D. (1987). "Empty Categories and Their Antecedents." Doctoral dissertation, University of Connecticut.

Fiengo, R. (1974). "Semantic Conditions on Surface Structure." Doctoral dissertation, MIT.

Fiengo, R. (1977). "On Trace Theory." *Linguistic Inquiry* 8, 35–62.

Fiengo, R. (1980). *Surface Structure*. Harvard University Press, Cambridge, Mass.

Fukui, N. (1986). "A Theory of Category Projection and Its Applications." Doctoral dissertation, MIT.

Fukui, N., and M. Speas (1986). "Specifiers and Projection." In *MIT Working Papers in Linguistics* 8, Department of Linguistics and Philosophy, MIT.

Grimshaw, J., ed. (1975). *Papers in the History and Structure of English*. University of Massachusetts Papers in Linguistics, Vol. 1. GLSA, University of Massachusetts, Amherst.

Grimshaw, J. (1979). "Complement Selection and the Lexicon." *Linguistic Inquiry* 10, 279–326.

Haig, J. (1976). "Shadow Pronoun Deletion in Japanese." *Linguistic Inquiry* 7, 363–371.

Hankamer, J., and I. A. Sag (1976). "Deep and Surface Anaphora." *Linguistic Inquiry* 7, 391–426.

Harada, S.-I. (1977). "Nihongo-ni 'Henkei'-wa Hituyoo-da." *Gengo* 6.10, 88–95; 6.11, 96–103.

Hendrick, R., and M. Rochemont (1982). "Complementation, Multiple WH, and Echo Questions." Ms., University of North Carolina and University of California at Irvine.

Higginbotham, J. (1983). "Logical Form, Binding, and Nominals." *Linguistic Inquiry* 14, 395–420.

Higginbotham, J., and R. May (1981). "Questions, Quantifiers, and Crossing." *The Linguistic Review* 1, 41–80.

Hiz, H., ed. (1978). *Questions*. Reidel, Dordrecht.

Hoji, H. (1985). "Logical Form Constraints and Configurational Structures in Japanese." Doctoral dissertation, University of Washington, Seattle.

Hong, S. (1985). "A and A′ Binding in Korean and English." Doctoral dissertation, University of Connecticut.

Hornstein, N., and A. Weinberg (1981). "Case Theory and Preposition Stranding." *Linguistic Inquiry* 12, 55–91.

Huang, C.-T. J. (1981/82). "Move *Wh* in a Language without *Wh* Movement." *The Linguistic Review* 1, 369–416.

Huang, C.-T. J. (1982). "Logical Relations in Chinese and the Theory of Grammar." Doctoral dissertation, MIT.

Imai, T., and M. Saito, eds. (1986). *Issues in Japanese Linguistics*. Foris, Dordrecht.

Jackendoff, R. (1971). "Gapping and Related Rules." *Linguistic Inquiry* 2, 21–35.

Jaeggli, O. (1982). *Topics in Romance Syntax*. Foris, Dordrecht.

Jaeggli, O. (1985). "On Certain ECP Effects in Spanish." Ms., University of Southern California.

Johnson, K. (1986). "A Case for Movement." Doctoral dissertation, MIT.

Kayne, R. (1980). "Extensions of Binding and Case-Marking." *Linguistic Inquiry* 11, 75–96. [Reprinted in Kayne 1984.]

Kayne, R. (1981a). "Two Notes on the NIC." In Belletti, Brandi, and Rizzi 1981. [Reprinted in Kayne 1984.]

Kayne, R. (1981b). "ECP Extensions." *Linguistic Inquiry* 12, 93–133. [Reprinted in Kayne 1984.]

Kayne, R. (1981c). "Unambiguous Paths." In R. May and J. Koster, eds., *Levels of Syntactic Representation*. Foris, Dordrecht. [Reprinted in Kayne 1984.]

Kayne, R. (1983). "Connectedness." *Linguistic Inquiry* 14, 223–249.

Kayne, R. (1984). *Connectedness and Binary Branching*. Foris, Dordrecht.

Keyser, S. J. (1975). "A Partial History of the Relative Clause in English." In Grimshaw 1975.

Kitagawa, Y. (1986). "Subjects in Japanese and English." Doctoral dissertation, University of Massachusetts, Amherst.

Koopman, H., and D. Sportiche (1985). "Theta-Theory and Extraction." Paper presented at the 1985 GLOW meeting, Brussels.

Kroch, A. (1974). "The Semantics of Scope in English." Doctoral dissertation, MIT.

Kroch, A., and A. K. Joshi (1985). "The Linguistic Relevance of Tree Adjoining Grammar." Ms., Department of Computer and Information Science, Moore School, University of Pennsylvania.

Kuno, S. (1973). "Constraints on Internal Clauses and Sentential Subjects," *Linguistic Inquiry* 4, 363–385.

Kuno, S., and K. Masunaga (1986). "Questions with Wh Phrases in Islands." In *University of Massachusetts Occasional Papers in Linguistics* 11. GLSA, University of Massachusetts, Amherst.

Kuno, S., and J. J. Robinson (1972). "Multiple *Wh* Question." *Linguistic Inquiry* 3, 463–487.

Kuroda, S.-Y. (1971). "Remarks on the Notion of Subject with Reference to Words like *Also, Even* or *Only*." *Annual Bulletin Number 4 of the Research Institute of Logopedics and Phoniatrics*, University of Tokyo. [Reprinted in *Papers in Japanese Linguistics* 11, 121–156 (1986).]

Kuroda, S.-Y. (1988). "Whether We Agree or Not: A Comparative Syntax of English and Japanese." In Poser 1988.

Lasnik, H. (1976). "Remarks on Coreference." *Linguistic Analysis* 2, 1–22. [Reprinted in Lasnik 1989b.]

Lasnik, H. (1981). "Restricting the Theory of Transformations: A Case Study." In N. Hornstein and D. Lightfoot, eds., *Explanations in Linguistics*. Longmans, London. [Reprinted in Lasnik 1990.]

Lasnik, H. (1985). "Illicit NP Movement: Locality Conditions on Chains?" *Linguistic Inquiry* 16, 481–490. [Reprinted in Lasnik 1989b.]

Lasnik, H. (1988). "Subjects and the θ-Criterion." *Natural Language & Linguistic Theory* 6, 1–17.

Lasnik, H. (1989a). "Case and Expletives: Notes toward a Parametric Account." Paper presented at the Princeton Comparative Syntax Workshop.

Lasnik, H. (1989b). *Essays on Anaphora*. Kluwer, Dordrecht.

Lasnik, H. (1990). *Essays on Restrictiveness and Learnability*. Kluwer, Dordrecht.

Lasnik, H., and M. Saito (1984). "On the Nature of Proper Government." *Linguistic Inquiry* 15, 235–289. [Reprinted in Lasnik 1990.]

Lasnik, H., and J. Uriagereka (1988). *A Course in GB Syntax: Lectures on Binding and Empty Categories*. MIT Press, Cambridge, Mass.

Lobeck, A. (1990). "Functional Heads as Proper Governors." In *Proceedings of NELS 20*. GLSA, University of Massachusetts, Amherst.

Marantz, A. (1984). *On the Nature of Grammatical Relations*. MIT Press, Cambridge, Mass.

May, R. (1977). "The Grammar of Quantification." Doctoral dissertation, MIT.

May, R. (1981). "Movement and Binding." *Linguistic Inquiry* 12, 215–243.

May, R. (1985). *Logical Form: Its Structure and Derivation*. MIT Press, Cambridge, Mass.

May, R. (1988). "Ambiguities of Quantification and *Wh*: A Reply to Williams." *Linguistic Inquiry* 19, 118–135.

Nishigauchi, T. (1986). "Quantification in Syntax." Doctoral dissertation, University of Massachusetts, Amherst.

Pesetsky, D. (1981/82). "Complementizer-Trace Phenomena and the Nominative Island Condition." *The Linguistic Review* 1, 297–343.

Pesetsky, D. (1982). "Paths and Categories." Doctoral dissertation, MIT.

Pesetsky, D. (1987). "*Wh*-in Situ: Movement and Unselective Binding." In Reuland and Ter Meulen 1987.

Poser, W., ed. (1988). *Papers from the Second International Workshop on Japanese Syntax*. CSLI, Stanford University.

Postal, P. (1972). "On Some Rules That Are Not Successive Cyclic." *Linguistic Inquiry* 3, 211–222.

Postal, P. (1974). *On Raising*. MIT Press, Cambridge, Mass.

Reinhart, T. (1976). "The Syntactic Domain of Anaphora." Doctoral dissertation, MIT.

Reinhart, T. (1981). "Definite NP Anaphora and C-Command Domains." *Linguistic Inquiry* 12, 605–635.

Reuland, E. J., and A. G. B. ter Meulen, eds. (1987). *The Representation of (In) definiteness*. MIT Press, Cambridge, Mass.

Rizzi, L. (1980). "Violations of the *Wh* Island Constraint and the Subjacency Condition." *Journal of Italian Linguistics* 5, 157–195. [Reprinted in Rizzi 1982.]

Rizzi, L. (1982). *Issues in Italian Syntax*. Foris, Dordrecht.

Rizzi, L. (1986a). "On Chain Formation." In Borer 1986.

Rizzi, L. (1986b). "Null Objects in Italian and the Theory of *pro*." *Linguistic Inquiry* 17, 501–557.

Rizzi, L. (1990). *Relativized Minimality*. MIT Press, Cambridge, Mass.

Rochemont, M. (1980). "A Theory of Stylistic Rules in English." Doctoral dissertation, University of Massachusetts, Amherst.

Ross, J. R. (1967). "Constraints on Variables in Syntax." Doctoral dissertation, MIT.

Ross, J. R. (1974). "Three Batons for Cognitive Psychology." In Weimer and Palermo 1974.

Safir, K. (1982). "Syntactic Chains and the Definiteness Effect." Doctoral dissertation, MIT.

Saito, M. (1984). "On the Definition of C-Command and Government." In *Proceedings of NELS 14*. GLSA, University of Massachusetts, Amherst.

Saito, M. (1985). "Some Asymmetries in Japanese and Their Theoretical Implications." Doctoral dissertation, MIT.

Saito, M. (1986). "Three Notes on Syntactic Movement in Japanese." In Imai and Saito 1986.

Saito, M. (1989). "Scrambling as Semantically Vacuous A' Movement." In Baltin and Kroch 1989.

Saito, M., and K. Murasugi (1989). "N'-Deletion in Japanese: A Preliminary Study." Paper presented at the Southern California Japanese/Korean Linguistics Conference, UCLA.

Sportiche, D. (1981/82). "Bounding Nodes in French." *The Linguistic Review* 1, 219–246.

Stowell, T. (1981). "Origins of Phrase Structure." Doctoral dissertation, MIT.

Stowell, T. (1986). "Null Antecedents and Proper Government." In *Proceedings of NELS 16*. GLSA, University of Massachusetts, Amherst.

Stowell, T. (1989). "Subjects, Specifiers, and X-Bar Theory. " In Baltin and Kroch 1989.

Tiedeman, R. (1989). "Government and Locality Conditions on Syntactic Relations." Doctoral dissertation, University of Connecticut.

Torrego, E. (1984). "On Inversion in Spanish and Some of Its Effects." *Linguistic Inquiry* 15, 103–129.

Torrego, E. (1985). "On Empty Categories in Nominals." Ms., University of Massachusetts, Boston.

Travis, L. (1984). "Parameters and Effects of Word Order Variation." Doctoral dissertation, MIT.

Uriagereka, J. (1988). "On Government." Doctoral dissertation, University of Connecticut.

Wasow, T. (1972). "Anaphoric Relations in English." Doctoral dissertation, MIT.

Weimer, W. B., and D. S. Palermo, eds. (1974). *Cognition and the Symbolic Processes*. Lawrence Erlbaum Associates, Hillsdale, N.J.

Wexler, K., and P. Culicover (1977). "Some Syntactic Implications of a Theory of Language Learnability." In Culicover, Wasow, and Akmajian 1977.

Whitman, J. (1986). "Configurationality Parameters." In Imai and Saito 1986.

Williams, E. (1986). "A Reassignment of the Functions of LF." *Linguistic Inquiry* 17, 265–299.

Index

Abe, J., 140
Abney, S., 208n20, 208n22
Absorption, 121, 189n22, n29
A-chain. *See* Chain
Ā-chain. *See* Chain
Adjunct-complement asymmetries, 17, 22, 36
Adjunct condition, 71, 89, 91
Adjunction, 84, 87
  condition on, 73
  successive cyclic, 81–83
  of WH-phrases to IP, 72, 83
  of WH-phrases to VP, 71
Affect-α, 59–60, 64–68, 74, 108, 117
A-movement. *See* NP-movement
Ā-movement, 106 (*See also* Wh-movement)
Anderson, M., 131–132, 159, 203n34, 208n20
"A-not-A" operator, 31, 190n33
Antecedent government, 14, 19–24, 73, 94, 106, 156–158, 209n30
  and adjunct movement, 29–39
  barrier for, 22
  definition of, 14, 24
  and government, 29–39
  and S, 22
  and Subjacency, 69, 184–185
  and VP, 21
Aoun, J., 3, 14, 17, 55, 69, 156, 158, 163–166, 185, 188n13, n20, 189n25, 191n5, 207n18, 208n18, n19
A-over-A constraint, 199n14
Argument-adjunct asymmetries, 48, 60–62

Baker, C. L., 10, 103
Baker, M., 129, 134, 157
Baltin, M. R., 62, 77, 85, 100, 141

Barrier, 69–75, 87, 102, 106
  and A'-binder, 102
  and inheritance, 74, 106, 197n1
  and oblique Case, 89, 91
  and VP, 85, 87, 106, 183–185
Barss, A., 89, 138, 140
Belletti, A., 23, 44–45, 145, 185
Binding, 24, 189n28
  Condition (A), 26, 110–111, 130, 140, 193n9, 198n6, 198n7
  Condition (B), 130
  Condition (C), 94, 163
  feature of NP-trace, 138
Blocking Category, 70
Bolinger, D., 172, 188n19
Bouchard, D., 189n26
Bounding node, 11, 189n31
Bresnan, J., 193n7
Bridge verb, 20

Case. *See* Inherent Case *and* Oblique Case
Case marker, as lexical governor, 42, 189n24
Cattell, R., 188n15
C-command, 28, 45, 189n28, 194n15, 198n6
CED. *See* Condition on Extraction Domain
Chain, 66, 70, 73
  A-chain, 66, 93, 157, 204n38, 205n44
  Ā-chain, 66
  composition, 98–99
  locality condition on, 93–94, 138
Chain-binding, 140–143
Chain Condition, 139, 142, 205n41
Chinese, 6, 30–36, 38–41, 43, 121–125
Choe, J. W., 13
Chomsky, N., 2–3, 7, 11, 14, 16–17, 24, 26–27, 29, 42, 46, 54–55, 58–59, 62–63, 69–78, 80–81, 83–85, 88–89, 91–94,